FOREVER AND OLÉ

The moral right of Georgina Carter Pickard has been asserted
First published in Great Britain 2020 publication Amazon

Interior layout design and formatting by Book Brand
Cover Design by mytealgiraffe.com

FOREVER AND OLÉ

A TRUE
SPANISH
ADVENTURE

GEORGINA CARTER PICKARD

For Jason

CONTENTS

To write this memoir I relied on my personal notes, emails and recalled upon my memory with the help of a timeline to how these events unfolded. In some cases I have compressed events together to allow a greater flow of the story and on some occasions omitted people and events if it proved not to be beneficial to the work. Almost all characters names and places have been changed or altered to preserve anonymity. At the time of writing any information provided was true, based on my own experiences.

PROLOGUE

Time had stopped. The office clock had struck the dead boring hour of four and I felt myself staring psychotically at the hands in an attempt to persuade them to fast forward to five.

I turned to my little loft-space window, my pale reflection stared back at me. I noticed the dark roots of my hair needed attention, the length too long to be comfortable in a ponytail any more. I longed for a glimpse of sunshine to lift my twenty-six-year-old spirit and inject colour back into my soul.

It hadn't stopped raining in Surrey for days and for early November I was surprised how warm it felt inside the office. Working life in a converted mill during winter was usually fraught with dampness.

On my desk sat a mountain of children's books, piled so precariously I thought a single breath might have sent them tumbling to the floor. Each one, embellished with different-coloured Post-it notes, scribbled with departmental instructions.

I was lucky enough to work on the best floor in the Publishing Company, the upper attic in Meadowbrook Mill, a former flour mill now reduced to quirky office space with sleek tangerine and indigo iMac computers and shelves straining with novelty books. The countryside views through the cottage windows were idyllic, framing the quintessential British countryside like a painting. A gentle flowing stream wound its way through a park and into a small village where the staff often retreated to a pub at lunch time. London was only a short train ride away, where I sometimes accompanied my boss, dragging a suitcase of new titles to our sales meetings, usually held at some swanky Mayfair hotel.

The Watermill held onto its charming 17th-century characteristics; exposed roof beams and tall arched windows made up of individual glass panes that were all original. Hand-crafted iron nails that had been embedded into dark oak joists centuries ago had long-since perished, leaving stained puncture holes. The curved crosspieces that offered effortless support showed cracks that only time could instil.

When I had sluggish days, days of wishing I was somewhere else, the mill's little eccentricities added fuel to my flame and made me want to build something of my own.

Darkness waited on the outside. I peered at my calendar, pinned on the wall and being careful not to disturb the toppling books I took a pen and drew an X through the date, the week was finally over. As I stood to collect my satchel and tea mug I took a moment to study the calendar. A colleague mocked how the marks on the calendar looked as if I were in prison, crossing off the dates I had served. I considered his remark a fair comment but I did not want to say anything that might give him cause to worry of my unhappiness at work.

The pleasant party sound of a popping cork came from the lower floor signaling its end to the working day that Friday night. I tightly wrapped my jacket around me as I prepared for the British dampness on the outside.

At the building's entrance, my colleagues were celebrating 'National Pickle day', a genuine excuse gleaned from the internet to delay working late on any printing deadlines. They each raised a glass, celebrating a colleague's ten-year commitment to the company, although the woman didn't look too happy about it and seemed to disintegrate into a mild shock that only I seemed to be aware of. With a smile, I apologetically declined the offer of a drink, I needed to call my mother in northern Spain as soon as I could.

Once home I barely gave myself enough time to peel off my jacket, before I hurriedly dialled the long phone number to Galicia. We chatted briefly about her week; how she and my stepfather Joseph had returned home from shopping only to find a horse tied to her front door knocker, the owner nowhere to be seen.

As I listened, I felt a sense of haste as if my thoughts might run away from me. The words spilt out. "Mum I'm thinking of a complete life change. Have been for a long time actually." There was a silence that made my stomach tighten.

"What kind of life change did you have in mind?" My mother sounded tense but intrigued. I heard the click of a lighter and her inhale deeply.

"Well, I feel like it's time I did something different, *somewhere* different."

"Georgina, what's brought this on?" she sounded concerned, her Norwegian accent always seemed stronger when she was serious.

"Nothing dramatic but it occurred to me today, the end of another month when I stood back and noticed my calendar was full of Xs, I realised I've been numb to everything. Life is passing by and before I know it, I might be sat at the same desk for a decade. Where's my life gone in that time?"

I imagined my mother nodding as she sucked on her cigarette.

"So if this is about taking control of your life perhaps you should think about getting a different job," she stated, hoping to put an end to my whining.

"The job isn't the issue. I've fallen into a comfortable, unadventurous lifestyle without actually realising I've trapped myself."

"So what are you going to do?" she asked, depleted of answers.

I took a sharp intake of breath so I wouldn't be interrupted.

"Perhaps it's time to leap into something big - move to Spain perhaps, somewhere like Valencia. I need to do a little more research but it seems very up and coming and somewhere that isn't loaded with eccentric expats yet. Possibly leap onto the Spanish property ladder, go from there."

"Or Galicia – you could buy a house near your mother?" She paused, and I could hear the hope in her silence.

"Not sure we're ready for somewhere that north and that rural yet," not wanting to squash her hopes.

"Well, you're still in your twenties, I suppose, so you've got nothing to lose. What about Jason, does he feel the same way?"

"I think he's sick of prison life more than I am."

1. QUITTING THE LIFE

Jason and I had met each other a few years previously through mutual friends while I was halfway through my second year at university. He was a year older than me and had recently started working as a prison officer in a high-security jail. He was handsome, athletically tall, with broad, muscular shoulders, had light brown short shaved hair and perfect teeth (which delighted my mother when I brought him home to meet her)

Three years later I moved out of my shared student house and into the fixer-upper three-bed terraced house in Surrey that Jason had bought, his first hop onto the property ladder. We had spent the start of the new Millennium eating fish and chips out of paper while sitting on a rug because we had yet to furnish the place. An open fire kept us warm as we waited for computers to crash and the world to end, as dramatically predicted by the media.

On weekends when Jason wasn't working, he undertook home renovations. A previous job working in a DIY store gave him some basic experience of plumbing, electrics and plastering. Anything he didn't know, he gleaned from books or the internet, increasing his basic skill-set from fixing toasters to building extensions. Once motivated he enjoyed his accomplishments wholeheartedly. It helped him disconnect from the struggles and stresses of prison, a career that as time went on was becoming exhausting and dangerous.

Almost every evening Jason and I would get very animated about the life we could be living abroad. We would draw sketches of properties we saw on the internet that was desperately in need of renovation and talk for hours about how we would redesign them. We romanticised about growing our own crops on spacious land. Picking fresh lemons for our ice-cold gin and tonics. This creative outlet was to be the start of many conversations we'd have on building our very own life abroad sometime in the future.

Two months after that phone conversation with my mother I couldn't suppress my desire of emigration. Standing in a local off-license on a dark rainy evening staring at bottles of Spanish Rioja, I was catapulted to Spain. I imagined sitting under the shade of grapevines in a floaty dress, retreating from the scorching sun and polishing wine glasses with a tea towel.

Wines I recognised from brief visits to Valencia were plastered with stickers boasting *Voted Best Wine of the Year,* deceptively influencing the UK over-inflated prices when, really, I knew it was decent Spanish plonk you could pick up for less than a euro - another consideration that ticked the relocation box.

The seed had taken root and we both decided that if we were going to have any future away from our monotonous lives, we should take the risk or forever be regretful.

Once our decision had been made to leave, everything else was simply logistics. In the spring we took a long weekend trip to Valencia, where an estate agent had arranged eight pre-selected properties we had seen online and supplied us with a modest apartment to stay in while we searched.

Most of the properties we viewed didn't inspire us and we were about to leave Valencia empty handed - until we spotted a white four-bedroom villa pinned to the notice board in the estate agents office that was a little over our budget. The agent hastily made arrangements to view it and as we pulled up outside the villa, the sun was setting over the mountains casting an explosion of orange and pink. Instantly we were excited as the agent pushed-back the hefty iron gates revealing a classically low level, white detached villa with a deep pool and a large plot of land with fruit trees. Fuchsia bougainvillaea adorned the property making it look ridiculously romantic. We took some time drinking in the details and assessed how our lives would be fulfilled here. I loved the house but a moment of doubt washed over me and I wondered if we were not just being naive and impulsive. It seemed like an unachievable dream, but there it was and we wanted it.

We made an offer which was accepted with a small deposit on a credit card – an absurdity in itself. The estate agent confirmed the property was free from debt and organised a *no questions asked* mortgage, and with a little extra from our parents, we were able to get our feet on the Spanish property ladder.

After that, it wasn't long before we sold the UK house, quit both our jobs and immediately felt the relief from the shackles of it. It took three more months of hectic organising, temporarily moving in with Jason's parents' and working our notice until we could close down our lives ready for a new beginning.

2. AN ENDLESS HOLIDAY

It was the summer of 2003 as we made our way through France, our most precious belongings crammed into the car with not an inch to spare. The aim was to split the journey up with an overnight motel stay in southern France allowing more than enough time to receive our furniture delivery the following day.

The next morning, as we whizzed our way over the Spanish border and headed south, I quietly reflected on our future; we were hurtling into the unknown and it was an exhilarating but nervy feeling. I flicked through a tourists' travel guide to learn some useful sentences, only to realise my pronunciation was terrible.

We agreed we would take Spanish lessons once we had settled in - I immediately felt our life was changing for the better already.

By late afternoon, we finally arrived at the villa feeling hot and weary, yet excited to see our new property. Leaving Jason to start unpacking the car I bounded inside to familiarise myself with the new place we would call home. I opened the metal-framed windows to release the musty air, scanned the kitchen cupboards and stood in our vast empty bedroom on the cool tiled floors, imagining how our first night would be spent here. In the far corner of the bedroom, I noticed a white candy-floss growth sprouting from the floor tiles that hovered like a low cloud. I curiously touched the spores and as I did, it collapsed into a fine heap of dust on the marble floor. I'd keep that information from Jason - at least until he'd had a cup of tea.

I skipped outside into the warm air to find Jason had received an update from the delivery driver, they were delayed by two or three days after a minor setback. I had visions of this 'minor setback' being our lorry laying on its side in a ditch somewhere in France, our strewn contents being picked through by a couple of locals.

For the next two furniture-less nights we made sleeping arrangements with what camping equipment we had; a pair of skinny airbeds, rolled-up beach towels and sleeping bags on the hard tiled floor.

In other areas lacking comfort, we were fortunate that the former owner had left behind household items we could use; a blue and white 1950s Formica dining set that would be ideal under the outside porch for *al fresco* dining, and a wooden table and mismatched chairs found in the garden suitable for inside dining.

We hoped to be lucky enough to uncover some more items in the shed, perhaps a wheelbarrow and garden equipment. But our discoveries were psychopathic-looking farming tools, twenty litres of unidentifiable yellow liquid - that looked suspiciously like piss and small pieces of rope tied into individual nooses - which I found rather alarming. I hoped we would never have a need for any of it.

Our new home felt so far away from anything I'd ever known. It wasn't just because we were finally free to do what we wanted; we felt like lottery winners who had escaped old lives. For a good while we stood under the intense heat of the sun and stared materialistically at everything we now owned; the spacious villa, the pool on its raised deck, the grounds, and the small plantation of orange trees. Even the large concrete driveway was so sizable it could be used as a basketball court, so to think that all of it was valued at half the cost of a flat back in Britain, was astounding. I sniffed and stroked the petals of exotic plants I had never seen before. Curious insects alerted by our presence, buzzed in the endless clarity of the blue sky. I could feel years of glum, English dampness evaporating from my skin, the warm injection I had been craving. The vast olive-tinged landscape and glorious cooking aroma's made our new home seem so stimulating. It was hard not to be impressed with my first real taste of Spain which could only get better.

A few hours later an overwhelming feeling of change kicked in and I felt the need to pick up a phone and speak to someone familiar, to tell them all our discoveries and reconnect but the absence of a phone line at the villa made that impossible.

While I busied myself with homemaking tasks, Jason had stumbled upon an old gas boiler - a huge money saving find, if he could find any gas to test that it worked. The boiler had seen better days and the more he tried to fix it, the more brittle pieces of metal broke off in his hands. He found an orange barrel with some left over gas and connected it, but still nothing. As his frustration grew he stormed past me, boiler instructions fluttering in his hand as he disappeared out into the dusty urbanisation. Five minutes later he returned with two identical, very short-legged men who had been working at one of the neighbouring houses. Both wore matching blue overalls and one sported a huge moustache and thick connecting eyebrows, making him look ridiculously like the Super Mario character. A cigarette, not much longer than the filter perched idly in his lips.

Jason had desperately tried to explain the problem but as the men approached the tatty boiler, one tutted, turned and walked away.

The remaining man, who seemed a more patient and kindly person obviously felt pity for us and gave the boiler his full attention for the best part of an hour. After tapping a few pipes, he dissembled the boiler, blew inside the parts to clear them of debris and handed them to Jason for polishing. Once reassembled the man wiped his hands from grease, took out a lighter from his overalls and lit the cigarette that hadn't left his mouth. He then flipped open the gas bottle switch and leaned into the boiler and listened for any hissing sounds. Jason and I exchanged glances and both took a step back. Nothing happened. The man looked utterly bemused and we relented that we would have to go and buy a boiler at the expense of two hundred euros. In the meantime, we would have to find a more inventive way of showering and cooking without gas.

As Super Mario left, Jason gratefully shook his hand and gave him a couple of beers as a thank you for his time which seemed very well received. Defeated, Jason heaved up the orange gas bottle to move it back into the cupboard when the hose fell loose, Jason looked up at me. The hose hadn't been connected properly in the first place. I smiled in delight.

That evening, after the gas valve had been properly secured to the gas bottle, we showered, ate and opened our first bottle of red wine under our terrace, finally able to relax and embrace our new lives. This was the moment we had been waiting for; to feel a warm rippling breeze on our skin as we sipped wine in each other's company. We agreed that we would have a nice long sleep, with a bonus lie-in, and tomorrow we'd be fresh to tackle anything.

By early morning the airbeds were so flat I thought a wild beast had crawled in through the window and jumped on my back, several times until it broke.

Our bodies hurt, we groaned as we awoke to the sound of our urbanisation. Noises seemed amplified in our new home. Barking dogs, cats meowing, people yelling, chickens, goats, skinny dirty sheep, and children screaming as they jumped into swimming pools. I had never heard so many dogs before in one place, a constant and repetitive hysteria. It was as if we were living next door to a dog pound. The realisation hit me then. How stupid my expectations had been to allow me to think we had moved to a kind of five-star paradise hotel where everything would be perfectly tranquil. I cursed myself for the lack of reality.

Our first big mistake was to believe it was a fabulous idea to relocate during one of the hottest Valencian months of the year – August. Our pasty white skin, sensitive lungs and eyes were used to a British tarpaulin of cloud and could not adjust in such an extreme climate. We had leapt from a tepid fourteen degrees to thirty-seven overnight, we felt like lobsters being fished from the sea and thrown in a boiling pan of water.

I had had the notion that it would be a lovely introduction to our new lives if we treated the first few weeks as a holiday. I had imagined us splashing about in the pool, tanned and fabulous in new swimwear, or sauntering around the beaches looking for tapas to try. But in reality, we gasped and choked on dry planet-Mars air and shielded our eyes from the flies and from that very bright and ridiculously hot thing in the sky. I noticed how our mood became temperamental in the heat, snapping like turtles at one another as we passed in the corridor.

In just six hours I had sweated through all the clothes I had brought in my canvas holdall, having made several changes throughout the day. I eventually ended up plodding about the house in my underwear, my wobbly bits dripping after me as if I were a tub of melted butter. It was too exhausting an effort to keep changing in the extreme heat. Almost defeated I rummaged through our bags until I found my white bikini. Determined to bring some sophistication into my new life I slipped it on and skipped up to the pool-terrace ready to turn on the tap to fill it up just enough to take a cooling dip. But when I reached the terrace I was confronted with a shallow pool of rain water that had putrefied into fetid green slime and was home to mosquito-larvae and snails. My optimism was beginning to run particularly low.

Two days later while we were cleaning the pool of algae, the delivery truck complete with cocky London driver, eventually arrived. We were relieved to be reunited with our clothes and furniture, ready to make our house a home.

A couple of weeks on, after the last of the boxes had been unpacked, our first visitors arrived; three friends from university along with my brother. It felt amazing to share the beginning of our new life with the people we felt so close to. The uni group had planned to travel further afield once they had spent enough time with us and so we were a comforting pit-stop which suited us nicely. In addition to them, an old friend of Jason's stopped by. Christopher was starting a new life in Valencia city, with a new teaching post and an apartment that was currently occupied. Until he could move in, we welcomed him to stay as long as he needed.

As the days pushed further on, nights became increasingly humid and alive with biting insects. I got used to ducking from hefty bugs as they propelled themselves towards the fruit trees.

The small group of friends that had begun with a casual stop-over, extended their stay. The atmosphere around the villa felt as if we all were on the same voyage to discovery, and it was amusing to see our friends' puzzled looks as they tried to interpret the Spanish culture, just as much as we were.

We sunk into heavenly evenings sitting on our porch, listening to travel stories over the gentle strum of a guitar. Persistent mosquitos nibbled at our necks so we sipped gin and tonics, one after the other, in the hope it would deter them from biting.

One unbearably hot early evening, the boys decided to cook up a barbecue feast. While they stood around the barbecue discussing cooking methods, a girlfriend and I padded our way up the stairs onto the pool terrace for a dip. Both of us falling breathlessly in love with the firework show from the direction of Valencia city and the views over Monrabana. The other villas looked magical with their lively, colourful lanterns while children and parents played at night in their gardens or dished-up evening meals.

We dropped our towels to the floor as we walked to the pool's edge and slipped beneath the silence of the cooling water. I floated a little while on my back to let the water mute my ears and as I stared into the darkening sky my mind drifted. For the first time since arriving in Valencia, memories crept-in from my past life. But before I could have any real hold on them they vanished. It was as if that part of my life was already a lifetime ago.

The aroma of charred meat from the barbecue made us feel famished but we were enjoying the pool too much to leave. A dog in a nearby garden began to howl followed by an eerie silence and a pick-up in the wind, and not a moment later - a monstrous fork of lightning struck somewhere in the distance. The boys, shocked at the crashing noise, rushed up to the pool terrace to find us still in it. Within a couple of minutes the calm sky had transformed itself into a suffocating blanket that moved towards us, threatening to extinguish our fun. Transfixed by the sheer luminosity of the flashes we were unable to peel ourselves away until the downpour leapt in a single long jump above us. What seemed like a year's worth of pent-up moisture dropped from the sky. Menacing lightning bolts drew their way closer and closer to our open pool. We screamed with delight and a little fear, while the guys worried about the barbecue being extinguished. We climbed out of the pool and ran from the torrential rain as it stung our exposed arms and legs. Wrapped in damp towels we shivered under the porch while we watched the boys huddle under one umbrella at the barbecue until it got too crowded. Our friends abandoned Jason, who stood prodding the food and getting drenched as he finished up the cooking. Unbelievably the rain did not deter the flies. We all stared, disgusted at the black mass of flies that took shelter on Jason's naked back. When he was done cooking we applauded him for duties under tough circumstances as he appeared through the rain with a plate of steaming meat like a barbecue hero.

We sat under the outside porch terrace and ate, talking loudly over the beating noise. I felt humbled, lucky to have such cherished friends sharing these new experiences with us under such a natural force.

3. BANANA FEVER

The tropical downpour didn't stop for the next twenty-four hours, still as hard and aggressive as when it first started. By the time the last raindrops fell and the sun emerged, every orange tree in sight was sparkling clean making it feel like we were living in a citrus advert.

In a bid to start landscaping our garden *and* to make use of the extra hands we had sitting around drinking all our imported tea, we made an agreement with a resident on the urbanisation to buy part of his banana tree plantation. The trees were owned by a British couple, the wife, a tribute singer going by the name of 'Shania Spain' who toured the clubs and hotels in Benidorm. The couple had recently split, and so the husband had put the house up for sale stating that we could take as many banana trees as we liked for one hundred euros.

Later that morning we secured bandanas to our heads, snapped on gardening gloves, and gathered what tools we had for the transplantation mission. Loaded with picks, spades, bin liners and a shiny new wheelbarrow we gathered our army and marched into Monrabana's very own Costa Rica.

When we arrived it was evident that the banana plantation had grown wildly out of control from neglect. The plants were tricky to transplant due to a wet and shallow root system. The owner had told us they had thrived in the Spanish climate and they should continue to do so - if we replanted them quickly without the roots drying out in the heat. Once established, we could potentially yield a few 'hands' a year, a lovely addition to our orange and lemon bouquet.

We stood like elves against the trunks ready to get stuck in and concocted a plan to select between a range of two and eight feet tall plants. The soil, sweet smelling and soft from the recent downpour, made the whole task an easier mission. We prepared bin liners with the soil first, filling them to cushion the roots when they sat upright in the wheelbarrow. Our friends, assuming we had done this before, waited curiously at the edge of the plantation for instructions. Then every one of us got stuck in. We hacked our way through fleshy roots, detaching younger off-shoots from their taller mothers. We dug deep into the ground, up to our elbows as we wiggled the plants free and wrapped wet rags around the roots.

Over the course of the day, in the searing heat, we managed to transplant over twenty-five, eight-foot-tall banana trees into their pre-dug holes in our garden. As our confidence grew, we made a disastrous attempt at extracting the bigger ones but they snapped like crayons, their trunks too long to transport them without the use of the car - which was just too tiresome a job to jog along behind and support the weight in the afternoon heat. It wasn't long before I had worked my friends too hard on the plant line. They leaned on their forks, sweaty and red-faced, squinting at their mosquito-bitten legs. I held back a smirk when I saw them standing together in a group, dipped in mud from head to toe.

A workers' union was soon formed, our friends were not impressed with my military approach as they moaned about being forced to work while on holiday. To try to claw back my friendships I emerged from the villa with a tray of ice-cold beers, which they eyed suspiciously as if it was a bribe for more labour. But I assured them that they had well and truly paid their way as we leaned back on the patchy earth and marveled at our achievements. We were thrilled to see the garden really taking shape thanks to our hardworking friends. They wouldn't admit it but they were proud of the effort they put into the project.

Two-and-a-half-months later most of the replanted banana trees had died. At first the trees were happy in their new home. We had cared for them endlessly, providing them with everything they needed so that they grew taller and sprouted little ones at their bases. One of our tallest trees even flowered and produced our first little 'nana' but despite our best efforts the climate wasn't humid or warm enough to sustain their growth. With our lack of experience we had planted the trees too far apart, so they couldn't huddle to protect themselves. Then rain came, accompanied by two days of relentless battering from high gale-force winds that left the delicate leaves shredded like a flag in a storm. I hadn't the heart to write to my friends and tell them that their best efforts had resulted in what looked like a field of giant dead leeks. We hoped the plants might have gone into hibernation early and would bounce back next year.

Jason and I carried on fixing up the house with a view to start advertising it for holiday rentals during the summer months for the following year. We were aware that our honeymoon holiday period was coming to an end and we had to start thinking about an income. We carried on painting and redecorating, ditching the Seventies decor for a lighter more modern look. The villa didn't require too much cash to get it looking presentable so decorating the bedrooms and the living room was straightforward. This gave us the opportunity to concentrate on the outside; an area of space we found ourselves spending all our time in, since the move.

Over the period of a week, we built an oval island in the centre of our plot, made up of yellow rocks we had scavenged locally. It gave the garden a focal point where gravel paths would lead up and circle around it. By filling the island with soil, scattering grass seeds and planting palm trees, the transformation had resulted in a tropical oasis in a short time.

We were uncovering surprises in the garden, plants and fruit trees hidden amongst a tangle of dried weeds. There were around ten orange trees, two lemon trees and eight almost-dead almond trees scattered around the back part of the garden but I didn't like to go wondering up there much, there were snakes I had seen them. As newbies to the area it would be useful to have local knowledge of the wildlife, someone who could advise us which spiders, snakes and plants were dangerous or not. Until we found that person we would have to keep our wits about us.

Behind the barbecue, between two orange trees, I stumbled upon an impressive spider web spanning around a meter in diameter. I only discovered this because my right arm brushed the edge of the web while picking oranges one day, causing it to vibrate and shimmer in the sun. My focus was drawn to its silvery threads, spanning out of my peripheral vision. Adrenaline pumped through my body, bringing me out in a cold sweat as I instantly knew that a little spider couldn't make a web of this size. Frozen and stiff I slowly turned to look into its center, there in the middle sat a spider that looked like a creature from a science fiction movie.

I couldn't believe what I was seeing, it was worth going in for a closer look. Curiously the body appeared to be formed of a thick, hard shell – unlike that of any spider I had ever known to exist. The walnut sized casing was the colour of buttermilk with tiny evenly spaced holes, three on each side, like pierced holes on a pie crust. It wasn't oval shaped all the way around but peaked at three progressively longer spikes towards its bottom end and balanced on fine ballet-dancing legs. The eyes were close together and slightly protruded – reminding me of a cartoon crab. I wanted to touch it, to feel the texture of the shell. I called Jason over and we took a series of photographs. *I was sure the spider was rare and the discovery would make us millionaires.* I thought to myself how lovely it was to have something this incredible living its life in our orange grove. But it also made me think twice about ever sticking my arm into an orange tree without checking first.

A little while later, somewhere else in the vast garden, Jason proudly lifted his garden fork and nodded for me to be amazed at his exotic find. An almost translucent yellow scorpion sat clenched in fear, ready for attack.

"Where did you find that?" I asked, knowing he had probably dug around for it in the dirt.

"Under that rock over there, it's the second one I've seen. Isn't it incredible?"

He prodded the scorpion with a stick to try and provoke it.

"Yeah, amazing," I said, unimpressed. "Leave it alone where you found it before it seeks revenge in your boots tomorrow."

Summer was drawing to a close and Monrabana became abandoned by most of its Spanish owners. Jason and I felt that we had settled in a little better, so one afternoon we accepted an invitation for coffee at our neighbour's villa. It was the perfect opportunity to make friends and gain that local knowledge we were after.

Pedro and Maria were smiley, generous people, each with masses of luxurious dark curly hair. Our introductions and small talk felt tense and awkward at first. They didn't exactly hide their look of frustration to each other at our terrible Spanish – for which I couldn't blame them. On reflection we should have prioritised Spanish night classes over Scuba diving lessons when we had the opportunity back in the UK.

Thankfully as we were new arrivals to Spain, Pedro and Maria understood that it would take some time to adjust and learn the language. So to get to know each other quickly, Pedro had loaded up a translation program on his PC. He had been excited to try it out and we were the perfect guinea pigs. He had stored the software on his children's computer in their bedroom in the hope that the children would take to learning English. He nudged me with a quick wink suggesting that perhaps I might want to volunteer for the role which I thought was a horrible idea, especially as I had seen the little terrors chasing their scraggy Alsatian around the garden trying to pull its ears.

To help keep the flow of communication open, we eagerly sat for the next hour, taking it in turns to type our questions and responses. But the program was one of those freebies you got with a PC magazine, so it was outdated and slow and despite Pedro's good intentions, it felt very awkward while we sat perched on tiny children's chairs in near silence. Pedro asked us why we had moved to Valencia and what we did for work. I typed in a few lines of text explaining our situation and the four of us leaned in, eager for this miraculous translation to bridge the cultural divide. Pedro and Maria read the Spanish translation and shot a look of horror at Jason. We read the text again and realised that it had been crudely translated implying Jason had worked in a prison for six years as a prisoner and not as an Officer. No wonder they looked concerned. We tried to make it better but we just made it worse. Pedro and Maria mouthed the words on the screen only to find that none of the sentences made any sense. We left shortly after, cringing at our awkwardness as we waved our goodbyes. United by the importance of language, we both vowed to learn some Spanish before we saw them again.

Over the next few days, Pedro and Maria kept their distance but kindly passed fresh eggs from their chickens over the fence. They advised us where to shop for building supplies and helped Jason work out the complexities of the swimming pool filter. It would be another string to Jason's bow but not before he had struggled to understand the obscure workings in the pump house. Jason was confronted with a million tubes heading in a network of directions, which I thought looked more like the complicated engine room of a submarine. Gurgling plastic taps, which sucked water from one direction to the other at the pull of a lever. Old brittle timers, wires and bags of used sand littered the floor of the low-lit pump house. Pedro insisted that Jason should spend some time backwashing the system, as this would clear the stagnant waste still sitting in the pump and blast out any hidden nasties.

As Pedro was spending time at our villa educating Jason with the replacement parts, we dragged him aside to show off our extraordinary crab-spider discovery. The spider was still safely nestled behind our barbecue, spinning a mummified fly in its vast web. I happily introduced our neighbour to the spider with a dramatic theatrical wave of the hand. Pedro's eyes swept from my hand to the hard exterior of the spider's shell. But instead of sharing our wonder and delight, he frowned. I felt a little worried at his reaction - he didn't seem pleased at all.

I wondered if perhaps it was a well-known dangerous species and we had been naïve living in such proximity to it. But then I reasoned to myself that it might be the only one in the whole world – *an undiscovered species!* Although, perhaps we had got a little carried away naming it after ourselves and imagining being interviewed by National Geographic.

Jason asked Pedro if he had ever seen a spider like it before, he hadn't but thought it was possibly dangerous, based simply on its appearance. We were unbiased about it – who were we to take something out of its own territory? Within seconds we knew the situation had been taken out of our hands.

Pedro bent down and picked up a dried orange branch, stripped its leaves and before we could stop him he whipped at the web in short strikes to bring the spider down. In the hope of a quick escape, the armored spider immediately dropped to the leafy ground and ran. Pedro jumped back with a yell, and in one practiced motion, he wielded the stick like a dagger and lurched forward stabbing the stick into the spider's hard casing, squashing it. Jason flinched at the cracking noise while I turned away, not wanting to witness the murder. Pedro, not even the slightest bit flushed after this unprovoked assault, threw his weapon into the long grass with the triumphant stamp of a bullfighter. Jason had turned as pale as the crushed buttermilk shell. We both swallowed our hurt and I muttered an apologetic *Lo siento,* to the mess at our feet.

4. FINDING OUR FEET

As time drifted on we spent our days doing more practical things like opening bank accounts and searching for insurance companies. Most of our investigation had to be done face-to-face as the world-wide-web hadn't reached our rural area and doing these things the old-fashioned way - on foot and in a language we hadn't yet grasped, was extremely frustrating.

Due to a lack of signage, we got lost in cobbled alleyways trying to locate our local tax office so we could pay our bin rates. Local residents helped us find the building and when we did, it looked as if most of the town had turned up that day too. After an hour of queuing, we shuffled forward to be received by a seriously stern face. We had done our homework by preparing our opening gambit in the car and practised our pronunciation until it sounded acceptable. The administrator wasn't going to go easy on us as she cross-referenced our papers with annoyance and after a few torturous minutes, took a medieval stamper and punched a blue illegible smudge down on our forms with dramatic force.

We knew of the common complaint about bureaucracy in Spain but this was the first time we had experienced it. Even opening a bank account required hundreds of pieces of paper, circular inky stamps and signatures. It all seemed ludicrously labor intensive and we hoped that in time, these things would get easier.

A few days later, we had again gathered up our bundle of paperwork and drove into central Valencia, where we sat waiting our turn in a magnificent government building, ticket in hand. The ceiling was gloriously high vaulted and echoed a cacophony of international voices being spoken around us.

Our task was to start the complicated procedure of applying for our own Tarjeta de Residencia - identity cards that were vital for residency and working in Spain for any prolonged period. It meant that we were on the path to integrating into Spanish life, so I was rather excited about getting ours.

After two hours of waiting our number was called. We walked up to a lady with short mauve hair, sitting in a booth. I was relieved to hear she spoke a little English. I politely asked for the application forms.

"No," the lady behind the glass rudely tutted, "You have to go in *that* queue," she scowled at me in disgust, while pointing to a long line of people that snaked outside the building's entrance.

"No, that cannot be right," I argued. "We were told to come here, we've been waiting for hours" My voice creaked up a notch in desperation. Jason looked over his shoulder to see if the heavily-armed security guards were moving towards us. The plump, hateful woman leaned into the partition glass as if I wasn't hearing her correctly, and bared several teeth

"Go, there! ¡Extranjero" My face fell, I flushed. I turned to face Jason. Had she just screamed "foreigner" at me? Anger raised its ugly head and I burned with frustrated fury. Jason ushered me away by my elbow, still keeping one eye on security.

The woman wasn't wrong, which enraged me even more. I was a foreigner and as a foreigner, I would have to learn that things were dealt with differently here. But what bothered me most was the way in which she had said it. From that moment on, I realised just how hard it was to be an outsider in such unfamiliar territory and how I would have to work hard to try and fit in as best I could if I was going to make it work.

We queued outside in the foreigners' line for a further three hours. Families from all over Europe stood waiting, smoking cigarettes, jiggling babies or straying from the crowd to stretch their legs. Bored and irritated, I felt as though I didn't care about the identity card anymore and resented how such things as paperwork could divide us. I felt a little lost, the illiterate foreigner in a city without my people. The friends I spent my days with, in my former life no longer played their part in this new world and without them, no job, no family around me, I felt suspended in a time where I was losing touch on who I really was. I needed to get a grip.

By the time we reached the end of the queue, which felt about fourteen hours later, during which time Jason had grown a beard - a tatty *Cerrado* notice had been propped in the window, a sun-bleached purple blind pulled down inside the cubicle. "How the hell can they be closed?" I whined to Jason.

The next day we drove back into Valencia and started the process all over again at the foreign office. This time we were there early enough to get a good place in the queue. We stood there, hand in pockets self-righteously watching other British people make the same mistakes as we had; turning up late, getting confused then irate and waiting in the wrong line.

Once our paperwork was submitted (and stamped to prove it had been submitted) we took ourselves home. It took a further two months before we received the call to collect our papers from the police station – another location we got lost trying to find. We were rewarded with our residents' cards and after all the effort it was nice to feel like we finally belonged.

5. SOMETHING TO WRITE HOME ABOUT

Under the shady white arches whilst sitting on a wicker chair, I penned a letter to my best friend back in the UK. I told her how I was missing spending time with her and how the transition to living in Valencia wasn't easy. I imagined her tutting whilst reading my letter, thinking I sounded spoilt.

But so far this life-change brought up challenges that I hadn't foreseen; the expectation that everything would happen quickly and easily wasn't realistic – especially in a country that ran things at its own pace.

I felt a dull ache when visiting friends left us to go home. I wrote, how not having a phone or internet connection had distanced us from everyone we knew, virtually plunging us into a solitary existence. It was a new life I had entered by choice that I would have to learn to adapt to.

I also wrote about how different life was in Spain, the cultural divide being far bigger than I had ever imagined and that was only the tip of the iceberg. I explained that Valencia was exciting, colourful and incredibly loud and in equal measures could be frustrating at times. How I felt a wonderful sense of discovery, freedom and safeness I hadn't imagined I'd experience and that our choices were ours, as long as we were both happy.

I hoped in time that our lives would be enriched and I would look back at the low days and realise it was all part of the change. I understood that transition wasn't ever going to be easy, especially in another country where you depended on your partner so heavily.

I wrote about my relationship with Jason and the challenge of spending so much time together when we weren't used to it, we thought we knew each other intimately but really, there was so much more still to learn. We were so dependent on each other for everything it sometimes felt as if we might split apart from the pressure of trying to make things work.

Some days I did feel like giving up but the precious moments made up for the pitfalls, like the blood-orange sunsets over the mountains and the freedom of a future that wasn't determined by anyone else.

I had found a new understanding about that thing we call *compromise* - and how it didn't always seem equally shared or how just a few hours apart could make the world of difference to our conversations. To know that sometimes you can't change a man's mood just because you want to and that spending too much time together could be just as damaging to a relationship as it was to spend too little time together. I was amazed at how, even though you could spend all your time with someone, you could still feel lonely.

And just like any good therapy session, writing these thoughts down gave way to a revelation of where things were going wrong.

By the time I finished the letter, I realised that we needed to make a lot of changes if we were going to maintain the balance of a normal, happy life abroad. For a start, I needed to be more independent and that included doing things on my own as I would have done back home. I couldn't expect Jason to fill the boots of other absent people in my life. He was only one person, capable of only so much.

We needed our own space, hobbies, friends and the Spanish language. Without those, we were just a young couple who had retired too early and we had much more planned than that.

6. BEWARE OF THE CAT

It was October and the oranges were beginning to turn from forest green to pale orange. Winter was approaching but the generous sunshine still warmed up the ground and interior of the house making it feel as if it were spring. The warmth was there without the suffering, and it put a zing under my summer-browned skin.

I decided I would explore the outer greenbelt area by going for a run. But because of my terrible sense of direction, I had planned that the safest route was to cut directly through the urbanisation and work my way outwards to the flat olive fields and loop back around behind the houses, towards home. I threw on my gym gear and put my hair up into a bun. Admittedly, I felt a pinch of smugness that I wasn't paying a gym membership like my friends were back home and I had the clean air and scenic views as a bonus.

But from the moment I left the villa, it was an uncomfortable experience. Bouncing along the path, I ignored the first few dogs gnashing wildly at their gates, drool hanging from floppy chops with the expectation of my leg in their mouths. Flies managed to get caught in my bun, causing me to panic as the trapped wings buzzed against my scalp making me yelp and rip the band free in one frenzied movement. I pushed my legs to work harder, even though I hadn't warmed up beforehand, just to flee. The gravel road became more uneven under my springing step and as my foot pushed off, the noisy crunch informed every dog, guarding every abandoned house in the area that I was about to pass their property. They charged manically about, barking as I broke into a sweat in fear that they might escape and chase me until I died from exhaustion. I had thoughts of my macho neighbours loading cartridges into their hunting rifles and half-cocking them, ready to fire because I had inexcusably interrupted them from their siesta.

I was thankful that I didn't see a human soul as I passed through the back end of the dusty urbanisation. The dogs' fierce barking, drifted into lonely howls behind me as I headed for somewhere open and green and quiet.

The next day, after a light lunch and a short siesta, Jason had heard a high pitched squeak beneath an almond tree in the scrubland area of our garden. Assuming a bird had fallen from its nest, he went to try to rescue it but instead had stumbled upon a wild, stripey kitten nesting in a pile of dead branches. Jason came running into the house where I was pulling on my trainers, weighing up the risk of heading out for another run.

He wanted to surprise me with his find but I rolled my eyes in protest - my interest in creepy crawlies had depreciated since the assassination of the spider. He confessed it was a kitten so immediately we crept over to the nest where I peered inside. It was small and vulnerable, it's glassy-blue eyes, pooled with tears. My heart broke as the kitten weakly cried with barely any strength in it. Had the kitten been abandoned by its mother, or was she out finding food for herself?

Immediately I wanted to save it but being conscious not to interfere with nature we wondered if we should wait a night to see if its mother would reappear. We decided that if she didn't return the following day we would take the kitten in and hand-rear it.

We waited through an agonising night. I stood watching at the window, praying for the mother came home but she didn't make a single appearance. I felt terrible leaving the kitten but I felt that I had to give the mother a chance to return before making assumptions. Early the next morning I crept towards the kitten's nest, there was no sound as I approached causing me to feel nauseous with regret for not rescuing it sooner. But as soon as the kitten heard me whisper, it cried its bird-like squawk, the relief I felt was immense.

It was still alone and starving, its mother hadn't returned and to make matters worse, flies had begun to lay their eggs along its bony spine – nature's opportunistic way of supporting life from another animal's imminent death.

Wearing labourer's gloves Jason gently gathered the kitten up from its nest and placed it in his palm. He thought its long, needle-like teeth, tall ears, tiger markings and protruding sharp claws had all the qualities of a wild cat. I laughed at his dramatic take on things, how aggressive could this little thing be?

We took the kitten to a local vet's, which looked like a third-world version of any clinic I'd ever known - it was as if we were in an underground bunker. The room had strip-lighting that discharged a blinding yellow hue and was sparsely equipped except for a stainless steel table in the centre and a waste paper bin. A glass-fronted medicine cabinet housed two empty vials and barely anything else. There was scratching coming from a room next door, the vet's own rescue dog which kept him company at work. Posters advertising medication for dogs paralysed by horrendous diseases caused by ticks and sand-fly parasites plastered the walls. I wondered if the vet himself ever grew used to those photographs or, if like me these horrific images might make an unwelcome appearance in his dreams.

Although it was depressing to be there, I was grateful it was a sterile environment and the vet could see us quickly. Jason unwrapped the kitten from its towel and placed it on the table where it shivered as its soft pink feet touched the cold metal worktop. The vet told us the kitten was male and about four weeks old; he was very dehydrated and would need special care to make sure he got its vitamins and regained some of its body weight. The kitten was given a booster antibiotic jab and we were told to come back to have his other jabs another day – the vet said he was out of meds and nodded to the empty cabinet. The rest of the information the vet gave us was lost in translation. I looked helplessly at Jason who was confidently nodding, without understanding a single thing. On the way to the pet store to pick up supplies, we pieced together the advice that we had understood and stocked up on all the necessary nursing items we would need to get him back to full health. A few days on, the kitten still hadn't used the litter tray so we grew concerned about his constipation. Another trip to the vet equipped us with a lesson in feline rectal stimulation involving a wet ball of cotton and some patience. We were taught how to emulate the mother cat by cleaning his bottom and to our relief, it worked a treat resulting in a mass evacuation causing us to cheer and the kitten to look relieved.

Within weeks the kitten had grown in length and had a fat healthy belly; his eyes were bright and mischievously happy. We, on the other hand, were weary. Tired from weeks of round-the-clock feeding the kitten demanded from us every two hours, day and night. We cleaned his litter tray constantly and placed a hot water bottle under a teddy bear to emulate a mother cat. I watched the tiny kitten sleep as he clung to the bear and my love for him took hold.

Unfortunately, the kitten wasn't as smitten with us as we were with him and before we knew it there was a wild side to him that started to emerge. He looked adorable but under that cuteness, there was a terrorist inside.

As the kitten grew stronger so did his aggression. When he didn't get his way - he got angry, his ears folded back, accompanied by a low warning growl, a head-tilt backwards, and even though no conflict had been initiated he lunged - claws out, teeth bared into the flesh of a leg, arm and even head if it was nearest. I considered the possibility that he might have been born with an illness, which might explain his aggressive behaviour and perhaps was the reason why his mother had abandoned him.

In contrast, he seemed balanced and happy but I guessed that was because he enjoyed torturing us. We prepared ourselves for feeding time by wrapping our arms and legs in towels and wore thick gloves as he scrambled and scratched his way to the milk formula, clamping the bottle with both paws and savaging the rubber nipple with his needle-sharp teeth. When the bottle was empty he refused to let it go as he scrunched his pink nose and growled primitively for more so that I had to scramble around for a refill to satisfy his insatiable hunger.

As the kitten grew he got further out of control, becoming stubborn and strong with little respect for his caregivers and because of this, it was hard to give him a suitable name to match his personality – (or at least a name we could call him in public). We sneaked along the villa corridor in fear of waking him from his nap. He would climb his way up the security window-bars and hang from the rails, jump onto shelves, smash glasses of unattended water and claw his way up and down the sofa. Like a trapeze performer, he wildly swung from curtains, shredding fabric as he abseiled down only to entrap himself with the frayed cord which tightened around his belly. When we tried to free him from being decapitated he would viciously attack our hands and arms.

He hid behind chairs and under beds, waiting for us to cruise by in our slippers when he would leap out for a frenzied attack on our vulnerable ankles. It wasn't a surprise that most of our friends held-off visiting, terrified to be caught in one of the kitten's violent outbursts and even when Christopher paid a visit - he checked to see if the kitten was around before setting foot inside.

Christopher had learned the hard way after the first incident when he had popped around to tell us how he was settling into his new Valencian life with the madness of fiestas, trumpets, and fireworks in his street. As he divulged his latest news, a cup of tea in one hand, his left ankle resting on his knee, the little beast jumped with the speed of a bullet through the gap in his legs, both paws extended forward as they mugged poor Christopher's face in a double slap. Before we knew what was happening our guest had yelped and involuntarily launched the tea from inside the cup into the air still grasping the cup firmly as the steaming tea rained down on him and our cream sofa. We all blinked in silence, our hearts palpitating with the shock of what had transpired – the perpetrator nowhere to be seen.

By the sixth week of adoption, we returned to the vet's covered in plasters hiding a multitude of abuse. The kitten never seemed remorseful about these attacks, although in between them he could be so loving we'd forgive him. The vet advised us to castrate him while he was still young. So for the sake of our sanity, and the fact that sometimes I felt like killing him myself, we agreed. As helpful as ever, our vet kept the kitten's testicles aside as evidence of having performed the operation. I was glad he did because for a long while I thought those little testes in the petri dish had been taken from another cat. It took many more attacks before he calmed and by that stage, I had resorted to throwing a glass of water over him when I felt he had really overstepped the mark.

The kitten's confidence only grew and even though he was still small he was sneaking off next door to pick fights with the neighbour's guard dogs, leaving me terrified that he would die in the mouth of Pedro's Alsatian. I caught him sitting on top of our neighbouring fence, claws out whacking the dog on its nose, incensing it to madness. It was then I lost my patience as Jason watched me having a furious rant, screaming at the cat on the fence to get down.

The kitten challenged me with his indifferent glare, pitying me for my pathetic love and so I told him to go kill himself if that's what he wanted. That cat chat didn't make any difference; that night he swaggered in late, looking like he'd come from a western saloon. All cocky, as blood dripped from two holes ripped in his left ear and a scratch that ran along the length of his big nose.

I took to a new jogging route, one that involved passing only a few houses with less risk of dog aggression and directed me up a dry grassy hill and over the back into dense olive fields. The expansive, uninterrupted view meant I could jog in any direction without bumping into a dog or person unless they were both feral. Returning from my jog one day I saw movement in the long grass near the entrance to our villa, making me leap to one side. My heart raced as I stood still to see what looked like a small tiger. When the animal appeared directly in front of me I couldn't believe the familiarity of it. It was as big as a dog, with huge pointed ears, long thick whiskers, familiar stripes, a pointy face, and an "M" marking on its head. There was no doubt that this was the father of our kitten.

This was reconfirmed when our kitten's fur darkened to black and dark grey tiger stripes, and its ears grew large and pointed. We finally had a name for him; Maximus – after the Gladiator.

7. DRIVING FOR INDEPENDENCE

The changes I had written about in my letters became a primary motivation to get our lives in order. I needed to make the transition from crazy-cat-loving-lady to a woman of independence. So I made a list of what I needed to do to achieve the balance. This consisted of making new friends, finding paid work, learning Spanish - and foremost, taking the advice from my family and getting back behind the wheel.

Driving in Spain was a new, terrifying experience for me as I lacked confidence behind the wheel. My past driving record wasn't great with many failed attempts before getting my licence at the age twenty-two. I am certain the only reason I passed was that my driving examiner became especially nostalgic while sitting inside my 1960s Morris Minor and those memories temporally blinded him to my driving skills that day.

My stepmother Lynda had urged me to drive in Spain and although I tried to fight it for a long time, I knew it would be impossible to live in a country so vastly spread out without a car. There were hidden dangers of living somewhere rural if you couldn't get to a hospital, especially as ambulances could often take a long time to reach rural villages. At some point, whether we liked it or not, accidents were bound to happen.

I worried I wouldn't be up to it. I took little steps going further out each time, with Jason at my side, encouraging me. We did trial runs to the doctors and hospitals and took the motorway to the airport. We took different routes to the beaches and shopping centres, all places I would need to go to on my own without being worried I'd get hideously lost. Once I did it, I loved every moment of the wide endless and empty roads, not to mention the crazy Spanish drivers. "Why do Spanish people seem only to be in a hurry behind the wheel and not in life?" I joked with Jason, who urged me to keep my eyes on the road.

Driving on abandoned rural roads was one thing but Valencia city was another. It took courage and forced aggression to make it over the first double round-about and from then on, it was how I imagined rally racing. The absence of lane markings threw me a little and as other drivers weaved in and out of lanes there was usually a moment where everyone tries to regain some order and fails. I noticed how almost every single car we stopped next to at the traffic lights had dents and scratches running along the side.

I loved the creative and insanely bad parking, there was something so spontaneous about it. As was the rebellious habit of not following all the traffic rules and the way people were so calm at the scene of an accident as if shouting blame was only pointless and exhaustive.

In built-up city areas, I thought the idea of leaving the handbrake off allowing others to push triple-parked cars out of the way - like some giant tile puzzle game - was a touch of genius. Then there were the illegal self-appointed parking attendants; the unemployed homeless migrants who creatively seek out a parking space, and flag you down in your time of need for a small amount of change.

It took me a long time to be patient at the painfully slow, ambling pedestrians, who would stop and debate the world's problems in front of your car as if you didn't have a destination to get to. Then there was the frustration of drivers not ever using their indicators, and the dangerous overtaking drivers from oncoming traffic; temporarily using your lane to overtake slow trucks, as they hurtled towards you. Every time this happened I gripped the wheel as if my life depended on it, preparing to swerve into a layby to avoid a head-on collision. It was all to be part of my ongoing driving experience.

8. SPANISH CLASSES FOR DUMMIES

The painfulness of the translation program at Pedro and Maria's had motivated us to take up Spanish classes the moment we could find one.

We enrolled ourselves into a group given by Lola, a native Valencian lady who spoke perfect English with a hint of cockney - an inflexion that had, no doubt rubbed off from her British husband. Lola had tanned long legs and an enviable figure. Her hair was auburn brown with such a glossy shine you could almost see your reflection in it. Once a week, eight of us sat around the large pine table in Lola's sunflower yellow kitchen. All the other group members were mature Brits aged seventy and upwards so it was common for most of the students to arrive late to class, delayed by doctor's appointments, or collecting last-minute prescriptions at the pharmacy.

A man called Jeffrey sat opposite us. He wore a hearing aid, which he didn't like to use, preferring to cup his hand behind his ear and say "pardon?" every time anyone spoke. He repeated this at least twenty to thirty times per lesson. Which grew tiresome to everyone in the group, including his wife Pat who screamed in his good ear which didn't seem to be any better. It was only when he realised he was a page behind in the textbook and his wife lost patience that he would eventually turn the device on. Margaret nervously fiddled with sweet wrappers and June talked about herself quite a lot during the times we were supposed to be concentrating on our verb endings.

And then there was Janet – or Dirty Janet as I liked to call her. On our first lesson, it was impossible not to notice Janet's disgraceful appearance. While the other ladies had made an effort in dressing nicely for their weekly lesson, with little earrings or a smidgen of lipstick, Janet looked like she had just stepped out of a slum – which incidentally she had not. She lived in a nice big house in an expensive area and enjoyed making chutneys from her home-grown produce. Her feet were filthy with dirt as if she had been using them as a spade and her toenails; long and as sharp as eagle-talons, were split and black from sun exposure causing everyone in the group to look away when she arrived in sandals. Dirty Janet wasn't just grubby in appearance, she was outspoken with her problems, broadcasting the discomfort of her runny bowel movements as we stood chatting with our classmates outside our teacher's house. We sympathised with Janet's woes, whether it was the fungus blighting her tomato plants or the flies that persistently harassed her toes, she was a negative force that everyone tried their best to avoid.

There was an audible north-south divide in our group, providing an interesting mix of accents among the class. We were the only couple from the south, the others being of Yorkshire decent and this caused much amusement within the class when it came to the variations of Spanish pronunciation. Dirty Janet was very open about her opinions towards people from the south, stating without irony that northerners were more likely to learn Spanish much faster and be more fluent than "you" southerners. This statement evolved into a class discussion during which we both sat there, open-mouthed, listening to fairly offensive reasons why we didn't share the same logic or intelligence - it was as if she didn't realise we were in the same room. The real irony, was that everyone was wasting their own time and money and not learning a single bit of Spanish. Thankfully Lola resolved this by promptly braking up the discussion and making each one of us conjugate a list of Spanish verbs.

At times I felt frustrated with the group and it must have been challenging for Lola to juggle with constant interruptions when she was in mid flow. With the extra chatter, we became increasingly annoyed that we weren't learning enough within the time frame. It seemed the classes were becoming more of a social club more than anything.

We gave it a chance and learned slowly, the additional homework allowed us to gain some understanding of the basics. Before long Jason's Spanish was developing a lot faster than mine, jotting down his homework in half the time that I could. I struggled to memorize the form of certain words and occasionally cheated by looking up the answer in the back of the book - which I knew was not the way to learn to a language, especially when it came to speaking it. A couple of the students were naturally gifted and our teacher did her best to challenge us all to suit our individual levels.

A lady called Rose one day surprised us all into silence when she read out an entire page of her weekend activities in near-perfect Spanish. Our teacher, watery-eyed with pride, praised her at the end of every sentence.

The others seemed passive, almost resentful against Rose, and formed a crossed-armed alliance. As Rose's Spanish words trailed off with a Northern English twang, the others looked as though someone had let off a bad smell in the room. From then on in my mind, I had named her Cocky Rose, but I hugely admired the way she took pleasure in her learning.

To test our Spanish language so far, we had gone in search of another gas bottle supplier after the old company had unexpectedly closed. Standing outside a co-operative building we rung the bell and waited at an iron gate with an empty bottle at our feet. A tall slim man in blue overalls came out to meet us but seemed hostile at the sight of our gas canister. He shouted and waved us away, as if not wanting our custom. We asked him to speak a little slower in our newly practised Spanish but this must have agitated him. He screamed a torrent of words in Valenciano, a usually lovely sounding language if the person talking wasn't spitting. He stormed off leaving us there waiting wondering if he would return. A few minutes later he re-appeared a little calmer and with a full gas bottle. Jason handed over the cash in small notes and waited for the change. The man looked at the notes and flew into another rage, pacing back and forth as he ransacked his pockets. As Jason held out his hand to accept the coins, the man purposely threw all the loose change at our feet with such force they bounced into the road scattering into the gutter. We couldn't understand such a reaction and wondered then if learning a few words in Valenciano might be crucial to our needs as well.

9. BREAKING OUR FIRST RULE

Not too long after Maximus had settled in and become calmer, a female short-haired ginger hunting dog with a white chest, white socks and a white tail tip, as smooth as a paintbrush wandered into our lives and wormed her way into our hearts. Her downcast features expressed her starvation as she waited at our front gate sniffing the air, rich with cooking smells. Her eyes bulged, her rib cage prominent as she scuttled around for scraps. We resisted the stray at first by shooing her away, our first rule of living abroad was not to take on such a tie. But as any expat with a heart will tell you, this is a rule that is almost impossible not to break.

Within a short time of settling in Spain, we had seen the terrible consequences of Spain's stray dog problem. The tiny number of rescue charities that do exist try their best to help the strays with the little funds they have. But this doesn't stop thousands of puppies being abandoned near the roadside or inside rubbish bins every year. Hunting dogs especially are a reoccurring problem in Spain as the owners can often lose one or two dogs during a weekend's hunt. We learned that some hunters purposely underfeed their hunting dogs a day or so before the hunt as this method is thought to gain a better reward. But as the dogs search for prey over large distances they can get separated from the pack and once lost, can suffer a terrible decline into starvation. If they are lucky and get back to an area where they can scavenge, they might be picked up by a kind-hearted local. If not those dogs will usually die in the rural wilderness or be run-over on the main roads.

Sometimes it seemed almost impossible to go anywhere and not witness a dog staggering in the road, delirious from starvation. I tried my hardest not to be affected by what I saw along the motorways in those early months but I always failed. At the sight of these poor creatures, I wished for death to come quickly in the form of a lorry if it would stop the suffering instantly for the poor animal.

For the lucky ones, they had limitless freedom and sometimes a kind soul to throw them scraps of food at night. These country dogs weren't ever bathed, de-ticked or wormed but they seemed content, coming and going, walking and hunting for hours as natural as life intended them to be without the shackles of man to restrict them. If I compared this to the lives of yard-bound dogs, tethered, starved and driven insane from biting mosquitoes and years of relentless isolation - the alternative at least gave them a chance of some kind of existence.

I saw with my own eyes what neglect could do and we tried on many occasions to diplomatically intervene at times. We hoped in some small way that we could make a difference but it always seemed to be a battle that was almost impossible to win. For me, it was probably the hardest thing to accept about being in Spain. Just knowing there were animals in our neighbourhood that were in the depths of such sorrow, day and night was utterly heartbreaking. It seemed that dogs were merely regarded as dirty wild beasts, or in some cases, they weren't regarded as anything at all.

When we took in the ginger dog, we had no idea if she belonged to anybody on our urbanisation. We gave her food and water, and her own blanket and then took her for a walk around the neighbourhood to determine if she had an owner. She seemed to have a compulsive need to eat, sniffing out old dog poo's that she would eat with delight. We asked anyone we came across if they had lost a dog, but no one seemed remotely interested in our plight – they looked at the dog with little interest or sympathy, repulsed at the sight of her scavenging ways.

We took her to our vet who we hoped could identify her by microchip but she didn't have one. He advised she looked too healthy to be a born stray – she was about two years old, and the most surprising news of all, *she was pregnant.* It was too late for her to have a termination so we would have to deal with her pregnancy. We hadn't been prepared for this at all.

Jason bathed her washing away years of filth and fleas. I fretted about a litter of puppies, worried how we would rehome potentially six or even eight of them, it would be a struggle to find good homes. After all, I had witnessed puppies – barely a day old with their eyes still closed - being handed out by unscrupulous men at the markets from a duffle bag in the city. It was frightening to think where they might end up.

We named our new dog Macey and helped her gain weight by feeding her with a rich vitamin diet. She gorged on liver and meat, fats, chicken stock with marrow, full-fat milk and our left-over dinners. For dessert, she ate blistered oranges that had fallen on the ground, and she quickly mastered how to crack almond shells with her teeth to reach the reward inside.

Although physically she seemed well, mentally she was obsessed with food, you couldn't pierce open a tin, or unwrap a baguette without her groveling and dribbling at your feet in desperation. As the cocky cat swaggered by in the garden, I observed as she weighed him up as a meal option. When they were first introduced Macey attempted to eat the kitten whole by gently testing his entire head in her mouth. After a few tellings-off, she realised we weren't offering her a snack. With some training using food as her reward, she soon complied and became a beautiful but greedy addition to our lives.

10. MEETING THE EXPATS

Sticking to my resolution of becoming an independent woman, I sharpened my outlook to making a start to our social circle. During our first four months, we had been solely in each other's company and that was wearing thin for both of us. We desperately needed some other English conversation and through our Spanish classes, we heard of a hippie bar called Bar Ché just outside Valencia that held a bilingual evening every Friday night, run by a Moroccan couple. With a clientele of all ages and Moroccan tagines to die for, it was supposed to be *the* place to meet a diverse range of people.

A small part of me felt unsure at first, I had images of expats from Benidorm in nylon shirts doing the conga around the pool table. Just because we spoke the same language did not mean we would make lasting friendships. However, Jason and I were desperately sick of each other so we agreed that this might be just what we needed and planned to go the following Friday.

The next day we were shopping in a busy hypermarket. It was a fiesta weekend so all the locals were crowded around the fish counter stocking up. Soggy deli tickets littered the wet, fishy floor, as housewives ordered tons of ugly mouthed Merluza fish and delicious fresh prawns by the bucket-load.

A tiny elderly lady with a pixie hairstyle and deeply tanned leathery skin stretched over a bony frame hurtled towards me as she leaned on her shopping trolley in a daze. Bumping my cart she smiled, revealing a tiny beautiful set of gleaming white dentures. I apologised profusely for the collision - as some British people do even when something isn't our fault - and we politely laughed at our recognisable accents, her husband joined us as he dumped a heavy pack of beer into their cart. He was tall, equally tanned, who I guessed to be in his late sixties. After a brief and oddly vague introduction, we established that Ruby and Barry had been living in Spain for six years and in that time gained some useful knowledge in the Spanish community. Barry described himself as a *Jack of all trades* and liked to help fresh arrivals to settle, by advising where to go for electricals and cheap building supplies. He connected British people to Spanish business owners advising 'tell the owner Barry sent you'. As he spoke it was impossible not to notice Barry's dodgy eye. While the right one looked straight, the other was so off course he might as well have been talking to someone behind me. I resisted the temptation to look over my shoulder. Ruby was very petite and would have once been very beautiful in her youth. It was hard to place an age on her as she had worshipped the sun and it hadn't been kind in return but I guessed she was in her late seventies.

Barry saluted to a white-haired couple at the far end of the supermarket he must have known and the couple simultaneously gave him a two-fingered response which made him chuckle.

Barry eyed us with a glint of superiority - an unsullied project standing before him. He told us that it was hard settling in, usually, the first year was the hardest with financial difficulties causing breakups and forcing couples to return to the UK. He seemed to enjoy being genuinely helpful and I imagined the fresh arrivals he had helped would have been grateful for his advice and in return, Barry and Ruby broadened their business and social circles.

Recommendations for places came thick and fast and just as the pensioners in our Spanish classes had mentioned, Ruby and Barry also frequented Bar Ché as a place to socialise.

"If you want to meet some British people once in a while we'll be drinking in the Moroccan bar with a load of others." He rummaged in his shorts leaning back to counterbalance his weighty belly and pulled out his mobile to take our numbers.

"The owners smoke a lot of the old wacky backy, so it's a pretty chilled-out place. Friday night around nine, if you're interested it's a nice place, isn't it, Rubes?"

Ruby eagerly rattled her tiny head in agreement, leaned forward and with her soft, smoky east-end voice whispered,

"We get a bit shit-faced" She giggled.

"I don't expect you to sit with us, there are loads of other people at the bar, probably around your age," Barry stated as he turned to me. "It might be a start as you're new out here?"

I noticed Barry had the habit of talking to my breasts but despite this, he seemed like a good man to know.

We genuinely thanked them for their help before saying our goodbyes. It felt comforting to be in the company of Brits who knew things when most of the time we felt so out of our depth.

That Friday night sometime after nine, Jason and I stood outside Bar Ché. A small door with illuminated red and green glass had been propped open with a brass statue of Ganesh. The fragrant smell of marijuana drifted out to the street. I looked across the square to the other bars and noted their complete lack of activity. From inside we heard roars of laughter, people singing, whooping and clapping. Unsure as to whether to go in, we waited for a signal.

"I think I heard a loud English voice then – this has to be the right place," said Jason.

"If it's not for us, we can always make an excuse and leave," I said.

We walked in and waited for our eyes to adjust to the reddish light. At the bar I noticed a smoky cloud clinging to the ceiling. Two grinning Spanish men were seated there, humming along to Cuban music. We were pleasantly surprised at the ambient mood and decent decor. Usually, Spanish bars tend to look as cold and unwelcoming as an operating theatre but this place was different and I felt immediately at home. On the right side of the room, halfway down, a shiny teak bar took the limelight, with polished brass beer pumps and complimentary bowls of olives and peanuts. Traditional Moroccan pigskin lamps stood on the bar, illuminating the wood to a soft, intimate glow. The walls were as fruity-red as Rioja and more ornate glass Moroccan lamps were suspended from the ceiling. Patriotic Spanish and Moroccan flags rippled on the walls, and behind the bar, a sizable marijuana leaf flag took pride of place.

Despite the popularity of the place, the bar was deceptively spacious. There seemed to be enough room for diners, thanks to a cleverly designed dining bench that ran along the wall opposite the bar. It looked as if the wood had been sliced from an ancient tree, each plank butted together making it one seamless long ripple that curved around the body of where the diner sat. It was layered with varnished so thick it amplified the wood grain inside. A wider den-like area at the back of the bar gave larger groups a more intimate place to gather around a cluster of tables – this became a new haven for all the British expatriates' who had descended on this unfamiliar world.

At the bar, a tall, long-grey-haired hippie weaved his way around customers with energetic ease. He hugged familiar customers as they walked in, warmly shaking hands and slapping them on their backs. When he noticed us he smiled a broad grin and walked briskly to greet us as if seeing long lost friends. We both ordered a beer and made ourselves comfortable on the bar stools.

"Oooh, hola guapos!" He looked from me to Jason and chuckled to himself. On his left bicep was a black tattoo of the Cuban revolutionist Ché Guevara in his trademark beret. Our new friend pointed a heavily-ringed hand at my blonde hair,

"Eh Germah?" he said with a strong French accent while pulling beer into a long tall glass.

"Sorry?" I mumbled.

"German?" he indicated at the colour of my hair again.

"Oh, I see, no, well, a bit but mainly English," I said wondering if we were going to be rejected.

"English! Ahhh, wonderfool, many English friends," he nodded in the direction of the back of the room as he worked a cork from a wine bottle. I glanced over to see a group of ridiculously bronzed, cackling ladies, fags between fingers, sparkly sequins, arms waving, clearly very drunk. The barman expertly loaded a round silver tray with drinks and flipped the tray onto strong, long fingers. I deduced from the number of drinks ordered that they were destined for the Brit table.

Once the barman had offloaded the tray he introduced himself as Zepo from Morocco. He opened his tanned hairy arms, bracelets of beaten metal clashed as he gave Jason a warm hug, then he patted my head and my shoulders as if I were a puppy and gave me a beautiful, warm smile. His skin was naturally bronzed and creased, which gave him an age of around the late fifties but it was hard to tell because he seemed so youthful in spirit. His long grey curls fell over his kind soulful eyes; he seemed so familiar, so incredibly likeable. I told him I adored the Cuban music he was playing; his eyes lit up and he requested I join him on the other side of the bar to choose the next playlist. We chatted to the Spanish men at the bar while we drank our beers, this was their regular hang-out and they loved to be part of the international mix. I expected that the pretty local girls might have been another reason they were drawn here – the girls sashayed in and out, giving the barman high-fives as they passed.

Thanking our new friend, we moved towards the back of the room to explore further. Framed photographs of a young Zepo hung throughout, mapping out a life of travel and heartache. Expertly shot with exquisite detail, the enlarged images revealed their own stories of Zepo living in Morocco surrounded by skinny camels and mountains of sand. Precious moments of an isolated sandy peak, the sunset mirrored in his aviator sunglasses. In other pictures, a small boy in dirty tattered clothes held a handmade toy from food cans, goats tethered to a parched tree and a black-and-white portrait of an old lady wrapped in a black mourning scarf, pain in her eyes as deep as the lines in her skin. These dramatic scenes and the people in them must have made a life-long impression on the barman. Zepo saw me studying the photographs and credited the work as Adrianna's - his photographer girlfriend who also worked at the bar a few days a week.

Barry stood up as soon as we approached the back of the room

"You made it then," Barry said, as he spoke to my breasts. We nodded and smiled. "I'll introduce you to everyone," said Barry as numerous eyes fell upon us through the red smoky haze.

After a quick introduction to Pat, Derek, Shirley, Barbara, John, Doreen, Jackie and Roger, Angie and Neil and of course reintroduced to Miss California Raisin herself little Ruby, I was ready for another drink. Some of the group welcomed us with heartfelt smiles, others nodded, unconvinced that we should be let into their circle. We must have been curious to some of these people, as conversations were reduced to whispers and the odd glance was thrown our way.

"And these two pricks are Lenny and Maxine," said Barry.

Sitting in front of us with their backs turned were the king and queen of the group. Lenny was wildly rock and roll, I could easily picture him signing groupies' cleavages. As the couple turned to face us I could see that he bore an uncanny resemblance to the Scottish comedian Billy Connolly and looked to be in his early fifties. His hair, the colour of tarnished silver, framed his long, tanned face as it lightly brushed his shoulders. He wore an earring and had a greying goatee and of course a statement white blazer with the cuffs rolled up. A thin gold bracelet hung loosely on his manly wrists and a tattoo of a rocket ejected an explosion of stars towards his jewel-encrusted fingers. His nails were flat and shaped like guitar picks - was he as talented as he wanted to portray, I wondered.

Under his dazzling blazer he wore a black shirt, the first three buttons left undone to reveal a shark's tooth necklace on a leather cord and expose springy chest hair that levitated up and down as he smoked his cigarette. He wore jeans but oddly no shoes, which I assumed was part of the Crocodile Dundee image he seemed to be trying to recreate. His tanned, bare feet rested on an unoccupied chair, his shoes nowhere to be seen.

"Well then, who's this *gorgeous* young thing?" said Lenny, in a strong Liverpudlian accent, staring me up and down.

"I'm Georgie."

"I WAS TALKING TO MY WIFE!" boomed Lenny, followed by a tremendous laugh that had everyone else roaring with excitable laughter and I suddenly felt as if I were part of some live audience show from the seventies.

I was pleased I didn't utter another word because just then his wife, Maxine - brushed herself against me, asserting her presence and parting her vamp-red lips in a surprising snarl. I politely smiled and kissed her cheek but felt like I had just met the devil. Maxine flipped out a shiny black concertina flamenco fan and shook back her jet-black hair, which clung to her face and neck. I noticed how profusely she sweated and wondered how much of that sweat had transferred to my skin. She wore a tight black dress over her curvy body and oozed so much cleavage it was as if her breasts were about to explode into a flamenco performance of their own. I spotted Barry keeping a very attentive eye on her chest as she jiggled her chair to make room for mine, trapping me between herself and Lenny. I was now part of a captive audience ready to hear this couple's story.

Both Lenny and Maxine were from Liverpool and had met each other in a pub shortly before they left for Spain. They weren't married but Maxine said she considered this a blessing as it kept Lenny on his toes. They referred to each other as husband and wife and boasted to be more in love now, than when they had first met, four years previously. Maxine went on to explain that she had a tough past that had changed her for the better. But I soon realised that as she told me her life story, it seemed more out of boastfulness than lessons learned.

She had been part of a well-known biker gang back in Liverpool, which didn't surprise me one bit. It wasn't hard to imagine her fueled with adrenalin, gritting her teeth as she straddled her fish-netted legs around a leather-jacketed rider. She had been involved in a few pub brawls, in which some people had been hurt, some got what they deserved, she said. Maxine gave just enough detail to engage me but I felt there was a lot more she wasn't being honest about. I was intrigued by the images of scattered bar stools, arguments in nightclub toilets and whipping hair during bitch fights. Women stealing other women's men - Maxine told me, were often the reason for these fights. I wasn't quite sure whether to believe it all but, fiction or not, she told a good story. She paused to wipe sweat from her brow and neck.

She admitted she had a fierce temper, which had often got her into serious trouble, and she had spent many a night inside a cold Liverpudlian police cell. She had been in a series of violent relationships of which, she admitted, she shouldn't have survived for being beaten so savagely. Now, gazing at Lenny with the eyes of a love-struck teenager she knew he would never hurt her. No, she would kill him first.

Lenny soothed Maxine by leaning across me, rubbing her legs, unaware of how awkward I felt between them. She seemed to bask in the glory of his public affection.

While the rest of the group got more plastered with cheap white wine and more animated with conversations of their own, Lenny decided to open up about his life too. In his mellow accent, he talked about his past marriages and the mistakes he had made with his grown-up children. How Maxine was his soul-mate and how they formed a yin-yang of completeness during sex. He seemed warm, flirtatious and spirited. A man who liked to live life through an immortal body, that wouldn't age or let him down. I was a little wary of his flirting, his over-familiar body language as he encroached my personal space in front of Maxine. From her stories, I was hyper alert that the woman had jealously issues and I wasn't about to get between her and Lenny in any capacity. In an attempt at female reassurance, I moved closer to Jason who was standing behind me chatting to Barry and rubbed his leg so that Maxine would clearly see there was only one man in my life. But she ignored the gesture and pulled me close so that her mouth was millimeters from my ear. Jason turned to me and without noticing the fear on my face saluted his beer in a 'cheers' motion. Maxine whispered intimate things to me about her sexual relationship with Lenny. With pure directness she spilled private details of their sexual activities, the sex toys they used around the house and garden and even in the car. *I made a mental note never to take them up on an offer of a lift.*

Her wiry, sweaty hair brushed my ear, repulsing me enough to jolt back a little. I hoped she might get the hint and stop breathing her exploits at me. But no such luck. Her voice now low and full of lust, she murmured how Lenny satisfied her needs and the extent of his sexual prowess. She held up both hands and mouthed "that's how many orgasms I have" indicating to all ten digits. I winced at what might be coming next, waiting for the next blow of graphic information. She wanted to go further, I could tell, she wanted to shock me. She watched for my reaction, the corner of her mouth playfully curled upwards. Afraid to offend her, I smiled as if this was an ordinary conversation to have with someone I had only just met, and remained passive. Perhaps content at having created tension between us, she released her cobra grip with a quick wink between girlfriends. Jason handed me a fresh beer which I gulped, bewildered as I tried to drown the images in my head.

On the other side of the table from us, Ruby vigorously shook the last drop of white wine from the bottle, her thin arms struggling with the weight of the vessel. She squinted into the bottle in hope that there was more until her equally wasted friend snatched it from her and tried to empty it as if Ruby wasn't up to the job. They both giggled like twelve-year-olds stealing from their parents' booze cabinet. "Zepo!" Ruby yelled across the bar, waving the empty bottle in the air for another. It seemed the ladies were halfway there to getting shitfaced already.

Breaking off a conversation with someone else, Lenny loudly asked me "Georgie! Do you know what's wrong with my wife's legs?"

I wasn't sure if this was a trick question – was there something wrong with Maxine's legs that I hadn't noticed earlier? I glanced at Maxine to gauge a clue. She wiped away a drip of sweat that was creeping down her neck and smiled a knowing look to Lenny, lowering her eyes to him and fluttering her eyelashes as if she was offering herself.

"Em, no I don't," I said, terrified at where this was leading.

"Well, Georgie, the problem with my wife's legs —" he paused for effect, "— is that THEY AREN'T WRAPPED AROUND MY NECK!" At his own joke (and one I was sure had been told a thousand times) Lenny burst into a hysteria of roaring laughter. Maxine rocked forward in her chair and nudged me until her tears of laughter merged with droplets of sweat and she had to dash to the ladies' room to deal with the mascara tidal wave.

Feeling revolted at the mere thought of Lenny's jokes, we charitably laughed our way around the room until we could escape as soon as we finished up our drinks. As we said our goodbyes to the group Maxine hugged me with the strength of two tigers and then threw a sturdy punch into my right arm. I couldn't be sure if this was her way of sealing our friendship or warning me to never overstep any boundaries now we had met. I fearfully smiled back, shaking off the throbbing pain in my bicep. Had I returned the gesture I have no doubt that I wouldn't have walked out of the bar the way I had walked in.

Ruby made her way towards us in a hurry as we were about to walk out of the door. I assumed she wanted to tell us something important before we left as she was almost running. But, "I need a piss!" was all she said as she wobbled towards us, rattling her bones at full pelt in fast little steps. She walked straight past the toilets and smacked, face first, into the red and green stained glass door panel. I wondered if she might have broken her nose but she simply giggled and wobbled off in search of the loo again.

We couldn't stop laughing in the car all the way home. The crowd at Bar Ché were the most eccentric mix of people we had ever met and now I was hooked with the place.

11. OFF THE TOURIST MAP

Before long we became regulars at Bar Ché, bringing along our friends and family whenever they were visiting. They too instantly fell in love with the atmosphere and the warm hospitality of the charismatic barman. During our visits, I wanted to find out more about the man, and we did through his extraordinary stories that had us captivated every time.

Zepo wasn't his birth name but nobody at the bar cared to know about the real man behind the scraggly hair. Customers loved the essence of his character and how that made them feel but their interest never went beyond that. His popularity caused an almost celebrity type of attraction as people of all ages trickled in until the early hours and Zepo was in such demand that it was a wonder he had any time to run a bar at all.

Unfortunately, there were times when the host's kind demeanour was taken advantage of. He could have thrown-out the customers who stole from him, blatantly robbing drinks from the fridge and even from behind the bar but it wasn't in his nature to confront those without a conscience. He was too trusting as he relied on the honesty of his clientele and some were too drunk to realise they were disrespecting the barman.

As well as being a devotee of the fragrant weed, or "za goot sheit" as Zepo liked to call it, he admired and took inspiration from the values of Ché Guevara. Zepo also felt deeply affected by peoples circumstances, and generously gave anything he could to help others.

I'm not sure how far he took his politics but something in that mountainous desert in Morocco pulled him back there every winter.

"The people of Morocco," he once told me "Are indescribably generous – it is the one place where my heart is truly free".

This is perhaps why he chose to dedicate the bar after his icon, Ché.

A short while into our visits Maxine and Lenny disappeared, it was a bizarre exit when everyone assumed they were sticking around. It was rumoured that they had moved further south towards Oliva, where Lenny was hoping to find gardening work but their quick disappearance left an air of suspicion around the bar and I wondered if they would ever make an appearance again.

The warmness from Zepo and his girlfriend Adrianna, made us feel like old friends every weekend that we stopped by.

I would always sneak into the kitchen at the far end of the bar to greet Zepo's long-term girlfriend and cook. Adrianna was French and didn't dress like your average forty-year-old chef. She wore her hair in a loose plait, dark tie-dyed dungarees over an oversized t-shirt and there was always the presence of a paisley-printed bandana, either on her head when she was cooking or around her neck if she wasn't. She topped off her hippie look with a variety of hats she had collected from her travels around the world.

Travel had drawn Adrianna and Zepo together in the first place; they had met in the desert of Morocco whilst exploring with friends. I imagined how romantic that first meeting must have been, the hammer-chest-pound of potential life-long friendship and love under a blanket of stars.

In her thirties, Adrianna had spent a large chunk of her travelling time following the backpacker trail around Asia and Australia and had picked up all her English language from fellow-travellers'. Sometimes when she said particular words the Australian twang got the better of her French accent. I loved to hear such a mix of high and low tones adding another dimension to her colourful soul.

Her facial features were peculiar. She always looked like she had either never slept in her life or just got out of bed, and it would be fair to assume she was just permanently stoned. She had a mouth that was always turned downwards, so when she spoke with her rich French accent she looked and sounded as if she were debating the world's problems. However, this seriousness was only conveyed on the bottom half of her face – all facial muscles and features above that turned upwards, smiling eyes, cheekbones round and full, her eyebrows kissing her bandana. These contradictions made her only the more interesting to me, as if she had been influenced by all the travelling she had done.

Adrianna was always pleased to see me, although sometimes it was hard to tell; when I popped my head into the kitchen, her mouth frowned, making me retreat the way I had come in but just as I turned to leave she would pull me back into the kitchen asking me to taste her latest Moroccan dish. She loved to experiment with her menus and her food was so delicious that it was hard not to salivate just from the kitchen aroma alone. Dining out was affordable at the bar and I often wondered if she wasn't undercharging the value of her talent. But that's what made Bar Ché so desirable; the wonderful cheap food and booze, the cosy décor and lively Cuban music. But mostly, it was the laid-back attitude of the hosts that brought different nationalities together, making bar Ché a place we wanted to return to.

The bar was at its most lucrative over summer, the outside tables in high demand for students wanting late-night meals. When we could get a table, I opted for the same dish almost every time; a tender shank of lamb marinated in a prune and pine-nut sauce served in a traditional conical tagine. I am sure Adrianna wished I was more adventurous with my choices but the lamb was too enticing. When she hired an additional cook to share the responsibilities, she would come and sit with us during her break and show us albums bursting with high-quality photography.

She shot mostly in Black and White Ilford film, in the days before digital made it cheap and instant. Her simple, classic style alighted a passion in me as I felt immersed in her intensely beautiful shots, a window into another world. Even a simple stormy sky landscape had captured a brooding depth that was enormously evocative. And the images of the people she met! - you could see how charmed they were by the woman behind the camera, the way a little boy in tattered clothes had thrown his head back in hysterics and how an old man affectionately smiled, his eyes filled with hope despite his obvious frailty. Adrianna captured extraordinary moments in life with patience and kindness in a way that only someone with years of travel behind them could. It was an impressive portfolio of work and she was touched at how much I appreciated her art when not many others paid an interest.

Zepo continued to trust my musical tastes with his worldly collection while he skinned-up carrot-sized joints behind the bar. Drug use at the bar was moderate and nobody seemed bothered by the clouds of smoke at a time when smoking inside wasn't prohibited. Smouldering incense and other ordinary cigarettes in ashtrays barely helped to disguise the powerful scent of marijuana.

On a couple of occasions we walked in to find two green uniformed Guardia Civil police officers having a beer at the bar during their shift. It unnerved me to see their matt-black guns strapped to their belts and I wondered if the officers' presence ever worried Zepo but he behaved the same with them as he did his usual customers, professional and relaxed, with a joint resting in an ashtray by the till.

We learned then, that it was legal to own a couple of plants for personal consumption and not long after hearing that, I noticed marijuana everywhere. Plants growing in front gardens and tomato bags on balconies. Students smoking on mopeds, couples smoking in outdoor bars, suited men smoking as they waited in traffic on their way to the office. It seemed so normal and acceptable.

Slowly we began to meet younger people at the bar – Dutch, Spanish and a couple of other young Brits. But there seemed to be a common theme which instantly put me off meeting the Brits – they only wanted your friendship to get something else out of you. Their opening gambit, usually a sales pitch of some pyramid-scheme they want you to participate in, which instantly turned me away from them.

As the summer became more hectic at the bar, Zepo hired temporary staff to ease his workload. He took on a Spanish couple – a tall and slightly bulbous-eyed twenty-two-year-old man from Barcelona called Marco and his girlfriend, a dark-haired porcelain complexioned girl called Anna.

Marco was slim and energetic with a hint of eccentric theatrics about him. He bounced flamboyantly around tables, massaged the male customers' shoulders, screamed when something excited him. He had a wonderfully elegant way of walking in his Cuban heels, pulling his elbows into his side. Anna, the more reserved and seemingly offish type, frowned at his hands-on approach but the customers seemed enchanted at the attention and exceptional service. As Marco didn't speak any language other than his own, he communicated to foreign customers through the art of mime. It was a stroke of genius trickery in my book and forced his customers to use what Spanish they did know to reply back. The more they were mocked the more they loved him.

Marco's favourite way to greet Jason was to run up to him and repeatedly slap him on his balding head while humming the tune to *The Benny Hill Show*, and run away again. It always amused me to see the irritated look on Jason's face and the pleasure it gave Marco. Another time he worked an entire shift with a fake rubber penis poking out of his trouser leg. It gave him little moments of joy to raise his foot upon a customer's chair so that the rubber cock and balls made an appearance. Marco loved the customers' reactions but Anna grew less impressed every time.

After spending some time at the bar a friendship emerged between us all and we took Marco and Anna up on an offer of a sightseeing tour. They took us to hidden waterfalls in Buñol where the famous *La Tomatina* tomato-throwing fiesta usually occurs at the end of summer. We climbed up to secret caves and jumped off ledges into the sparkling emerald water below and strolled through wooded parks taking photos of historic abandoned churches. And while we scrambled our way through thick foliage, we came upon crumbling ruins that we dreamt of restoring for our next venture.

On another occasion, we met Anna and Marco at a funfair where we watched the locals buy canvas hammocks and launch wooden balls at coconuts for prizes. We tried our hand at 'shooting ducks', the mechanical targets moving too fast for our air-powered rifles. I fired the gun with great satisfaction only for the plastic bullet to deflect on the metal duck, shooting myself back in the eye. Jason convulsed with laughter as he pointed at my weeping eye, unable to believe my bad-luck rebound.

Additional trips took us to a bull farm where we gazed over a fence to watch cute baby bulls trotting around in their pen. We dipped our feet in green lagoons and listened to the intense noise of mating bullfrogs nestled within swampy reeds. We even braved our first bull run in the streets of our local village. The pounding weight of mighty beasts thundering towards us and veering around corners and into narrow streets. Young boys attempted to be macho in front of their friends by confronting the bulls as close as they dared, only to retreat in squeals when the bulls came too close. One teenager threw a plastic chair at the bull that bounced off, and even though I knew it most likely wouldn't have hurt the bull, it still made me furious at the intention of hurting it.

On a cloudier day, we met up with our friends in the outskirts of a traditional Valencian village, where we were taken to an Aladdin's cave of Spanish antiques. The shop was conceived from a small existing cave where the internal rock had been painstakingly carved to form a high oval ceiling.

Once inside, with a nod from the owner, we scattered ourselves around the trinkets and glass cabinets, all the while observed by the shop owner who had a permanent look of disapproval. He seemed to take an instant dislike to our young and inquisitive minds. I ran my hands over rich dark oak furniture lined with blood-red fabrics and traced my finger along the carved arm of a stunning baroque throne. Gold trinkets and candlesticks looked dull in the poor light of the cave; oil paintings dramatised religious stories of torture or wealth. Jason stood by a life-size bullfighter in full traditional costume and examined the craftsmanship of the stitching. Anna blushed as she spotted Marco under a niche archway, attempting to dance with a medieval suit of armour. We departed before the shop owner could show us the door with a stern finger, and made our way to the nearest coffee bar.

Spending time with Marco and Anna proved to be invaluable to us. We practised our Spanish, they learned some English swear-words, and we got a real taste of hidden Spain - off the tourist map. There was nothing synthetic about the environment and culture we were experiencing.

Late one Saturday night we met up with Marco and Anna in a bar. Marco wanted to take us to a special club he knew well, informing us that the owner was an old friend and could get us in for free. Guests were invited by personal recommendation only, which seemed so secretive I wondered what we were getting ourselves into. We squeezed into Marco's yellow Seat and drove out beyond the bright lights and into rural darkness. I was a little confused, what kind of club would be situated outside the city and away from transport links? We drove into a tree-lined side street, past rural farm buildings and up a dusty track road. Eventually, after what seemed like an hour's drive into no-man's-land, we rolled into a wide parking area. A few cars were present but it certainly didn't look like a place where we were going to have a jolly night out. I wondered if there had been a miscommunication.

When we got out of the car the air was cooler. I heard music but couldn't place which direction it was coming from. In the darkness we all walked towards a building – all I could see was a very grand and private mansion that was covered in thick foliage. Marco excitedly skipped forward toward the house, as we trailed trustingly behind him.

High on the roof, an orange neon *Harley-Davidson* sign pulsated in the darkness. Underneath another sign read *Blue Biker Bar* in dazzling blue neon, accompanied by a shiny chrome motorbike engine that was hanging from glistening chains.

Just as I was wondering if Marco had brought us to an electrifying gay club, two familiar faces emerged from behind another car. A bouncy Zepo dressed in his trademark skin-tight black jeans and slender grey t-shirt looking like a rock star and beside him, an exhausted-looking Adrianna wearing a porkpie hat and purple hippie slacks, who greeted us with her warm and familiar downturned smile. It was wonderful to see them in different surroundings other than Bar Ché.

Adrianna explained that the building, formally a normal, residential home been converted into a nightclub that only permitted exclusive guests recommended by trusted friends. Its deserted location was key to its success – as it had to remain under the radar because it wasn't a legally-run establishment. This secrecy made the mansion only the more alluring. I stared up at the foliage camouflaging the building and wondered how anyone could convince themselves it *was* a normal, residential home. Weren't the blazing neon logos an obvious enough sign?

As we approached the huge set of leafy garden gates, I noticed a cluster of abandoned motorbikes leaned heavily on their stands. Scratched helmets lay cuffed to the wheels with little respect for the safety they might bring.

Marco excitedly announced our arrival over the intercom and immediately the iron gates extended inwards revealing two chisel-jawed bouncers. They recognized Marco with a nod, and we walked through like royalty.

The mansion was as dramatic in splendour as it was kitsch.

Tropical flowers and palms flooded the grounds. Planted with such expertise it was as if, we had stepped into a five-star honeymoon oasis.

Earlier arrivals were dotted around sparingly, the very essence of an architectural model brought to life. White fluorescent tube lights spiralled around tall palm trees into the night's sky. Immaculately manicured lawns provided grassy islands with pub benches, where groups of good-looking students sat and drank cocktails in their smart-casual attire. Some wandered the cobblestone paths, wine in hand following a route that led towards an impressive Grecian-style swimming pool by the right of the mansion.

My eyes were on stalks, and I was set adrift. I noticed how the submerged pool lights made the surface shimmer in silvery glitter. At one end of the vast pool stood a pair of white marble pillars, illuminated by spotlights in the floor. Grecian pillars in any other garden would have looked ridiculous but here they only added to the magnetism of the place. At the other end of the pool, a more subtly lit bamboo structure hosted another lounge area of soft sofas and low bamboo coffee tables.

Whilst wandering around like Alice in a Blue Biker Wonderland, I had inadvertently detached myself from the rest of the group. Drawn by the sight before me, I had difficulty believing this was a genuine, functioning club and not part of some reality television show. As I strolled around the tiled pool area, I saw a group of beautiful girls - possibly models, wearing tiny white PVC skirts and matching bikini tops diving into the glistening swimming pool. One of the girls casually submerged herself into the water, still wearing her skirt. I watched as she made her way from one end of the pool to the other in a single breath. The strands of her long dark hair slicked to her back as she glided over the black and white mosaic tiles. When she silently emerged up at the other end and propped herself up on the pool edge, not a smudge of makeup had absconded from her eyes and her skin looked almost dry.

I stood there with my mouth gaping as these slim tanned bodies slipped around each other. I was living inside a man's creation, someone else's fantasy. I smiled to myself and wondered how many teenage boys would give their right arm to be standing where I was now. Feeling a bit overwhelmed (and overdressed) I realised it was time for a drink. A quick scan around had me heading for the bar, which was where I found Jason staring in just as much disbelief.

To facilitate the bar, part of the exterior wall of the mansion had been removed, the weight of the upper floors supported by three impressive columns that lead to a generously-staffed, eye-shaped bar. The bar was situated so that one side could be accessed by garden drinkers and the other from the dance floor - an area that had previously been the enormous living room until its conversion for more useful, raving purposes.

I tried to imagine the person behind the fantasy. Who was he? A big-time football player, a hotshot banker or maybe a young internet entrepreneur?

We bought some pricy beers and wandered around the landscaped paths until we came to a wrought iron spiral staircase wrapped in fairy lights, leading to a small terrace. We climbed the ornate steps, drinks in hand and gazed at the view. From the mezzanine, it was apparent just how wonderfully isolated the mansion was from other villas. I appreciated its secrecy then, my initial suspicion overridden by pure atmospheric indulgence. We managed snippets of conversation between loud songs that pulsated through the platform. A few drink-rounds later, feeling more relaxed, we all made our way to the dance floor. The DJ exchanged places with another, bringing a fresh playlist of Spanish hits we had got to know so well. While we were dancing, Zepo jumped in to show us his moves. For a mature guy, he still had *the moves* and out-danced the rest of us until we were exhausted and he kept going.

Marco weaved past me and as he did, screamed in my ear.

"El Jefe ha llegado!" - The boss has arrived!

Through the bobbing heads, I raised on my tiptoes to get my first peek at the infamous club owner as he was circulating the bar. I was astonished that he was a lot older than I had imagined. Spain's very own Hugh Hefner in his Playboy Palace. The mansion owner greeted his guests as warmly as Zepo greeted his at Bar Ché, so it seemed no surprise that the two of them were old friends according to Adrianna. As guests retrieved drinks, the owner moved around the floor receiving almost star-struck looks from the room. His hair was scraped back in a short ponytail, sleek grey strands taking over youthful black ones. He looked elegant in his comfortably-fitted black shirt and jeans, a long silver pocket chain looped from his back pocket to the front. For a man of his maturity, he had a quality about him. The face of an old cowboy movie star who never loses the ability to charm. His handsomeness - once beautiful - had weathered in time. The girls didn't seem to mind that he leered a little too long at them, some were clearly smitten by the attention as they trailed behind him and he glided through the crowd charming the guys' with the same warm greeting. He checked in on the bar staff, perhaps to see if all was well before making his way towards our group and falling into Zepo's open arms, exchanging in an affectionate back slapping ritual and finally being introduced to us as, Toni. Zepo grinned fondly as Toni asked us what we thought of his paradise raising both palms upwards and simultaneously we all nodded in approval and promptly received an invite to future parties.

We talked and danced and grew tired. None of us had noticed that night had dissolved into day and at six o'clock the next morning we made our way back to the car park, sleepy and dehydrated. I looked back at the house – above the neon Harley-Davidson sign, a shadow of movement caught my eye. A silhouette of a dancing couple in one of the bedrooms made me wonder if old Toni had got lucky that night.

***

The months pushed on, and Jason and I became more focused on long-term plans for our time in Valencia. We were happy with the friends we had met and enjoyed exploring our new surroundings. But at times it seemed that our life here didn't have much stability to it. Just as we had made friends, Spain's unstable economic situation forced a change so that people needed to migrate and find work elsewhere. Before we knew it, Marco and Anna's jobs had finished along with the season. As autumn emerged, Bar Ché closed and its owners packed up their tatty old Jeep to head south to their beloved Moroccan desert. Marco and Anna soon discovered that after a few weeks of each other's unemployed company they were mismatched after all and decided it was best to break up. Within a few days, they had packed up their apartment and left separately to find work in other areas of Spain. The last we heard was that Anna had disappeared on her moped, making her way north to Barcelona and Marco tried to find work locally but found it difficult and he too drifted away. It seemed unlikely either would return to Valencia any time soon.

As Marco and Anna made new plans to start over separately and our friendly bar owners had another exciting journey ahead, we were left feeling a little abandoned. It was with real sadness that our friendships were uprooted when they had only just been secured. It wasn't easy to make friends when we didn't have regular jobs and a good grip on the language. It left us feeling frustrated and we missed our friends back home.

Despite our loss, we were feeling more settled in the country and Spanish life became our "normal". We noticed that a new closeness was beginning to emerge between us too, a closeness that holidays and weekends alone hadn't been enough time to bond us together. Our constant proximity to each other brought often conflicting challenges so it was easy to let minor irritations blow up into something monumental, but we were finally getting to know and understand each other's true and honest selves.

We had flittering nerves about our future in Spain. However deeply we worried about our unchartered future, we tried to remain positive. We told ourselves that as long as there were opportunities here in Spain we could still make things happen.

12. CHRISTMAS DAY PUPPIES

It had been decided that we would spend Christmas with my parents, in Galicia - a nine hundred and fifty-kilometre scenic journey north-west that would take around nine hours.

We assured ourselves that the trip would be good for us, and the distance from Valencia would give us some perspective on what to do with our future.

The next evening, while my mother and Joseph agreed to watch over the menagerie we had brought with us, Jason and I treated ourselves to a night out in the delightful historic town of Betanzos for some traditional Galician food. It felt so familiar being back, for the reason that every summer during my teenage years my parents had driven to this hidden medieval village in their VW Camper van from the UK. My stepsister and I had squabbled over handsome, tanned boys on mopeds and ate pistachio ice cream under the carved stone arches of the cafes. I remembered how often I had lost direction in the eucalyptus forests, usually to distance myself from the arguments with my stepsister and how being temporarily stranded and alone in those deep forests never seemed to bother me, a curious teenager exploring the world.

Jason and I parked ourselves at a high table in a cobbled side street where we sipped wine and the nostalgic feeling shrouded me once again as I recalled the memories of good family times. I remembered when my mother remarried again and how her marriage to a Spaniard had opened my cultural perspectives. New siblings, a language with many regional dialects and a country that produced such interesting and varied foods was exciting to me. I was introduced to strange cured meats, fish and cheeses and my parents allowed me to sample regional wines occasionally. My stepsister and I had giggled every time my parents asked us to set the table for lunch, with bread, pâté, jamón, "And don't forget the *titty* cheese," they would say, referring to Queso de Teta - a plump mound of soft creamy cheese that peaked on the top and tasted divine. I felt rather sentimental sitting at the same spot under the twinkling lights as an adult with Jason, listening to the Latin vibes coming from the restaurant.

I boldly ordered the octopus which had been bubbling away in a large copper pot. Its chewy texture made eating it hard work, but I loved Galician seafood and the dish had a subtle flavour, more delicate than its extraterrestrial appearance would suggest. The first time I tried pulpo I was thirteen and had to give it a few attempts before I was truly happy to eat it. Octopus looks rather horrifying to the average British person, with its purple outer skin and fleshy rubbery interior. It's one of those foods that you're aware it may become a choking hazard the moment it enters your mouth so you weigh up the risk of trying it and hoping your dining partner will be competent at the Heimlich manoeuver, should you need it.

Once the octopus is cooked, it is hooked out of the boiling cauldron and roughly grappled by a rubber-gloved cook as if it still might be alive, it's firmly held down, hacked up and served on a wooden plate with a dash of olive oil and a sprinkling of salt.

I couldn't resist attaching the suckers to my tongue and wiggling the tentacles at Jason as he sliced into his Galician steak. We raised our wine glasses to the familiar chant Joseph had taught us, "¡*Salud, Amor y Dinero!*" to health, love and money.

We returned to my parent's village a couple of hours later and all seemed quiet from the outside. However, in the living room, Maximus was tearing around my mum's newly upholstered sofa and, as if that wasn't enough to irritate her, he had spent the best part of the evening sitting behind her head on the sofa so that he could batt her hair clip. This pleasurable taunt had kept the cat occupied for hours at my mother's expense. Too afraid to move from the sofa she sat, frozen, mocked by a cat she was never going to like. We joined my parents in the sitting room but as soon as I sat down nausea came over me.

My stomach groaned. I felt the octopus writhe and flip itself over inside. It was too late a thought but perhaps it hadn't been a good idea to mix pulpo with three large glasses of Rioja. A cold sweat followed. I ran upstairs to the bathroom, my stepdad shouting after me, not to strain myself.

It's rather hard *not* to strain oneself whilst vomiting up a purple sea creature. Aggressive contractions pumped the rubbery chunks forward with every heave; undigested suckers dotted the toilet bowl at an alarming rate. Staring at the creature that made me so ill, I knew I would never look at an octopus in the same way again, my appreciation for it had now been replaced with repulsion. I took a few gulps of air and appreciated the relief before heading back downstairs. I felt sure that pulpo was not meant to be eaten by non-natives. These Galician's must have the stomachs of Vikings.

Unable to speak from the soreness in my throat I flopped in the doorway waiting for the sickness to dissipate. I watched as my mum poured Jason a glass of wine while he soothed an irritated Maximus back to a calm state. The kitten, still offended by our earlier departure on a night out, had more assaults planned. Maximus lunged, teeth bared, attaching himself to the left side of Jason's jaw bone. With piercing strength, he hung from Jason's agonised face as we looked on helplessly. After a few grisly seconds, Jason managed to detach and fling the kitten onto the sofa. Maximus gave Jason a backwards glance, before hopping down and sweetly curling around my ankles. I heard my mother mutter, "I hate that cat" as I defensively scooped Maximus into my arms.

Two days later on 25th December 2003, at approximately seven am Christmas morning, Macey gave birth to eight plump puppies each packaged in their amniotic sacs. Jason vigilantly stayed by her side as she birthed them, none of which bore any resemblance to her. Half were chocolate-brown and had abnormally short stumpy tails. Three others had a mix of black and tan markings and normal-length tails. And then there was the last one, small and jet black - the runt of the litter, whom I fell in love with instantly. Jason was over the moon with the new arrivals but I worried for them the moment they were born which wasn't helped by the fact that Macey wasn't an overly maternal mother – retreating into the corner to avoid them suckling.

The surprise birth had happened in the hallway of my parents' house when we hadn't anticipated her to deliver for at least another week. The remaining placenta that hadn't been cleaned-up by Macey had somehow made its way halfway up the walls, much to my mother's annoyance - indicated by her rolling eyes, although she didn't complain once.

On Boxing Day we nibbled on Spanish turrón, cheeses and marzipan cakes, while we sat in my parent's sunny courtyard basking in a patch of sunshine. The puppies were all tucked up and quiet giving us a moment to catch up over a fresh pot of coffee.

My parents had moved to Spain a year before us. They wanted to enjoy their retirement and for Joseph it was a matter of rekindling his love for the place he grew up in before he fled to London as so many others did in the sixties.

With his Spanish-London accent and Al Pacino looks Joseph announced, "When they're ready, we'll take the biggest one you've got," referring to the puppies. He had been quietly selecting one as a guard dog.

Joseph licked along the liquorice gum strip of the cigarette paper he was rolling, sealed it and then tapped the end twice on the table before lighting it - his head sharply cocked at an angle.

"Watch how they develop, if there's a dominant one that stands out, I want it. It can scare the shit out of *him*," he thumbed towards the ugly grey cement house opposite. My parents had an ongoing land dispute with a vile and idiotic neighbour and Joseph thought the threat of a guard dog would be a good way of stopping the neighbour from flinging dead rats and dog shit onto their pathway each day.

We talked about the property market in Spain and how our lives needed to change for the better. My parents had been developing properties for most of their lives and knew enough about the Spanish market to give us direction if we felt we were ready to buy in a different location. It was fantastic to have their support and enthusiasm to pick us up when we felt a little lost.

A day later, we all were beginning to grow weary of the demands of the animals and the mess they caused. The puppies wriggled and constantly spilt from the overcrowded basket as Macey avoided feeding, not helped by the cat who had taken up residence in the same basket for warmth and the dog did not dare throw him out. My parents stepped delicately around their house to avoid any fatalities and understandably they grew impatient with the mayhem so we decided to depart early for Valencia to avoid any fallouts. My parents seemed relieved at our decision to leave although my mum tried her best not to cry as she always did when we departed. In the blue-grey light of dawn, we did a last-minute headcount and, with ten animals secure in the boot of the car, we headed back to Valencia through the beautiful snow-capped mountains of Madrid.

13. A POTENTIAL PARADISE

A few months into the New Year we decided we would sell the Monrabana villa and move on. Although we had enjoyed the previous summer, the house was proving insufficient for our needs. The urbanisation had its faults too; the barking guard dogs had become unbearable to the point of being unable to sleep throughout the night. The gravel roads, street lighting and telecommunications were all pending completion – the promise of these services looked as if it was never going to materialise. I grew tired of typing-up emails on my home computer, storing it on a stick drive and having to drive to an internet café just to send it. Internet on our old mobiles was primitive too and we concluded that a move would give us more options for improving these things. Besides, the Monrabana house was only ever meant as the first step on the property ladder in Spain and we were free to go where we liked.

Macey's puppies were growing at an astonishing rate and chewed their way out of everything, including their purpose-built kennel that Jason had constructed from reclaimed wooden doors. This was situated in a dry, warm area by the storerooms and offered plenty of shade and garden play areas, in addition to giving us some distance from the mountain of waste they deposited every day. The pups soon got bored and regularly broke free of their shelter to explore, potentially putting themselves at risk of injury. One particular puppy, a female bruiser – independent and assertive - ascertained places of weakness in the pen and broke through it. As soon as Jason had secured the breach and walked away the resourceful puppy found a way to beat his repair. We updated my stepdad, Joseph with this news and he was so impressed with her devious ways, he requested to keep the dog aside for him.

The dog was named Coco, because of her chocolate and caramel fur and wildly instinctive personality.

When the remaining seven puppies were old enough and weaned from Macey's ragged nipples, we placed them in a cardboard box and made an emotional journey to a dog rescue centre. Jason and I had both been debating, arguing and dreading what to do with them. The very small amount of people we knew, already had taken in stray dogs and understandably didn't want any more. Through our research, we found a reputable establishment knowing that puppies were more likely to be rehomed than older ones. The staff assured us that most of the pups would be trained for work purposes and wouldn't be put down. It was even likely some would be trained as police dogs as they appeared to have Alsatian characteristics. We paid the rescue home a contribution towards their keep and handed over the box of squirming puppies. The staff cooed and pulled the puppies out of the box one by one and as we walked away I forced myself not to look back. I felt as if I was the worst person in the world, but our attachment would only deepen should we put it off. As I put on my seat belt in the car I sobbed with guilt at how wrong it felt to give them up. Three days later my parents came down from Galicia to collect Coco and although I felt sorry to admit it, I felt enormously relieved to have just Macey and Maximus in the household once again.

A month later we popped out for our usual coffee and food shop in our nearest town. The streets were chaotic with market traders and locals queuing at the Churros pastry stall. We casually walked by an estate agent's window and stopped to glance at the properties on offer - which had become somewhat of a habit since deciding we wanted to move. There was only a small selection this time, mostly horrid boxy apartments that never seemed to sell.

Then a house at the very top of the agent's window caught my eye. It was a cream, four-bedroom, two-storey, detached country house with wooden shutters, located in a place we'd never heard of - Chulilla. It was surrounded by pine trees in dense woodland, in a mountainous area of natural beauty. My heart leapt at the price – it was affordable and in desperate need of modernisation. Barely able to contain my excitement, I knew instantly this was the opportunity we had been waiting for and we had to go and view it.

We stepped inside the doorway and introduced ourselves to the estate agent who offered us a Marlborough Red cigarette, we declined and he lit one up for himself.

Vincente was a short, smartly dressed handsome man with smiling brown eyes and boyish features. He insisted we spoke English with him as he needed the practice due to an increase in British clients. I looked around and noticed the lack of a computer, and soon after that, I noticed the lack of an office. The entire space of the estate agent's premises was as small as a cleaning cupboard and was barely able to accommodate a desk, two chairs and a wastepaper bin. A calculator, along with a pile of mobile phones, seemed to be the only presence of technology.

We pointed to the house in the window.

"We would like to see this house in Chulillia," I said, not quite knowing how to say the name.

"*Choo Lee Ya,*" the estate agent corrected me. "In Spanish, the two L's are pronounced as a Y, so it's *Chulilla.*"

"*Choo Lee Ya,*" I repeated and asked again if we could see the house now that I had got the pronunciation correct.

"You want to see that house? Are you sure?" Vincente said without a hint of a salesman's skill.

"Yes, we would like to see it today. Is it far from here?" I said eagerly.

Vincente took three quick successive drags on the last centimetre of his cigarette and dropped it on the floor. He squinted the way a TV detective might as he exhaled a plume of smoke, smothering a framed photograph on the wall of a little girl's Confirmation. I was startled by her Technicolor pink cheeks and boundless curls.

"Not far, twenty minutes. But first I must tell you, that the property does not have a boundary." Vincente paused as if hoping this might put us off. He was possibly the worst salesman I had ever met.

I looked at Jason, a little confused, then back at Vincente.

"You mean it doesn't have a fixed legal boundary or it doesn't have a fence?" I asked.

"No, it does not have a fence, wall, or anything."

I couldn't see why this was even being discussed. Impatience nagged at me. "That's OK, we can put a fence in. But it must have a telephone line, I can't live without that, does it have one?"

"I am not sure, but we can go now, I have keys somewhere. It is the owner's second home, the husband was old, a doctor, but he died…" Vincente abruptly stopped short of the end of his sentence as he rummaged in a metal cash box until he pulled out a set of keys from a hundred others.

I wondered if this might be fate's way of finding us the perfect house. Without even planning it, our market and coffee morning had turned into a dream house viewing.

In Vincente's old banger we headed up the CV35 dual carriageway towards a place called Ademuz. I thought about the mountain hideaway we were about to see. From the aerial photographs in the estate agent window it looked secluded but not totally isolated as there were five other houses a hundred meters or so apart scattered on the side of the mountain. Each house was surrounded by dense woodland at different heights. I thought it looked utterly magical in its wooded surroundings and we hoped it had masses of potential as we were looking for a development project. It was stuck in a seventies time warp, however, unchanged from the moment it had been built. I tried to imagine how all the rooms looked, how much work there was to be done. The estate agent gave us very little information as he threw the car from left to right climbing further into the mountains. I put those fears to the back of my mind about the old doctor dying and hoped that Vincente wasn't about to tell us he had died in the house. Would that put me off even if the house had potential?

We drove towards the hidden village of Chulilla. As we glimpsed between the blur of olive trees, it became apparent that the village had developed around expansive volcanic mountains and impregnated itself into the rock-face. An oasis born from a scar, deep in the mountain crevice. It was hard to believe given the location, just forty minutes inland from Valencia city. Even though our current house was only a short drive away we had no idea this place existed and unlike other parts of rural Valencia, which can be unimpressive, blighted by a scattering of industrial buildings - this was far from that. The further we headed into the shadow of the mountains the more I wanted to explore. We passed agricultural fields of leafy vines and crooked olive trees and as I wound down the window I was instantly hit with the persistent odour of onions. We veered around tractors on windy roads and I was struck how non-commercial it was. Local farmers were bent double in terracotta fields, harvesting crops like a scenic oil painting.

I was instantly impressed by the precision of the stone terraced walls and how the trees were saturated with heavy oranges. Palm trees, yucca and cacti plants were abundant everywhere. And then there was the intoxicating smell, a mixture of orange blossom and pine that no air freshener could replicate.

"What a fantastic film location this place would make," I commented as we drove past a monumental jagged cliff face, an impressive backdrop to any production. The estate agent pointed to a pair of red squirrels as they leapt from a tree, then twirled around it, in a cartoon chase.

"The house is up there at the top, with some other villas," said Vincente, pointing to nothing in particular but towards a steep part of the pine forest high on the mountain.

"Is it possible for us to see the village, quickly? You said it wasn't far from the house,"

"OK," Vincente shrugged, in a not-so-bothered way.

We veered around a bend, past a rustic-looking restaurant, and a place called Tony's Bar. We drove into an area of uniquely built villas, all slightly different in style, facing towards a deep Jurassic valley and a river flowing below. I imagined the residents would never be disappointed with the view from their windows. A moment later we passed through a pretty whitewashed medieval village. Houses unsteadily stacked, some in the process of being renovated. Each property was plastered with snow-white emulsion and adorned with a variety of bright flowers.

Crowning the top of the village was an ancient medieval walled castle. Islamic and Roman in origin - we were told, dating back to 13th century. Once it had been the protector of the village, now all that remained was the crumbling dungeons and lookout turrets, its ascending path worn from decades of tourists seeking a glimpse of its past.

In the distance, we could make out rock climbers clinging by dexterous fingers. They climbed up the burnt-orange rock face of the gorge before gently slipping the rope, gliding to the bottom. The river below these prehistoric walls had in time, carved its own path. Pooling in a wide expanse creating a beautiful blue lagoon. There was so much to feast the eyes on, and probably years of exploring to do.

Vincente turned the car around and we drove out of the village, climbing a road with such a steep incline I feared the car might roll backwards when Vincente dropped a gear.

"This mountain here is called La Muela- meaning 'the molar'- like a tooth," He went on to explain that the mountain was flat at the top and the foot populated with detached weekend homes. The road levelled out for a few meters around a sharp bend before rising up another steep incline. The terrain was so uneven the car violently rocked from side to side causing me to bump my head on the window. I wondered if this access road was a settled landslide.

As we approached a dense area of pine forest the road flattened and Vincente pulled the car to the side.

"We are now more than four hundred meters above sea level," he stated, matter-of-factly.

As soon as we arrived at the house I felt absurd happiness. The villa was spread over one level but deceptively had the look of a two-story country house from the front. Only, the lower floors were large storage rooms that had been built into the rocks.

As expected the house was neglected, dead plants had impregnated their roots to the outer walls and there were bare patches where the plaster had fallen off around the windows.

We walked around the exterior of the property while Vincente fiddled with the door lock. The garden was an untamed plot of borderless land - the parameters marked by yellow spikes at each corner, making it clear where the boundary lay. There was plenty of potential surrounding the property; car-parking, wood storage, space for a large swimming pool, barbecue and sun lounging. Most exciting of all, at the far back of the garden we noticed a cluster of Jurassic boulders that had once fallen from the top of the molar. Tree's had grown around them and leaned dangerously at angles. Heavy rain had washed channels into the mud around the rocks causing the area to retreat in a sunken pocket. If the trees were thinned a little we could build a cabin hideaway.

The garden had three terraced levels – small enough to manage, unlike the dry crust of unmanageable land we had in the Monrabana Villa. As well as hundreds of pine trees populating the area there were fragrant bushes of rosemary and wild thyme. They were leggy and dry from nature's neglect but with some attention, they could be revived. The garden had many possibilities for landscaping – I just wasn't so sure about tackling the mound of soil that someone had piled up in a heap behind the house and hoped the doctor wasn't buried under it.

We joined Vincente inside the house and I walked around the

property in a state of almost deranged, pleasure. In the lounge, my heart skipped a beat on seeing an expanse of panoramic windows with tatty colonial shutters. Vincente educated us on the traditional styled arched ceiling, listing the raw materials that had gone into creating each perfect curve between the beams.

I stared lovingly at the drab interior, imagining what tones would bring the features back to life. To the right of the windows, four more shuttered doors lead to a large exterior space of a terraced balcony - the size of a lounge that faced the dusty track road and mountains beyond.

The three of us stepped out onto the balcony. There was an odd scene here; rows of yellow wooden school chairs all faced the same direction as if they might have been occupied only moments before. We all fell silent assuming the belief of something paranormal. Perhaps it was best to not overthink my theories of cult meetings or séance gatherings high up on this mountain. Vincente lit another cigarette and motioned for us to take ourselves around the rest of the house while he made a phone call.

We looked in on the kitchen, small and narrow, decorated with yellow corn-on-the-cob illustrated wall tiles coated in coagulated fat. The cupboards and worktops were all outdated, there would be nothing to salvage here.

I took myself down the narrow corridor, peeking briefly through all four-bedroom doorways. I found Jason tapping the wall between two impractically small bathrooms and hoped he was working how to knock the rooms into one. The plumbing situation was complicated. By the looks of it, someone had taken a sledgehammer to the sink in a rage until it slumped to the floor, its pipes straining and grossly bent under the weight. I remembered Vincente's reluctance at showing us the house, to begin with, and wondered if this had been the reason why. Most buyers would not want to tackle this much work.

The décor was hideously oppressive; smothered in dark green

patterned tiles in one bathroom and dark blue tiles in the other with a coloured suite to match. We moved on, making our way to the large bedroom situated at the end of the corridor. The bedroom's white walls had yellowed with time. An ugly pair of striped orange curtains hung eerily to the floor, torn and scarred as if a wild dog had tried to claim them. The sunny mountain landscape view from the window was lovely, however. I took in every detail of the landscape and sighed at the thought of how marvellous it would be wake up to.

I was distracted by a frighteningly large and grotesque lacquered wooden crucifix hanging on the wall above a sagging double bed. Jesus's lifeless body hung from nailed wrists and bled above where the occupants had once slept. The bedroom, which I assumed was the master suite, was sparsely furnished, with just a chair by the window and a copy of the Bible under a shade-less lamp on a table. The room was completely drained of all colour and it struck me then that it couldn't have looked more like the bedroom from *The Exorcist*. The authenticity of this was confirmed as I tiptoed over to the bed and saw what could have only been a pool of dried blood on the middle of the mustard bedspread. I stared in disbelief, half expecting to see the blood coming from Jesus himself. Was I crazy to disregard this house of horrors as a potential paradise?

Apart from the apparent evidence of mass murder in the bedroom little else could dampen my spirits and love for the place. It had so much potential in an area that was stunning, peaceful and surrounded by nature.

Jason assessed the crime scene on the bed and tried to reassure me with, "It's probably nothing, a nose bleed or something." He shrugged, seemingly not bothered by the discovery and peered into the dark built-in wardrobe. I reasoned to myself that *if* this had been someones next-to-final resting place there couldn't really be a nicer more peaceful place to be in.

I tried to calm myself from the excitement, I certainly hadn't felt like this with the first house. We conspired, sharing our ideas and thoughts away from Vincente's ears. Jason seemed as besotted with the villa despite its flaws as I was. It certainly had the potential for the perfect restoration job but with one difference – we would keep the house for ourselves and would not sell it.

We couldn't imagine our lives without it and so from that moment on, an adventure was stirring in the pine-scented wind.

Throwing his cigarette onto the balcony floor and grinding it out with the tip of his shoe, Vincente looked up as we joined him. He seemed pleased with himself.

"I have good news. I called the telephone company and they can put a phone line here within a few days, if you still want the house, that is?"

14. ALL OR NOTHING

We were astonished when, a few days later our silly offer, hugely under the asking price, was accepted. I couldn't believe our luck.

Meanwhile, the Monrabana villa got an exterior facelift with a fresh spray of white paint and in keeping with doing things the Spanish way, we put a hand-painted 'Se Vende' - Sale sign on the gate so the locals could pop in. I spent a few days dressing the rooms for photographing and translated all my sales copy to hand over to the estate agents.

Although the market was a buoyant one, we still needed to do much of the groundwork ourselves. Estate agents seemed to do so little, that at times I wondered how they ever managed to sell houses in the first place. My frustration levels bubbled away. I was appalled when I ended up having to help one estate agent turn on a computer because she didn't know how; she looked horrified when I handed over a CD with my own selection of photographs, her baffled face hidden behind a mask of fury as she huffed and puffed and tutted at me, making me feel as if I was a huge inconvenience.

It took around a month for the house to be properly advertised with no fewer than thirteen agencies around Valencia. We hoped and waited for a quick, pain-free sale.

Over the following four months, we spent our time doing odd jobs around Monrabana. Tidying the house and picking up the mess that the fruit trees constantly dropped. We lost hours cleaning and waiting for estate agents to turn up with their clients, only to be left waiting until the sun went down with no apologetic phone call. One Spanish estate agent in particular, who could have passed for Danny DeVito's body double had cancelled viewings so often that even he was finding it hard to come up with excuses. When the last of his clients cancelled he knew he had to go ahead with the viewing in order to keep us happy. He turned up an hour late, wearing a promotional straw hat for Amstel beer, which looked like it had long since lost its shape under a steamroller. The agent didn't bother to introduce his client to us – an equally short lady in a coral knitted sweater who waddled around the garden looking slightly lost. The client, it turned out, was not a client after all but the agent's own mother. We found this out because we asked her what she thought of the villa, she told us that she wasn't interested in buying a house; her son had just promised her a drive out for the afternoon followed by lunch.

My father and stepmother Lynda came out for a short break so they could visit Chulilla and see for themselves why we had fallen for the place. We took them to the village and they too were enchanted by it, their excitement fuelled our confidence in knowing we were making the right decision. Their holiday was good timing for us as it meant we could have extra hands painting the balustrades on the pool terrace while we were still waiting for the villa to sell.

During a particularly hot day, we took the first step towards winemaking and under the shade of the terrace, we crushed ripe red grapes in a shallow bucket with our bare feet. Both Lynda and I felt profoundly disappointed at how unromantic the process was, compared to those vineyard scenes in films. We squealed at the odd sensation of what felt like cold snails squirming between our toes while swatting away the flies that were attracted by the vinegary smell. Jason put the brew away in the dark to ferment but I had already gone right off the idea of actually tasting it but at least we could say we had tried.

We couldn't do much else but remain patient and positive for the right buyer and meanwhile make plans for our new adventure.

We conspired over our wild business ideas and made drastic additions to the layout of the villa. We were so motivated by the Chulilla house; our first thoughts were to turn the villa into a retreat, thanks to the quiet location but then other ideas took hold as we considered the hiking and climbing opportunities.

Winter drew in slowly at Monrabana with many pink-cocktail sunsets blushing the sky. I had expected it to approach with a swift and mean hand but we were gently eased into an uncomfortable coldness that penetrated from the tiled floors upwards. I had no idea that Spain even had much of a winter – another fact I should have looked into before we relocated. With no central heating, the house was as cold as a cave and no matter how long the log fire had been burning, it seemed to make no difference to the temperature of the room. We moved our sleeping arrangements into the lounge so we could have the benefit of the log fire and piled on blankets, socks and hats. We were quite happy though and it was far from the wet and frosty winters back in Britain. We had new dreams to set our minds to, as the olive wood crackled and burned out halfway through the night.

The Monrabana house took a further month of intensive viewings and a price reduction before it eventually sold. Finally, we had a deposit from a Valencian couple who both put on such convincing poker faces I would never have thought they would end up buying it. Thrilled to have sold our first property abroad we celebrated with a bottle of Cava, happy to have made a small but tidy profit. Once again our lives were propelled forward at a fast pace – 'all or nothing' was how things seemed to go out here.

With a swift and nerve-wracking purchase at the notary office, the Chulilla mountain house - our second project was ours.

That same day, as the old doctor's wife, Mary reluctantly handed over a set of her keys, she placed her long elegant fingers on Vincente's arm and whispered into his ear with an irregular request. She wanted to follow us back to the house to collect a few of her belongings and say farewell, one last time. The agent, who was a good family man and didn't want to seem unkind by pointing out the lateness of this request, agreed, as long as we were all right with the arrangement. As we had a few days to move our belongings with our buyers, we were in no great hurry to disagree.

It became a remarkably weird afternoon. However much we wanted to show our excitement and rummage through our new house, we had to be sensitive to the owner. We understood that although this was to be a big positive change in our lives, it was also a giant leap forward for the widow to let it go having had many happy years with her husband and children.

The house was in an uncomfortable state and yet amongst all the neglect, Mary released small mournful sobs as she walked from room to room, unhooking decorative plates from the walls.

As Vincente didn't want to cross any awkward threshold between the seller and buyer he stood outside the front door on neutral territory, smoking casually. Jason and I both tried to look relaxed with our hands in our pockets, floating around in the background.

I felt a little guilty for our presence. I noticed how rigidly Mary held herself, and I wished for her sake she could have had someone, a friend, or daughter may be, to support her. She might have thought she was strong enough for this moment but there was a vulnerable softness in her eyes that her heavy eye makeup failed to mask.

She took her time, placing her hands on the door frames and walls as if to steady herself or perhaps to feel the texture one last time. She took in the distant mountain views from the balcony and swallowed hard, choking back tears. From the far side of the living room, I observed her regain her stiff composure, opening her purse to place a tissue back inside before straightening the cuffs on her cardigan. Mary turned and walked towards me, managing to give a small, grateful smile as she passed. I smiled back and, although I didn't have the words in her language to do so, I wished her all the happiness for her future.

As the widow prepared to leave, Vincente translated that it was Mary's wish that we promise to look after her house. We walked them out and after they left, Jason rushed back inside to get acquainted with our new villa. I stood there alone beneath the trees, in a silence so profound it was hard to adjust to it for a moment. Not one barking dog. Just the soundtrack of nature – birds and red squirrels dropping chewed pine cones onto the dry ground. How *rare* to be in a place where there are no human sounds. I understood then how difficult it must have been for Mary to spend time alone here. I tried to imagine the contrast between this home and her apartment in the city. At least there would be a certain chaotic soundtrack to comfort her.

It felt fantastic to place the first few tins of paint on the living room floor and snap on the rubber gloves the next day.

I tackled the Exorcist bedroom first. Although the vendor had thankfully taken most of her possessions away, she had kindly left behind the blood-stained bedspread and the ragged curtains. I half-closed my eyes and held my breath, not wanting to inhale any dust and swiftly I rolled the rags into a bin bag. The widow had left something worth keeping, however in the storerooms below: a few nice pieces of wooden furniture that I could recycle and use elsewhere – a wicker chair, a couple of bedside tables and a rustic Spanish dresser.

While Jason had started work on the bathroom a week later, I drove to the local Ecoparc to check if anything interesting had been discarded. The discovery of our local recycling centre was very exciting and due to the fact that the council couldn't always have it manned, it was a great place to go treasure hunting and not be challenged about taking things away. Previously in Monrabana I had stumbled upon a crater full of dumped household items whilst out running, we dragged an antique Dutch bevelled mirror, windows and some wooden shutters from landfill and upcycled them.

This time I left empty-handed and headed back to the house

where I found Jason on his knees leaning into a square hole in the bathroom floor, elbows deep in excrement as he used a soup ladle to scoop the waste into a bucket. The smell was so offensive it sent me running back outside, his only protection was a scarf tied around his face to keep from gagging. Whoever had installed the toilet hadn't bothered with such technicalities as sending sewage further away. Instead, a small cement chamber kept the festering stools out of sight just a foot down from the tiled floor.

From outside the bathroom, I could hear Jason gulping for air and uttering the words "filthy", "rotten" and "bastards" over and over again.

He rushed past me, warning me to get out the way before he covered us both in faeces. He deposited the mess to a muddy pit in the garden, the foul foaminess of it drawing our greedy dog Macey to sniff the air curiously.

Over a short time, our scribbles on scraps of paper soon came to life. In the searing heat, Jason got to work on the new kitchen extension. He opened up the walls to the back garden and constructed a brick extension, twice its original size. We used our dump finds; shuttered doors and windows to finish off the country retreat look.

Further projects consisted of building an en-suite bathroom in the master bedroom. A new two-step sewage system to the villa's 'Pozo Negro' cesspit and the construction of a covered porch seating area by the front door. We hired a building firm to construct a swimming pool with an extra lap length on one side.

It was a big chunk of our money but well worth the investment. These renovations made a huge impact on the footprint of the house, where we could spread ourselves around in different areas without disturbing one another – a luxury retreat in itself.

To finish, we redecorated in natural muted tones to match the forest environment using colours with names like Kenya, kelp, Natural twine, Bamboo and Seagrass against clean white ceilings and colourful Nordic textiles. The villa had been transformed from a tired Seventies house to a luxury mountain retreat and the revived antique furniture I had found in the shed and dump added a country feel to the natural tones of the walls and tiled floors.

As we settled, friends and family came out to visit us to see it for the first time. They were in owe of the view, the silence and the wildlife. We sat outside on the balcony drinking wine while tucked under woollen blankets as darkness claimed the fading light. We watched as bats took flight to catch mosquitos and geckos moved into position. Patiently we waited and watched the dramatic lightning storms ride in on a humid night so we could coo at the blue strikes of light. When the rumbles crashed in, we pretended not to be scared and sometimes when the crickets stirred and the bullfrogs croaked, it felt as if we were on safari.

During that summer we became a little more acquainted with our permanent neighbours Isabel and Nicolás – A friendly middle-aged couple who had lived in Chulilla for the last fifteen years, although Isabel was English and was fluent in both languages.

It was nice to spend some time with them over coffee and be asked to sit with them at fiestas and join them for paella or their children's parties. It felt refreshing to be with genuinely happy people and even though they had busy lives of their own they always made time for us and so we could feel part of village life.

When it wasn't so hot, I took Macey running with me through the quiet orange plantations. She wasn't always the best companion, tripping me when she got the scent of fallen fruit or a discarded sandwich. We took a shortcut towards the mountain range through a steep and stony valley and out into a cultivated area of orange and fig trees. It was often at this point I lost the dog completely - she hunkered low, scavenging citrus delights, and remained there, scoffing, until my cries fell silent and she ran to find me in fear of abandonment.

We heard rumours of other nationalities living in our remote village, and I was curious to hear how they had ended up here. I hoped to bump into one of them on market day when the town square was transformed from a ghost town to a mass of tables piled high with muddy, locally produced seasonal vegetables. Other stalls filled the square too, an abundance of fruit, clothes, lace and antiques that dotted the village with noise and colour.

I searched among the stands, stopping to browse at a vibrantly-coloured South American stall hoping to spot a potential friend in the crowd. But I failed to find a single person around my age to befriend. Where had all the twenty-somethings gone? I could see smooth-skinned tanned teenagers, sitting on the steps to the town hall, nibbling on sunflower seeds with their friends and a group of mature gentlemen seated on a bench, elegantly draped in pastel coloured sweaters. But where were the age groups in between?

In desperation for female company, I invited some older, local Spanish ladies to the house for tea and cake. Teresa was a local resident and was known for being somewhat depressive but her two friends, Frances and Carmen who I had met at a local fiesta seemed friendly and kind, which was enough for me to pursue a friendship. I was thankful the two ladies accompanied Teresa – the more the merrier, or at least that was the idea.

The ladies were in their mid-fifties, although they seemed much older in comparison to anyone I knew back home of that age. They seemed happy for the invite and I hoped that Teresa wouldn't be her doom and gloom self.

From the outset I struggled for conversation, not because of the language barrier – they spoke perfect English and liked to practice with me. But we were worlds and ages apart. They all talked at once, over each other, interrupting without apology, and the volume increased with excitement. I was used to this, having grown up with a Norwegian mother and Spanish stepfather, which brought its kind of domestic madness that not many of my friends could relate to. If my friends stayed for dinner, they often sat wide-eyed in silence as my family, far from dull, debated world issues and danced to The Gypsy Kings.

I served the ladies my favourite homemade carrot cake and poured my guests instant coffee. I knew the processed coffee would be frowned upon, especially since I tried to disguise its true nature by serving it in a cafetière.

My new friends grimaced with their first sip, *I never was any good at making coffee* but I was grateful they didn't mention how terrible it tasted to my face.

They tucked into the cake and paused. For a moment a mild panic rose in my chest that the cake was as bad as the coffee.

"Has the cake been made with oil?" Teresa asked the other two ladies.

"Don't be silly, of course, it has," Francis answered on my behalf.

"Well, it's different, not normal," said Teresa, shaking her dark, rusty hair, pretending not to enjoy it as she devoured the lot.

They chewed and stared like a herd of cows and left me feeling like I was teetering on the edge of some village-fête cake competition, my '1st place' ribbon just out of reach.

"Actually, it's made with butter," I added, to bring myself back into the conversation, "And I've never heard of baking with oil before, is that traditional here?" I asked. They all looked perplexed and didn't engage.

Teresa smirked. *No oil?* She shrugged and finished off their cake before I had a chance to sit and eat mine, I was struggling to make this friendship work.

The conversation flitted from village land stories to the old regime of Franco and the development of Spain's economic situation ever since. It was a period that in reality wasn't that long ago but one I knew little of to give any valuable or credible input. I was curious about Spain's past and knew some history, mainly from stories Joseph told me about the atrocities his Jewish relatives suffered during the war. My naïve questions either went unanswered or were answered indirectly with a long diatribe that struggled to hold my interest. I remembered the Spanish literature that Joseph kept in his glass cabinet in Galicia, a hefty book translated into English that we often referred to as the shelf-breaker. I would ask him if I could borrow it and gain some perspective before my next social gathering, maybe. As a penalty for the loan, it was likely that Joseph would want to discuss each chapter to test my new-found knowledge.

The three women chirped away as they discussed whether the new synthetic mop heads cleaned better than conventional cotton mop heads. I sniggered into my cold coffee, causing Teresa to throw me an icy glare. I thought they were joking over their housewives' dilemmas but they were deadly serious. They fussed over the price of plastic-covered table cloths and commented that if I were to keep my new cream kitchen clean, I would need to clean it every day without fail. Housewives of the nineteen-fifties sprung to mind and without thinking I flippantly replied that I had more exciting things to do in Spain than be permanently attached to a sponge. They looked at me as if the Pope had just died. I tried to laugh off my comment but it was too late, I had alienated myself.

At what felt like hours later, I cleared the cups and plates away from the three women and they got up to leave – the day had been long and I hadn't realised how exhausted I felt. What a disastrous afternoon, I thought to myself. The world I had grown up in, seemed futuristic by comparison.

As they stood to leave Teresa asked me how the renovations were coming along. Pleased she finally seemed to be taking some interest I offered to show her around. But if she was impressed with the changes she didn't show it. She skulked from one room to another barely registering the renovations. All our hard work deserved some kind of compliment, even if it wasn't heartfelt. Francis and Carmen trailed behind us, politely skimming their eyes around and nodded approvingly, which I appreciated, although they didn't utter a word. Teresa remained silent until she was halfway out the front door and looked back at me.

"Oh well, I suppose it'll be nice —" she paused for effect, "— *when it's finished,*" she nodded at her remark as if that was the final word, collected her friends and walked off home.

As I watched the women close the iron gates behind them. Carmen and Frances waved back in secret so Teresa couldn't see. I seethed through gritted teeth as I waved back.

"It *is* fucking finished," I muttered.

15. EXPLORING CHULILLA

I was beginning to think the rumours weren't true and I'd never find a true friend, someone I could laugh with, someone nearer my age. The idea of other nationalities mixing amongst the Spanish community could only make the area more culturally diverse, and it gave me a sense of comfort knowing that if other foreigners had succeeded in settling here, perhaps we could too.

Keen to make friends and not waste any more time, I tracked down 'La Casa Serena'. A home and guest house to a worldly couple I had heard about through our neighbours. I wasn't entirely comfortable having to track down prospective friendships but these circumstances were different; I was in a different country without the usual advantages of meeting people through work, so it was up to me to make the effort.

Hoping not to appear too much like a stalker, I found myself standing nervously outside a heavy pine-lacquered door, staring into the hollowed-out eyes of a grinning terracotta sun. The guesthouse was situated off the main village square, among a cluster of whitewashed houses on the cliff edge of a green valley. I was impressed with the effort and warmth ingrained into the façade. A smattering of pretty summer flowers in pots, pink and yellow, white and blue, aligned the length of the building, making the other houses shrink unbecomingly in comparison. Bright artwork had been painstakingly hand-painted around the doorway, indicating this couple were arty and fun.

I bravely rapped on the door, noticing promotional information in the window: stickers boasting 'No. 1 best bed & breakfast in Chulilla', logos of well-known travel websites and an impressive list of spoken languages. I swallowed hard, feeling quite intimidated. Two men opened the door and despite my unannounced visit, kindly offered me a drink inside their guesthouse which was warm and welcoming. They introduced themselves as Alex and Kazimir; immediately I could tell there was a quirky and interesting quality to them that I had been longing for in new friends. We chatted a little about how life was in Chulilla and what had brought us here.

Alex wore circular pink-tinted sunglasses and had small laughter creases at the corner of his eyes. He had a slim build, a subtle tan and his short greying hair contrasted with his fashionable brown-red stubble. Originally from Britain, he articulated with a soft, relaxed tone and seemed to be an intelligent and mischievous man who could see the truth in things. I noticed how years of living in Spain had influenced his body language, as he spoke, he gestured with his hands, which I thought was lovely.

Kazimir, Alex's partner was Slovakian with a strong build and an infectiously warm smile. He had a T-shirt emblazoned with the Slovakian flag and wore slippers which for some reason immediately made me feel at ease. Together they ran the guest house all year round and Alex also taught English at public school in the adjacent village, as well as private classes at students' homes. After our brief chat, I left. Rock climbing guests were expected and I didn't want to interrupt their hospitality.

I felt genuinely pleased to have met Alex and Kazimir and hoped there might be a friendship there. The couple appeared to be happily settled within this rural community – they were already living like locals and we still had a lot to learn.

A month later, with the midday sun fully blazing, we had gathered a small group together to go exploring and find those secret locations that were impossible to find without local knowledge. With the guidance of our Spanish neighbours Isabel and Nicolás, their two teenage daughters and another local couple, we explored all the hidden locations Chulilla had to offer.

First on our list was Fuencaliente - Hot Springs. We squished into two cars and drove over a rocky, narrow ledge, teetering high on a mountain road. I grasped the window frame and peered at how close to the ledge we were. The road was only the width of a car, and I silently prayed we wouldn't encounter another vehicle. I imagined our car plunging into the deep dark stony depths of the ravine, never to be seen again. After what seemed like an endless drive at – thankfully – a snail's pace, we disembarked and stretched our legs, before clambering down a smelly, boggy unmarked trail. It amazed me just how tucked away these places were. A bundle of bamboo had been cut and laid down on the soggy ground as an attempt to make the crossing safe. But the bamboo had rotted and sunk into the swampy mud, making each step dangerously slippery. I skidded a couple of times disturbing flies and midges as I grappled to balance. We moved towards the crashing sound of a waterfall where I longed to soak my baseball cap and cool my burning scalp from the sun. As we walked behind a curtain of bamboo, the noise intensified.

We came to an opening and got our first glimpse of this precious wonder. There were, in fact, three separate waterfalls, one after another in a row. Water cascaded over the top, dropping like shimmering gold coins as they caught the sunlight. Bulbous lumps of velvety, acid-yellow moss, clung to the volcanic rock, allowing channels of water to drop loudly into the flowing water below. A fig tree, rooted in a crack to the side of the waterfall, romantically arched its trunk to face the sun, heavy with sweet, ripe teardrop fruit, its roots delicately caressing the icy water.

The scene before us seemed prehistoric and I had no words but a feeling of childlike impatience to be immersed within it. We kicked off our shoes and clasped our toes around the icy pebbles, eager to gain better access to the waterfall. Each following the other in turn, we slowly moved through the water, bracing ourselves for the horrible moment when the freezing water would reach our delicate parts - Nicolás and Jason knowingly nodded to one another and winced in anticipation. Once in, up to our hips and numb to the cold, we all marvelled at the beauty of the lagoon, the biblical offering of free fruit and the small fishes nipping at our toes. We could have been in the Brazilian rainforest for all we knew. It was our secret paradise.

Encouraged by Isabel and Nicolás to stand waist-deep under the deluge of the waterfall, we moved under its immense pressure, the shocking coldness thumped our backs and pummelled our shoulders. The incredible force pushed my body downwards into the water and pinned me to the spot as I screeched at this relentless and surprisingly painful massage.

After everyone had their turn standing helplessly underneath it and emerged with pink shoulders, we followed Nicolás as he moved towards the back scaly wall under the waterfall. I tentatively touched the crystallized slimy surface and shuddered as my heart tried to pump warm blood to the rest of my body. Nicolás turned to both of us with a mischievous glint in his eye.

"You can't see it but behind this wall is a cave. You must swim under the water to get to the other side, want to try?" he shouted over the downpour. I didn't like the sound of this - I had heard of potholing and I had never liked the idea of it – but Nicolás had brought us here, and so far no harm had come to us. We nodded in agreement, we didn't want the adventure to stop now.

After Nicolás had taken a dramatic gulp of air and disappeared under the wall, Jason paused to allow Nicolás a moment to resurface before ducking under himself. The rest of our party who weren't into caving had already made their way to the other side of the river and back onto dry land, warming themselves in towels and lighting cigarettes.

Taking a deep breath I dropped under the water with my eyes wide open, hands out in front, searching for obstructions. I kicked forward towards opal light, and before I had barely broken into a swim I emerged into the cave.

Blinking fresh water from my eyes I saw a blurry Nicolás standing proudly, waist-deep in the water. Jason floated in a circle on his back, staring at the ceiling. The cave was dimly illuminated as sunlight reflected through the water and bounced off its deep, soft, sandy bottom. Unlike the consistent flow of the water outside, it was still in here, with a serene, milky glow that reflected upon the ceiling, giving just a hint of incandescent light.

I realised it was warmer too, perhaps it was the string of warm bubbles that rose from the sandy bottom or maybe from the sun's rays on the rocks above. Jason pulled me towards him and pointed up at the stalactites hanging from the ceiling. Our voices echoed around us and I felt a childlike wonder from the excitement of our discovery.

A long, smooth rock at the back of the cave, provided a perfect spot to rest and examine the details of our surroundings. Nicolás informed us that the cave was linked to another via a dark tunnel. Eager to explore further, we climbed to a higher platform of rocks, feeling our way forward, trusting our toes and fingers to guide us in complete darkness. I had an unnerving thought that my fingers might run over the face of a bearded man in hiding. Thankfully my hands made contact with a boulder instead which we had to slide over on our bottoms, hoping not to snag our swimwear to get to the other side. It was a relief when my toes connected with a soft, sandy patch as we crept forward. My heart pounded with exhilaration as we were welcomed by a blue glow that beckoned us into the adjoining cave. This cave was a lot smaller, and colder due to the exposure of its own separate waterfall. We stood behind the thunderous cascading flow - as if looking out of a one-way mirror. The shimmering water shielded our euphoric whoops and hollers from our friends waiting on the outside.

That unforgettable day at the hot springs, reinforced how much more there was yet to discover in our area and beyond. We urged our friends to show us more and they couldn't have been more enthusiastic to comply.

During another, slightly less dangerous exploration with our new friends Alex and Kazimir, we ambled down more ankle-twisting paths and through jungles of bamboo to reach our next location, aptly named The Emerald Gorge because of its mineral green waters.

Like a jewel in the crown, its sparkling location was home to a more visible crop of animals. Large carp and trout swam freely in the green open pool at one end where dragonflies and kingfishers hovered. We saw a green snake bolt from our presence and in a moment of sheer luck, a foot-long iguana crossed our path, pausing long enough for us to photograph its dazzling blue and yellow scales.

High volcanic grey walls channelled the river, just wide enough for a dinghy to pass towards a cascading bowl of rocks at the end. As the water was very much active, the flow provided several undercurrents which, if you weren't a strong swimmer, could easily drag you from the calm end to the hazardous rock cluster at the other. What appeared to onlookers as a gentle drift, felt more like being sucked into a whirlpool, while mysterious lurking entities stroked and grasped at your legs.

Adjacent to the gorge, there was an enormous rock wall with a small opening leading to a corridor that held its own secrets. We crouched along the low tunnel walls, shuffling as we stepped over rocks on the wet floor. When we reached a bend halfway, we were rendered into complete darkness but like all prepared explorers, Jason handily kept a small torch under his hat which he used to light the way. The immediate illumination startled bats and large spiders - *which we soon realised jumped*, causing us to run for the exit, in a thrilling escape.

The day trips allowed us to get acquainted with our new friends too. Alex had lived in Spain for three years before a chance meeting with Kazimir in Valencia one day. They had both strolled around the twisted stone pillars inside La Lonja – the old Silk Exchange building opposite the old market. A magnificent 15th-century building of late gothic architecture with its exuberantly ornamented doors and high vaulted ceilings. Alex recalled how their connection had been instant as they sparked up a conversation over an appreciation for UNESCO world heritage sites, travel and adventure.

These excursions soon became part of our weekly outings. We got used to the scary mountain roads, but our car suspension didn't. It took us a few treacherous journeys to navigate around the collapsed cliff edges, sometimes stopping to move small fallen boulders. We loved how we were part of the ever-changing natural landscape, and rewarded by the beautiful mountain top scenery that took our breath away on every single visit.

16. DISCOVER CHULILLA TOURS

It was on one of these outings, whilst crawling through an ancient Roman aqueduct, scuffing my bare knees on the tunnel walls, that 'Discover Chulilla Tours' was born. We had seen enough stunning locations to come up with the idea of running our own excursion business. If we turned all this local knowledge into a business opportunity, we could both organise and run a daily package tour. The idea had materialized with perfect timing. Our savings were running low and we were both feeling twitchy with nagging financial concerns. With all the amazing water-themed locations Chulilla had to offer, it seemed obvious to us that we had to at least give it a go.

For a week I worked through the cool evenings building a website, a blanket wrapped over my shoulders as I sat hunched in low light at my computer till the early hours. Jason rolled away from the cold draft as I crawled under the bedsheets beside him each night and sank into an exhausted sleep, my mind far away from lagoons and caves.

As the sun's rays began to heat through the pine trees, we used the mornings to sit in the garden and scribble notes and talked through ideas on how to publicise our venture without exploiting the locations. The business wasn't entirely legitimate; we were aware that we should seek permission from the local council to run the tours. But the deadly bureaucratic red tape was bound to stall – if not completely kill – our new venture so we remained under the radar and focused on our small British market.

Although we were only twenty-five kilometres away from an

expatriate community, we still had to bring our village and the tours to the attention of holiday-makers and retired couples that lived nearby. We aimed to advertise to mainly British visitors because there was a lack of things to do in rural areas. Our target audience were families of permanently retired Brits, who were desperate to coerce their children and grandchildren off their sun loungers to explore the *real* Spain rather than a plastic theme park further south. We planned for the tours to start as soon as possible but would run the waterfall tours through the hottest months of summer when the lakes would be refreshing rather than arctic. We would provide either a cooked barbecue or a lunch hamper at the end of the tour at a scenic site, with extra refreshments along the way to keep everyone happy. But more importantly, we needed to buy a second-hand Jeep, so we could carry a group safely off-road in mountain conditions and through overflowing rivers.

Jason settled on an ex-council, battered Land Rover Defender 110 he had found online in Madrid. He hired a local Spanish welder to make a roof rack and ladder and tinkered away for weeks making foot-bars and customising it for the comfort of our guests.

He then tested the Land Rover's performance in each location on trial runs. Clambering over rocky mudslides scouting-out replacement options if a location should be cut- off from a rise in the river levels or dried up from drought. The vehicle ably gripped rocky edges up and down rough tracks, sailed through streams and conquered mountain roads, proving to be the ideal off-road transport for our new venture.

We distributed leaflets at a small selection of expat bars, Bar Ché, internet rooms and on stalls at British-run car boot sales. We talked to the owners of a small British supermarket who were happy to help and left leaflets with our new friends at the guest house. I even made uniforms for the pair of us: white t-shirts, shorts and swimwear branded with our logo. Everything was in place – we just hoped all our hard work would pay off.

Throughout winter, bookings slowly trickled in with flip flop wearing holidaymakers. Bookings increased and by the time June had arrived, it became apparent that the heat was here to stay giving us ideal conditions to start our first watery tour. From one Brit bar to another, news spread of our existence, proving to us that we had cornered the market. We were elated to overhear our names mentioned in snippets of conversation. It seemed that gossip could never be underestimated, especially in the strange and small expatriate world. As the sun took us hostage, more bookings came in. We were establishing ourselves which felt like the best outcome we could have hoped for.

If there was a spare seat on the tour, I would tag along to assist Jason. We were a good team, fulfilling our roles; Jason navigating over rough tracks and narrow lanes, with live commentary, whilst keeping us safe from the steep mountain drops. And myself among the group, getting to know people and hearing their other holiday exploits. In turn, our clients were curious about us, they didn't know many younger brits in these rural areas so they were curious about our plans.

The tours were exhaustingly hard in the heat and by the late afternoons' our energies spent, we had to cool off at home in the pool or flop on the balcony for a siesta.

One glorious summer's morning we packed the Jeep with food, blankets and inflatable rings as buoyancy aids. We buckled up four pensioners in the back of the car and made our way to the Emerald Gorge. Despite my warnings of the difficult terrain for a group of their age, they still insisted on this location. They waved my worries away, arguing that despite being seventy they were all fit and healthy, and no obstacles would hold them back. Within five minutes of our trek walking along a steep gravel track, Grace, a slim and chirpy lady, had collapsed in a heap on the rocky ground. Both her knees had spontaneously buckled, almost as if someone had hit her in the back of the legs with a cricket bat. Blood trickled from perforated holes in both knees. Her husband Arthur, spat furiously as he lectured her about her capabilities on such uneven ground. Embarrassed for her, we set about abandoning the tour but Grace, giggly and red-faced, insisted on carrying on as we hauled her lightweight frame off the dusty track.

Worried about any kind of personal liability law-suit, I took her elbow to offer support. We walked on and gained a slow but rhythmic pace on the downward winding path which led to the entrance of the river. Once again, in an impossible coincidence, Grace's knees gave way with cataplectic weakness. It was odd, the way they could no longer lock properly. Grace plunged forward towards the edge of the cliff, nearly taking me with her and I managed to keep her from going over by gently lowering her to the ground. Ranting and raving for a second time Arthur decided to call it quits on the tour, which started a row between them. The rest of us listened to her heartfelt pleas that she didn't want to spoil anyone's day. I had hoped she would take advice and abandon the walk, but she was persuasive and bargained with her husband and friends until they relented.

Once Grace was upright and supported again, we moved on in silence, but the enjoyment had vanished, the outing now overshadowed by concern. Grace relaxed her weight into mine, leaning harder on me as we ambled at a slow pace towards the entrance to the gorge. She took liberties with the support I gave, her entire body growing floppy as if she were a doll.

My back started to ache as her head rolled uncomfortably on my shoulder – this felt more like a visit to the infirmary than an excursion. Breathing softly, Grace rolled her head and looked up at me. She smiled cheekily, and it was then I realised her dysfunctional limbs weren't the result of age or dehydration but intoxication from gin. I could smell it on her breath. I counted to five, my fury dispersed, and we ambled on.

After helping Grace gently over boulders and fallen branches, like a fragile infant we finally reached the rock pools where we could rest. I felt exhausted. The group steadily paddled in the shallows while Jason remained cross-armed and watchful, in lifeguard mode. After a few hours of soaking up the sun and eating our lunch, we headed back up the track and thankfully Grace, had sobered-up, even managing to walk by herself. I mouthed to Jason that it was *his* turn to carry her if it came to it.

Safely back in the Jeep, I worked on patching up Grace with the medical kit we kept in the car. She had more scratches by now, from passing prickly bushes and bouncing off trees. Green bruises were starting to appear on her arms where she had toppled and I had haphazardly grabbed her when she had almost fallen to her death, but she didn't seem bothered.

It was a huge relief to arrive back at the village where we could relinquish our responsibilities.

From Grace's injuries, it would have been fair to assume we had kidnapped the tourists, tortured and beaten them before throwing them back to the curb. Grace looked as if she'd spent five nights wandering a cactus-ridden desert rather than having been on an afternoon's outing.

As soon as their sandals hit the pavement I slapped the back of the Jeep to instruct Jason to make tracks.

It wasn't a hugely lucrative business but it certainly helped with some bills and, although the constant chatting could be tiring, we loved the work. I enjoyed being with our guests, hearing the whoops and shrieks as we bumped dramatically up and down in the Jeep as if we were on a real safari ride. The catastrophe with Gin Grace forced us to hunt for another, more suitable location for less able groups. We got better at persuading over-ambitious folk to take gentler tours by making them sound more exciting. The reality was that the heat exhausted most of our customers before we had even loaded the jeep, so the less active, the better. We drove further upriver to a flatter area, that was not as beautiful but by no means less attractive to the tourists. Minimal walking, meant barely any accidents as we chaperoned them from the Jeep to the safety of a tartan blanket at the edge of a wide river. Our clients were able to sit happily with plates of food on their laps, watching fishermen throw lines in blissful dappled sunlight.

Sometimes if we had encroached a wasps nest or snake burrow, Jason had to move the group to another location, we adapted to changes as they happened and put our clients' needs first.

As the popularity of the tours increased I picked up a second-hand convertible Suzuki Jeep so I could also pitch in when needed, whether it was a matter of hauling all the gear in my car or making sure we had cleaned up the rubbish after ourselves, we both put all our efforts into the business to make it a success.

Very occasionally we had the *El Grande* tours – these were the money earners but didn't come along very often. They consisted of a large group, made up of two or three families from all ages and were happy to take their vehicles off-road, following us in a convoy.

However, not all guests were suited to outdoor pursuits and it was their partners who pushed the not-so-willing ones to embark on one of our trips, even if that meant facing a phobia. One afternoon we took a lady called Shelly, her husband Dean and their three teenage kids on the Emerald Gorge tour. Shelly was vocal about her hatred for nature, insects and rivers - so the gorge was probably the last place she wanted to visit. The nearer she got to the location, the more her resentment grew towards her husband for making her go. The couple argued about the security of her white glossy designer handbag and Shelly was so worried it would get stolen that she vowed to not let it out of her sight. Once we reached the gorge, rather than leave her belongings on a rock by the side of the lagoon as everyone else had, Shelly clung onto the bag as she braved the depths of the river and I helped her into the inflatable ring. The rest of the family barely held it together to see Shelly in the water clutching her glittery sandals and handbag screaming "This is ridiculous! Why am I doing this?" with furious resentment that seemed to thrill her husband and kids the more upset she got. Once all of us had joyfully ridden the current to the end of the lagoon and Shelly was calmer, we had two ways of heading back to land - either back up-stream against the current or the quickest route through the bat-infested dark watery tunnel. Dean persuaded her to take the tunnel and we all sloshed through in single file. Shelly trailed along at the back yelping and whimpering in bursts convinced something was touching her, Jason thought it was best not to mention the residents in the cave to add to her anxiety. As we neared the exit some five minutes later Shelly emerged hysterical, covered in spiders, of which she had a phobia of. She sobbed all the way back to the jeep clutching her handbag as her husband and kids were bent double in hysterics. We felt sorry for her but at least she would have some great stories to tell.

17. EURO, EURO, EURO!

While keeping up with the tours and the renovations on the mountain house, I was also taking sewing commissions from our friends at the guesthouse. From our kitchen table, I created one-off cushions to match their interior palette, and with any leftover fabrics, I made additional textiles that I could sell. These along with a few upcycled antique pieces from the dump and a wire rack to display handmade greeting cards, was enough stock to furnish a stall at the local car boot sale.

Living in the mountains didn't allow us to mix with many Brits apart from the tours, so it was always good to meet people where we could and make new contacts. I only wished that the car boot had a better turnout than the dozen or so cars but it was a new concept that needed time to grow. The British organiser's hoped that the foot traffic from the existing Spanish food market in the adjoining field would bring fresh visitors, making it a bustling marketplace.

Retirees successfully sold tropical plants they had cultivated and the promotion of new independent business ventures seemed well-received to the many buying Brits, who used it as another social outing. It struck me how early in the morning these folk would gather into herds and drink endlessly in the midday sun. As the location was rural, everyone drove home – despite how much they might have consumed before lunchtime.

The car boot sale was a strange phenomenon for the Spanish, so it was amusing to watch locals tentatively rummage in dirty boxes before giving the stall-holder a look of disgust and walking off. They were suspicious of old tat but with the potential of finding treasure, Spaniards gave it a go and seemed to enjoy the rummaging and bartering process. I loved to observe two cultures coming together, once a good deal was struck the delight was palpable. It wasn't too long before the locals joined the Brits and set up their own stalls, some rivalling the other horticulturists and bookstalls. This created some snobbery as car boot etiquette hadn't quite been adhered-to. The absence of trestle tables gnawed at beady-eyed expats who watched on as heinous items that should have been discarded, was turfed-out onto a crusty tarpaulin. Some objects looked as if they had simply been raked-up from a garage floor; matted pieces of animal fur, old romance novels, piles of old tape cassettes and on one occasion a stack of filthy porn mags - their pages curled and well-thumbed through. At least only a small proportion of items were fit for the bin and there was enough of an eclectic mix with something for everybody.

I made friends with a retired Spanish seamstress, whose stall I had visited a few times. There were second-hand items on the table but her speciality was selling traditional hand-knitted children's clothes made to an exceptional quality. She told me she enjoyed the interaction of meeting other creative people and had got her husband involved by making wooden pieces of furniture. She explained that during her grandmother's life, her family had to make do through the civil war, reusing items until they had worn down to nothing. This taught her that having things on display in the house was like showing off that you had money - at a time that was considered bad taste to flaunt it. Today, the idea of buying anything second-hand other than antiques seemed almost repulsive to her generation.

It was an interesting historical insight for me, and I listened carefully to learn more background on it.

"After all of those struggles, we don't have to have second-hand things anymore," she said looking about at the other stalls.

And then her eyes lit-up at an old ceramic bowl on the corner of a nearby trestle table

"Oh, just a euro?" she asked.

One sunny car boot morning, an unfamiliar British couple in a flashy new Range Rover pitched up next to us. They rapidly unpacked kitchen items that looked almost new and had enough greeting-card stock to fill a shop. The cards repeatedly slipped from the mountainous stack on the table onto the ground, causing an almost delighted rage in the man, as he jumped to the rescue.

I looked at my revolving card tower, containing a hundred and seventy hand-illustrated cards in smart packaging and hoped I'd sell some next to this bargain lot.

The man was around fifty years of age and was obviously military in his pristinely dressed and ironed outfit. He held the kind of upright posture my parents always nagged me to adopt. His square jaw was dotted with a day's growth of rugged stubble, his crop of thick white hair clipped neatly at the sides. Desert boots and a kaki coffee flask accessorized the look along with pair of bifocals that hung on a string.

When he wasn't running about energetically as if anticipating a last-minute greeting-card panic-buy invasion, he stood motionless, hands-on-hips squinting across the barren horizon. His wife, an attractive blonde in her mid-forties, slowly emerged from the car and staggered off in the direction of the facilities. He placed his hand on a hip pouch and pulled out what looked like a walkie-talkie.

"Frequency two, Harriet, don't forget we need to keep in contact!" She muttered something back, and continued on her way.

As the sun positioned itself with its killer midday rays that we couldn't escape from, familiar faces passed by our stall. Ruby and Barry looked ridiculously more bronzed than ever. They glanced over and gave us a wave before joining their friends at the bar tent.

Ruby was already drunk if her stagger was anything to go by. I spotted Dirty Janet from our Spanish lessons walking around with a live rabbit under her arm - I presumed she knew it was there and it hadn't just formed like the mould on her toes. It was common to see Brits rescuing puppies and rabbits at the car boot and I was pleased about it. The poor animals sat dehydrating in the sun in small cages and at times I asked the owners to put down water for them, although they usually ignored me much to the intense scrutiny of the other stall holders.

A couple of hours later with a few euros in the pot, we got talking to our car boot neighbours, we established they had prominent careers in the army. The wife, Harriet had taken early retirement due to an accident that damaged her vertebrae. Her husband - Stuart worked for the forces and was still in active service until he decided to retire. Harriet was the quintessential army Major's wife. Her manners were impeccable, as unflawed as the saltwater pearls she wore around her neck. When she spoke she pronounced each word with a low and husky voice that had me transfixed as if I was being told a dark secret. They seemed an oddly paired couple; while Stuart was more energetic than a schoolboy, Harriet spent much of her time stationary because of the pain in her back and remained quiet and reserved.

In the short time we spent with them our new car boot companions were good company, kind and spirited and Stuart seemed particularly keen to keep in contact and take a tour with us. Before we packed up and left for the day we exchanged details, the couple were genuinely pleased to have met us in this environment of weird and wonderful people.

We felt so content in the mountains that our visits back to London became less frequent. Besides, we didn't need to, we had a gentle flow of visitors throughout the year who we took out to the city, the beaches and our little medieval village.

New friends Stuart and Harriet that we had met at the car boot, lived just outside of Valencia and we had kept in regular contact. Stuart initiated most of the meetups, whether it was a tour with us or meeting up in our village for drinks. We were invited to the couple's house to talk about their self-build on a plot they had just bought, it was a dream they had planned for years and they wanted our thoughts on the ambitious layout. We appreciated the growing friendship we had with them and although we had met other couples, none seemed to be as eccentric and entertaining as Stuart and his wife. A realisation was dawning on me, however, perhaps we were finding too much comfort and safety in seeking out other English-speaking people?

I wondered if we weren't limiting ourselves in the country we had come to explore. But surely it was possible to have the best from both worlds? As long as we didn't submit to the expat bubble and spend our days paralyzed by drinking, I was sure we would be OK.

18. GALICIA, 'THE KINGDOM OF SPAIN'

After the summer had ended and the tours had ceased with it, we progressed into another brief, crisp winter. As we emerged into a bright new year ahead, we had a plan to get stuck into a significant property development. An ambitious project that would occupy both of us in a full-time, nine-to-five job. Something - unbelievably, I was starting to miss.

We needed to keep projects moving *and* if we could get a mortgage on the Chulilla house to fund our next project then we were good to go. There was another reason for this too, we had thought that by immersing ourselves within a Spanish community it might give us the push we needed to grasp the language a lot faster than we were.

After some research, we soon discovered that the housing boom in Valencia had priced us out of the area very quickly. If we were to take on a restoration project we would have to look towards an untouched region of Spain. After several telephone conversations with my mother and stepfather, we considered that perhaps Galicia might be the next best option and it seemed a natural step if we wanted to have their hands-on support during the build.

We took the nine-hour drive north-west on a viewing trip, absorbing the transitional landscape along the way. Madrid was a wonderfully vibrant city but the destitute tented slum areas on the outskirts startled me, a surprising reminder of how many immigrants desperately wanted a future here. The further north we drove, the more colourful the country became in the landscape, language and unique properties. Abandoned stone ruins - some quite spectacular - lay waiting for someone to bring them back to life. These places were a lot cheaper than most small villas in Valencia and we would keep the costs down by doing the work entirely ourselves. The decision was helped by the fact that I knew some of the areas of La Coruña already from family holidays. It was still a risky and daunting prospect but what better place to get the taste of real Spain, integrate with the Galician people and educate ourselves about this region.

Along the journey, I reflected on how Galicia seemed to be one of those places shrouded in mystery, a great Garden of Eden with its forests, hidden ruins and wild horses. It isn't known for its blazing sunshine all year round; it certainly isn't the place you see many retired German or English expatriates sipping sangria, baring white legs and trainers, nor is it flat and dry but mountainous and fertile, mist rising from the earth as it warms.

This is because Galicia's Atlantic climate ensures the presence of moisture, even during the holiday months, where it feels – to me at least - like Britain during a perfect summer. Unlike Valencia the average rainfall in Galicia can be well over a hundred days in a year – compare that to Valencia's average of forty-odd days if you're lucky, to relieve the dryness.

Curiously, some areas in this region have microclimates, especially true of my parent's village in the mountains where it rains without fail throughout the night. Impenetrable forests that form into steep valleys, green grazing fields with healthy-looking cattle, undulating mountains, rivers and streams all crease the landscape causing no doubt as to why this region has been labelled 'The Kingdom of Spain'.

As we drove further north, passing through small busy towns I noticed how Celtic symbolism proudly presented itself on buildings and tapestries.

Joseph taught me a little about Galician nationalism, or *Galicianism*, as it's known. A growing ideology, which seeks to recognise Galicia as its own independent nation and maintain its strong heritage with immigration control, language and traditions independent from the rest of Spain. Combined with the wetter weather and landscape, this is perhaps the reason why Galicia has always felt, to me at least, unconnected from its neighbouring regions. It is hard to believe they are part of the same country at all.

As we neared our destination through more undulating terrain, traditional wooden-clad huts with slate roofs appeared – bearing a resemblance to Nordic buildings; painted in smokey-blues, barn reds and greys as well as in traditional Galician colours: Galician forest green, chestnut and off-white. Another relic of Galicia is the hórreo, a slim-built wooden hut perched on carefully carved slabs of granite. These were traditionally used to house and protect precious grain from hungry mice and rats. Nowadays, they are used mainly for storage.

Galicia in the most north-west part of Spain, couldn't be further from Valencia in both a geographical and historical sense. There is a known saying in Galicia 'You can grow anything from a stone' meaning the poorest seed can be cultivated because of the nutrient-rich soil. Galicia is one of the foggiest, wettest and most wild places I have ever known but if you ever manage to fly over Galicia, or drive through it, you'll understand why we can forgive the weather. Because when the sun breaks through the heavy clouds and warms up the eucalyptus trees, it is a place of legend. It is as if man has not yet touched it and ruined it.

When we arrived exhausted at my parents' house we were given coffee and cake along with the latest village gossip before having a short nap from the long drive. That evening as we trawled through the local property papers we spotted an impressive stone farmhouse for restoration. Stone houses in this region were becoming increasingly popular with property developers, city-families and business professionals, all wanting a summer retreat and weekend project.

Speaking in thick Galician, Joseph booked an appointment directly with the owner over the phone the next morning. To my English way of thinking, it felt a little uncivilized not using an agent as a middleman but it was common practice to scout privately and book viewings this way. My parents made a habit of this, even if they weren't looking to buy, it made exploring the region far more interesting.

"After the viewing, we'll all go to a local bar for coffee and cake," said my mother who loved to poke her nose inside people's houses.

Joseph looked at my mother with adoration, content that she had embraced these cultural activities. Jason and I had ideas of settling in Galicia permanently if this property development worked out. We were even open to the ambitious possibility of opening a casa rural guest house, like the one our friends Alex and Kazimir owned in Chulilla.

The next morning Jason and I drove towards a place called Dos Rios passing pretty stone villages and wonky grain stores. We dipped up and down mountain roads passing horse-driven carts and it was a welcome sight to see black and white Friesian cows chomping grass in plentiful fields. We drove through almost uninhabited hamlets, apart from a few farmer types who felt the need to stare in a threatening manner as they worked in the potato fields. I found myself caught in an absurd glaring war – it was as if the locals had never seen a foreigner before, although perhaps they hadn't. Stunning palettes of oily greens and browns caught my eye along with the heavily budded baby blue hydrangeas that grew in abundance and sagged to the floor from their weight.

As we entered into a more lively area that housed bars, a community centre and a small tobacco shop, I noted the current trend for restoring stone houses. We passed two beautifully completed ones, both with carved wooden balconies and impressive stained-glass windows.

As we neared the house we were about to see, I spotted a sign for the infamous pilgrimage route that would eventually lead to Santiago de Compostela - a further forty-minute drive away. The road dipped and we dropped down to a village that seemed suspended in the past.

My parents had arrived early, giving themselves just enough time to scout the area that at first glance was profoundly rural. I wondered if there was more to it than scattered farming plots and a gathering of beaten–up stone and concrete houses. It was quiet but for the sound of pecking chickens, meowing stray cats and a farmer slashing crops in a vast field which broke the deafening silence.

We immediately spotted the vendor who was a stout elderly gentleman by the name of José Ramón who stood waiting patiently outside a small stone church called Iglesia de Santa Maria.

He held a gigantic iron key and gestured towards a considerably sized stone farmhouse next door to the church. Joseph and José Ramón chatted animatedly in their collective language as Jason and I excitedly assessed the house we were about to see. Keeping an open mind about it, we were told that at some point in its life, someone had haphazardly thrown lumpy cement at the chunky stone exterior - presumably to prevent it from collapse. It was built on two floors and had been formally two separate dwellings on a large footprint – a priest's house on one side and an animal barn in a lower section on the other.

Once through the heavy front door and inside the hallway, it took a moment for us to adapt to the cold, dark and extremely damp interior. José Ramón flicked a switch to the one solitary light bulb in existence, that had barely enough output to light a cupboard. No other rooms in the house had electricity so a torch was necessary and revealed a long corridor of panelled wood that ran from the floor to the ceiling. This handcrafted wooden wall with a solid barn door at its centre seemed to have been hastily constructed, looking as if it was imprisoning a dangerous secret on the other side.

Purveyors of keeping our minds still *very much open*, we shuffled through the barn door, covering our mouths and noses from a sudden acrid stench. Three steps down and we were standing on solidified cow waste in a cattle pit. Someone had lit a candle - from here the solid stone construction was more evident, though mismatched rocks had been shoved in muddy gaps, and didn't quite fit into the stone jigsaw. The stone was exposed as much from the outside as it was inside. In comparison our Valencian villa was built from breeze-blocks and smothered in cement or plaster, we didn't get to see the bare materials of what it was made from, unlike the solid stone in this building.

We stepped back out and into the old kitchen, this raised my hopes and I felt a flurry of excitement. It was an amalgamation of two entirely different eras. Mid-century Formica furniture contrasted with a medieval, stone-carved sink and an unyielding stone trough – the size of a bath.

Joseph told us these troughs had been used as a form of refrigeration for meat in the old days. His grandmother had used one, and he remembered the smell of the bay leaves she used to scatter in with the salt to dry cure the meat. The method was to drain the pig's body of blood. Wash it down, butcher it and cover it in salt for preservation. Joseph pointed to a little drainage-hole on the curved bottom of the trough, which would have been plugged with a hand-whittled cork. A sturdy cupboard made from heavy chestnut had been constructed above the trough, where meat could also be hung to dry out without flies getting in. But the most impressive piece of old history in the kitchen was the lareira in the corner. A wide-open chimney on a raised platform of flat stone slabs. Supporting its hefty weight, were three neatly carved floor to ceiling posts at each corner. It was a marvel, a thing of Galician traditional beauty.

The room looked a little like an old English country pub,

with its Tudor-style beams, window shutters and low light. My mother was already eyeing up the fireplace, inspired to mix up some experimental paint colours once she got home. Two benches sat beneath the stone chimney flume. I couldn't understand why the benches were on top of the flagstone platform where the fire would be. Joseph explained, again patiently, that as the main hub of the house this was where the occupants would spend most of their time, cooking and chatting, keeping warm with the fire at their feet.

"You'd better get used to wearing a dust mask if you're going to clean up these beams, hah!" he said as he walked off. I felt a flutter of pride thinking how wonderful it would be to own such a project. The beams, four large thick tree trunks and around twelve thinner ones were so black with soot they would keep anyone busy for months. Hundreds of years of smoking, curing, cooking and grime had left the old chestnut barely visible.

The four of us eagerly accompanied José Ramón upstairs where he explained that at some time in the fifties the upper floor had been converted into the village school. This brought up a fast discussion between the pair of Galician's and we couldn't grasp a word. Joseph's whispered to us that he thought the conversion hadn't been done well, although he didn't quite suggest this to José Ramón. A thin layer of cement had been poured crudely over the floorboards to stop the foul stench rising from the once active cattle pen below. But the cement was so thin it had cracked underfoot revealing rotten boards or in some areas no flooring at all. Two melamine desks were placed in the centre of the room, one for the teacher and a smaller one for young students. The lick of pastel-green paint on the crumbling walls didn't do much to improve the conditions – to me, it resembled a bullet ravaged militant hut in a South American village. But *still*, it held a certain rustic charm. Tall shuttered windows and a generous ceiling height gave the room an air of rustic sophistication that felt promising.

We left my parents for a moment and walked through a series

of rooms to the back of the house that faced the garden. In a long narrow room that would have been the fourth bedroom, we delighted in the beautifully carved beams and more of the same wooden flooring. But then we noticed the entire back wall of the house was leaning outwards at an alarming angle. It seemed the roof had collapsed in places and there was nothing to brace it. Joseph and my mother joined us and we all fell quiet for a moment. Joseph contemplated the restoration job and optimistically suggested to Jason that if the roof was replaced, it would secure the wall to stop it bowing out any further. My mother and I weren't so sure.

The proprietor raced ahead opening shutters to light our path into the priests' living quarters. It was here we spotted, *the mother of all tree trunks* that supported the roof and dominated the bedroom. Spanning the entire width of the room, the supporting beam was a magnificent brute but a complete and utter head-hazard for anyone above the average, ancient Galician head-height. Like a Catholic vault from another time, uncomfortable looking beds, meter-long rosaries and crucifixes all etched their presence in the room. We stepped delicately down the ramshackle staircase to the lower floor, Joseph warned me to stop stomping as I went, or I'd fall through.

The house had a historical life within the community which I found fascinating but it had been uninhabited for over thirty years and lacked all modern services. Even the toilet waste pipe didn't go to the cesspit. Instead, it deposited excrement to the barn and all who might live there.

Despite all of this, we could see the enormous potential. Either as a fixer-upper or as a bed and breakfast if we had the funds. We wanted to show our interest to the vender so gave the nod of approval to Joseph.

José Ramón guided us into the light of the garden where my mother hurriedly lit up a cigarette as if it had been days not minutes since the last one. Doing his utmost to negotiate a deal with his best poker face, Joseph tactfully questioned the owner on our behalf, about the neighbourhood, questions of debt on the house and the possibilities of dividing up the surrounding land to bring down the price of the property. It was at that point that José Ramón seemed reluctant to let the property go as tears welled up in his eyes. After all, three generations of his family had been born in the house and most probably died there too.

As they continued their conversation, the rest of us walked around the parameter of the land and into an outbuilding the size of a double garage, where I got all excited to see left-over timber.

In the garden, we came upon a gnarly grapevine that we were told was over a hundred and fifty years old along with a fully-loaded lemon tree. Six foot off the ground, a traditional hórreo grain store rested majestically on granite slabs, facing the distant mountains like a sacred tomb. There was so much here! A wealth of projects to play with.

It was then I spotted it, the inflexible negative that manages to turn something of potential into an instant put-off. I stared in disbelief at the black granite coffin-housing estate. Of *course*, there was a mausoleum next door overshadowing the garden, why wouldn't there be? Doesn't it come as part of the package when there's a church next door? It was time to evaluate our commitment to this place.

So *this* was the rub, a Catholic cemetery, or as some might see it, the site of two hundred deceased residents, overlooking our potential project. There was a shoulder-high wall between the graves and us so feeling curious to see more, I walked back through the house and out to the street at the front. I noticed an alley between the house and the church so slipped down the narrow passageway, my shoulders brushing the sides as I emerged into a churchyard. Three dark walls loomed around me. I felt overwhelmed by so many people having been buried in such a small area. Each of the deceased had been stacked up in rows of fours, as if in a storage warehouse. Which essentially it was as long as your living family kept up the rent.

Each grave was marble or granite-fronted with long family names inscribed on gold plaques and most were embellished with silver hoop rings. Some held marble vases for flowers, others the ghostly face of the deceased had been immortalised into a porcelain pendant. I thought it was a ghastly idea but must have offered the grieving family some comfort.

Joseph, who had been silently observing my discovery from the other side of the garden wall, stood with a familiar look of apprehension. A liquorice roll-up hanging from one side of his mouth. He nodded at the graves with an audible,

"Hah! You won't get me in one of those," he cocked his head as he relit the cigarette and mooched off.

It was the empty *ready and waiting* compartments that disturbed me more. The family names of the ones yet to die, inscribed with greedy anticipation. Putting those thoughts aside I rationalised that at least there wouldn't be any noise complaints from them while we did up the house *and* we'd have front-row seats to funerals (I had been told the Galician's love a good funeral).

The grave yard-filing-cabinets and the daunting amount of restoration didn't put us off completely. That same afternoon, after two rounds of tepid espressos in a smoky bar we struck a deal with José Ramón and the house, was to be ours. Perhaps it was down to the caffeine overdose but we felt that this was a fantastic deal. We hoped that our bank manager would see the same potential and be as pleased with the purchase as we were.

Exactly three weeks later Jason, Joseph and I sat nervously in the local Notario office and waited for the vendors to turn up. After what seemed like an hour, José Ramón and four other family members filed into the room, quietly acknowledging us. The solicitor gave us paperwork to look over before signing and then made a quick nod to Joseph before exiting the office, leaving just us and the vendors alone in the room. This was the moment when the mood changed to serious matters. Black Money was often the term used to avoid paying large tax sums when buying and selling a property. The vendors and buyers agree on a lower amount for the official paperwork but the actual amount is topped up in cash 'under the table' away from legal eyes. This practice works in favour of both parties and is commonplace in Spain, although we had heard that some notaries were refusing to allow it and it was likely to be phased out. Jason passed our envelope of cash to the vendors where it was counted. Silence, followed by a short discussion and crestfallen faces. The money was shuffled back into a pile and passed to José Ramón for another recount. I noticed sweat beading on Jason's forehead as he counted along, his lips moving in silence. José Ramón barked at Joseph but it sounded more like an accusation rather than a question. Joseph blushed,

"They are saying you haven't got all the money?"

Jason and I broke into a panic as José Ramón slid the money back to Jason to count for himself. As he frantically began, he splayed notes all over the table. I needed a stiff drink as I sat there helplessly knowing that in a few minutes the Notario would reappear expecting our business to be tied up. In the panic Jason lost count, sweat dripped from his forehead onto the table. I laughed a little, trying to ease the tension, and hoped my smile would pacify those glaring faces – it was as if we had tried to con them and they were furious.

"It's short" Jason agreed as the colour drained from his face. I grabbed the padded envelope we had used to carry the money in, and shook it in a desperate attempt that any remaining money might still be inside – and thankfully there was! We all sighed in relief as a few 500 euro notes drifted onto the table. In return, José Ramón handed me the gigantic key to the stone farmhouse. The old stone house was ours and it was going to be our biggest project yet.

19 "DO YOU WANT TO SEE MY BULLETS?"

Back in Valencia, sitting under Stuart and Harriet's porch one late afternoon, we discussed the overwhelming project that lay ahead. They poured wine and sucked on olives as they listened to our ideas and concerns.

I liked their positivity and creative minds but it dawned on me as I watched them together, what an extremely eccentric couple they were. Stuart more so, with his persuasive, engaging banter. He could spontaneously derail a conversation in an instant with a joke. He was the kind of person who, on a night out, could upstage an entertainer - much to everyone else's embarrassment but his own.

I gained an understanding that it was part of Stuart's personality to be charming and flirtatious. He often projected a sexually frustrated undertone, through his anecdotes. His wife, the voice of reason, seemed well practised at pacifying his boyish energy. It was an interesting cocktail, where an evening with this couple could never be boring. Being in the company of our new friends, was enough to help us forget the daunting months of renovation and rough living ahead.

That same evening, to celebrate our house venture, Stuart had booked a table at Michael Angelo's Pizzeria. A family-run restaurant, a two minute walk away from their house. After a delicious pizza and an embarrassing interlude where the Major loudly involved himself with a couple on the table next to us, we wished our fellow diners goodnight. Stuart insisted that before we go our separate ways, we stop by back at theirs for a nightcap. It was a nice suggestion and even though Jason couldn't drink because he was driving home, we thought it would be rude not to agree.

It seemed though, Stuart had other ideas than just a thumb-sized shot. He jovially convinced me to hop onto his new leather reclining armchair to 'test' the various positions of the furniture. This resulted in me being thrown on my back blatantly in front of his equally drunk wife who didn't seem to bat an eyelid at his lingering hand on my knee.

"Do you want to see my bullets?" Stuart asked. I agreed, but only because I assumed he would leave the room to get them. Before I could move, he flipped the chair upright and hastily ushered me into his office. Inside the small room, the walls were adorned with pictures of vintage aircraft and shelves dedicated to military memorabilia. Stuart came up close and handed me a brass canister that I thought was a vase.

"It's a shell casing, it's huge isn't it!" He bellowed, his eyebrows playfully danced and I couldn't help but find him amusing. A moment passed and I realised then how alone we were and how perhaps, it wasn't the best situation to be in. I never felt truly threatened by his flirtatiousness - it was just part of the act of who he was. I was more conscious of how my absence would look to Jason and if he might wonder where I had got to. Maybe Stuart had seen my hesitation because before I knew what was happening, he swiftly kicked away the office doorstop – a diffused landmine - so we could be alone. Was he playing me? I suddenly felt like he was disrespecting my relationship with Jason. As the door slowly closed off my escape, I muttered an excuse for the loo and lunged through the gap in the door leaving Stuart on his own. Once in the bathroom, I sat on the loo seat feeling drunkenly-light-headed and confused. Deep down I knew Stuart was harmless despite his flirtations but I did blame myself that perhaps my friendly demeanour had possibly been misunderstood.

I gathered our coats from the hallway and found Jason in the lounge, being closely entertained by Harriet. I gave Jason the *time to leave nod*, and we quickly left giving Harriet and Stuart quick hugs as we departed.

Once in the car, I explained to Jason my close encounter and we laughed off the idea that Stuart had any romantic illusions for me. I was young enough to be his daughter *and* they were almost parental figures to us. We concluded it was just a silly drunken moment. One that Stuart probably wouldn't even remember. We left it a few weeks before we saw Stuart and Harriet again. But when we did, the couple offered well mannered, friendly company with a good dash of humour. There weren't any further awkward moments so we put the whole bizarre scenario behind us. Or so we thought, until the next time we met…

20. ON THE CARAVAN HUNT

Over the following days, we busied ourselves trying to locate a second-hand caravan to live in on-site for the Galician project. It seemed an impossible task. They were mostly mouldy and overpriced, each viewing more depressing than the last. Eventually, after a month, we tracked one down south of the country in a Costa paper. The ad boasted, '*Streamline 18-foot, 3-berth, Abi Jubilee caravan, great condition*'. We scrambled to the phone immediately.

After a brief chat with the owner Jackie, we arranged to view the caravan the next day. It was a long drive in the southern heat so we were relieved when we arrived at the designated meeting place - a petrol station near a popular tourist village. But it soon became apparent that Jackie was a no-show. Feeling furious after the distance we had driven, I called her and she sheepishly redirected us to another location – a *further* two and a half hours drive south. She explained that she had miss-pronounced the first village but was too embarrassed to call back and correct it. I had the feeling that this was all part of an elaborate scam but we had committed ourselves by coming this far. Reluctantly, we pressed-on into dry, unfamiliar expat territory. We passed desolate villages and tiny farming communities' and before long there was nothing at all. Finally, we arrived near a battered road sign that Jackie had mentioned and parked up outside the only house in the area – a grubby-white detached villa with black window bars and no sign of life. There were so many tumbleweeds rolling by that I half expected to see an armadillo scuttle across the parched ground. There, in the corner sat a caravan and it didn't come as much of a surprise that the caravan was as nondescript as the place it was sitting in.

Ten minutes later – trailing a cloud of dust, an old maroon banger hurtled toward us, smoke pouring from the exhaust. Jackie jumped from the driver's seat and strode purposefully toward us, as she lit a cigarette. She wore a purple dress that embraced her thin, deeply tanned body and for a second I imagined she could have been Ruby's younger sister.

In the time it had taken for Jackie to arrive, Jason had inspected the caravan by crawling underneath it. Both tires were flat to the metal rims, leaving a stack of bricks to support the back while the front rested on a stone wall. I could see Jason's irritation rise. It was a long way to come for a turkey.

As Jackie smoked, Jason and I circled the caravan, peering into cracks and tugged on disconnected wires. I thought the caravan looked acceptable from the outside. It was modern and spacious from what we could see through the large wrap-around windows. But he grimaced at such a high asking price if the caravan wasn't in working order. The front had two expansive double-glazed windscreens - unfortunately with a brick-shaped hole through one of them - a flaw that hadn't been mentioned in the ad *or* during our telephone conversation. Once inside everything looked as it should. I was happy with the layout, the storage cupboards, the pull-out bed looked comfortable and the little kitchenette was clean. There was a gas hob, an oven, a fridge and a sink. And best of all – no mould infestation!

I was feeling quite good about it, but Jason was unsure. Jackie exhaled a plume of smoke from her nostrils, which reminded me of an angry bull I'd once seen in Valencia. She became agitated, checking her watch and her surroundings, which gave me the distinct feeling she might be on the run from someone. While Jason inspected the caravan a little more thoroughly, I asked a few general buyers' questions;

"Do you have all the paperwork, is there a toilet-cartridge, does the water pump work?" to which Jackie shrugged an unhelpful, "Dunno."

We weren't willing to pay the advertised price – that would be ludicrous in its condition – but we did want to leave with a caravan and hopefully before dark. But I wasn't comfortable parting with any money if Jackie didn't have the paperwork, so I pressed her on the issue. She stated vaguely that the papers were *somewhere else* and she wasn't sure if she could even find them, as she had moved several times over the past month.

My suspicion grew, who *was* this woman? Did she even *own* the caravan? I took a breath and looked down at my feet. I was about to walk away from the deal but we had come so far and we didn't want to go away empty-handed – this was our last resort and we couldn't start our project without it.

Jackie realised I was having second thoughts and tried to pressure me.

"Can't we just hurry this along, you gonna take it or what?"

Why was she so uneasy? It was making *me* nervous. She huffed and turned back towards her car and I wasn't sure if she was going to take off. She grabbed a packet of cigarettes from the dashboard, took one out, lit it and dialled a call on her mobile.

I briefed Jason on what I now thought was a dodgy situation but to my surprise, he had come around to the idea and seemed impressed with the caravan after all. Apart from a few faults that would have to be dealt with, it appeared on the surface, to be a good buy. It was impossible to know the depths of any issues without testing the electrics, something we couldn't do on its pre-existing flat battery. Jason and I agreed that if we could knock the price down and the paperwork was intact, we'd go ahead and take it. Jackie had been half-listening to our conversation while on the phone, and for the first time allowed herself to smile slightly.

Jackie snapped her phone shut and flicked her half-smoked cigarette into a dry grassy patch, I was sure would ignite. Her nostrils flared with irritation as she pointed at me.

"Right, if you want the paperwork you'd better come with me into town – then we might be able to get down to business." She stood, hands-on-hips, directly waiting for an answer.

Go with her on my own, to a place, I didn't know? I didn't like this one bit. I could foresee tomorrow's headline:

'KIDNAPPED BRIT, FALLS FOR COSTA CARAVAN SCAM'

Jason, clearly not worried about putting me up for collateral, nodded in approval for me to go off with this woman. He went to the back of our car and dragged out a foot pump so he could get to work on the caravan tires while we were away.

In Jackie's 80's British-registered, untaxed Fiat we bumped off into the wilderness of the desert with smoke pouring from the exhaust. We passed a wooden shack, an abandoned plough and a set of wagon wheels. With no markings on the tracks or even road signs, I couldn't tell where we were heading. I was relieved when we reached the main street but it was still as deserted as any western movie set. We drove on, trailing dust into the hot air as we went. Still thinking that Jackie could turn out to be a dangerous psychopath, I made polite conversation. At least she seemed to have relaxed a little. Perhaps her mood had lightened with the prospect of payment coming her way. She lit another cigarette and held it in her lipstick-smeared teeth while she fiddled with the air-con - which had packed-up long ago from the evidence of dust on it. I shuffled my feet among the food containers in the foot-well while she gabbled on about drought.

Ten more minutes of strange conversation later, Jackie threw the car in a haphazard parking position in front of a dilapidated red brick building with a flat tin roof. She jumped out and I trailed behind her trying to keep up. Inside the building, I noted dark corridors of bedrooms. Ceiling fans wafted down smells of damp newspaper and urine as I stood in a reception area amid two long burgundy plastic-covered sofas. On the table, a selection of grubby faux leather folders with what appeared to be a menu inside – only I couldn't see a restaurant. Convinced I had been brought to a desert brothel I remained standing. I didn't want to confuse any punters and get into any more trouble.

Jackie introduced me to a large man behind the reception counter whom she called Jon. He was Dutch and was like a father to her, she explained briefly before running off in search of the caravan paperwork. Jon had a creepy sideways grin and disturbingly huge hands – the kind that might be used to handling chloroform.

Jackie must have been swallowed up into one of the dark corridors because just a few minutes of waiting for her seemed like hours. The ceiling fan ticked and whirled as Jon kept a close eye on my movements. When I caught his eye he pretended to fiddle with something behind the counter. I scanned the waiting room for secret cameras but couldn't see anything. I heard doors slam and got a whiff of urine again. It was so repulsive I decided to wait outside in the heat instead. A man came out of the brothel and gave me a little wink as he got into his car. *Great*, I thought to myself. *He thinks I work here.* Jackie finally reappeared with a flimsy folder under her arm and shook her car keys at my nose.

It was a relief to arrive back at the caravan to see Jason covered in dust, looking a little happier now that the caravan was upright on plump wheels.

"Right, let's go over the paperwork, I'm sure you'll be wanting to make lunch soon," I said, nodding at the shoddy white villa we were all standing outside. Sheepishly, Jackie turned away from the house. "Couldn't we just settle up now? You have all the paperwork. Check it over when you get home" she said with a weak smile and I knew something wasn't right.

At my unease, she blurted out.

"This isn't my house."

I paused; Jason looked up from inspecting the battery unit.

"*Right, OK*, so whose house is it?" I asked

"A friend but he's away right now; he permitted me to store

the caravan after the brick incident, thought it would be safer out here." she stammered.

"Is the caravan yours?" I bravely asked in a high-pitched voice, preparing myself for a *how very dare you* reply. An unconvincing

"Yeah" escaped her lips. I didn't know what to believe. However, the brick story added-up and the registration matched the documents we had from the brothel. I suspected the caravan wasn't hers to sell, but it wasn't stolen either as her name was on the documents, which was all I cared about.

So I concluded with my lightning detective skills that Jackie must have been running from her ex-husband, whom she had mentioned bitterly, and wanted to keep the money for herself. We had offered a fair price – reduced because of the damaged windscreen. And she begrudgingly wrote a receipt, in-case we got stopped by the police on the way home. Jackie snatched the cash out of my hand so fast I felt as if I had been nipped by a jackal. She jumped back in her car and sped off leaving a cloud of dust. We were left with the feeling that if we didn't hurry and get moving, someone might come back and stop us from taking it.

The sun had fallen below the horizon by the time Jason had connected the caravan up to the car. And by then, he realised the caravan's rear lights weren't functioning at all. After an already stressful day, we were in for a tense drive back towing a long load in total darkness with absolutely no indicators or brake lights. Thankfully the roads were quiet and we eventually arrived home safely, undetected by police or angry ex-husbands.

The following morning, Jason delved into the bare basics of the caravan and discovered a mess of burned-out electrics. We enlisted the help of an electrician friend who stripped it back and rewired it. In the process, a mouse's nest under the cooker was found. The critters had nibbled through everything including small chunks of marijuana stuffed behind the sofa.

Two weeks later with all the electrics finished and some added home comforts, the caravan was ready for its biggest mission. We only hoped it would stand up to the tough Galician weather and be our solitude during tough times. With just over a week to go before we left, we had a lot of organising to do. I had advertised our villa for holiday rentals online and bookings were already beginning to pour in for the summer. All that was left to do was to find a couple to handle the change-overs, cleaning and maintenance. Someone who had people skills with our English speaking clients.

After a few interviews, we found the perfect couple for the job, Freddie and Brenda. We liked them instantly and knew they would be capable representatives for our Rural Retreat holiday let business while we were slogging away in our northern haven.

21. A NIGHT TO REMEMBER

As a farewell and good luck gesture, Harriet and Stuart had kindly organised a delicious Thai dinner party at their lavish villa. They convinced us of the practicalities of stopping over for the night so we could have a drink and get to know the other guests. With four double bedrooms, they certainly had the room, so it was arranged without too much inconvenience that we would sleep in Stuart's old bedroom while he moved to the spare guest bedroom next door to ours. The bedrooms and the family bathroom faced each other on the spacious marble landing upstairs. The largest was Harriet's room with a luxurious super-king-size bed, with expensive-looking Egyptian cotton bedding fit for a queen. Stuart joked that even though they had separate rooms he had 'visiting rights' on occasion.

We arrived that evening a little late; the other guests, two couples, a mix of both Spanish and English were already settled under the outside terrace. Armed with drinks, we took a seat and got to know the other couples. Harriet, slightly flustered, promised us all a feast that night – she had been marinating the meat for two days and was excited for us to taste her first Thai curry after having being taught in a culinary school a year before. The accident with her back had since left her in agony and she was unable to stand for long periods, so until now cooking had been kept simple or left to her husband.

We weren't let down, the curry was probably the best we'd ever had, and everyone had second helpings, followed by lashings of dessert. Stuart poured more wine and we leaned back with full and satisfied stomachs. It had been such an enjoyable evening, where conversation flowed as much as the wine and our hosts had been attentive to everyone's needs.

At the stroke of midnight, Stuart checked his watch and stood up from the dinner table. I wondered if he might make a speech but instead, he wiped his freshly-shaved chin with his napkin and excused himself, declaring it was his bedtime. *That's a bit odd*, I thought to myself, *wasn't it strange to retire to bed before your guests?*

Harriet didn't seem to mind her husband's early retirement and wished him goodnight. I wondered if it was hard to shake the regimented standards the army had instilled in him.

We carried on drinking and chatting to the other guests for a couple more hours while Harriet packaged-up left-over curry as party favours. I realised then, that the other guests weren't staying over for the night but had ordered taxis to come and collect them.

We pitched-in, helping Harriet clear the piles of dirty dishes. She was as drunk as we were because her debilitating back pain seemed temporarily cured as she glided to the kitchen with ease in her long silk skirt. Even witnessing her lift a coffee cup most days had seemed to cause her agony.

"I think my husband has arranged it so we'll go out for late-morning brunch together, does that suit?" Harriet sounded even more eloquent when she was plastered.

"Sounds great," We agreed, "and thanks again, Harriet, this has been a lovely evening," I slurred, slightly embarrassed by my drunkenness.

We insisted on helping her clean up the rest but she shooed us away to bed. Halfway up the stairs we paused to look back and saw her polishing off the dregs of red wine the other guests had abandoned in their departure.

Blurry-eyed from too much alcohol, we brushed our teeth and giggled into the bathroom mirror. I had forgotten to bring anything to sleep in, but it was a sweltering-hot evening anyway so I could cope without. We slipped between the crisp, clean sheets and drifted off in a drunken haze.

What a perfectly lovely evening that was.

"Wake up," whispered Jason. "I said - wake up!" I felt my left hip being shaken softly.

"Stop it, go away," I said feeling irritated.

"Wake up, something is -" Jason paused.

"You're hogging the sheet again," I said pulling it up to my chin, as I turned to face the wall.

"It's Harriet, she's... well... *she's in bed with us!*"

Now *that* got my attention – but I knew that would be ridiculous. I giggled a little at the thought.

"- and she's *naked, totally naked!*" Jason squeaked.

I opened my eyes and turned to look at him. He looked terrified. Slowly I sat upright and peered over behind Jason's back. Sure enough in the moonlight, I could make out the curvy figure of a blonde woman huddling into his back. The sheet barely covered her naked hip and smooth pale thigh.

I started giggling, and couldn't stop.

"It's not funny, why are you laughing?" Jason looked sternly at me.

"What if this whole thing is a set-up? Stuart might walk in any minute. Perhaps this was *his idea?* Or if it isn't, he might think this was *my* idea. I might have to fight him! Wait a minute – what if they're swingers? Oh my god, this is *all too fucked up!*" panicked Jason.

"Shh, she might hear you!" I felt hysteria rising in my chest again and suppressed my laughter with the back of my hand.

I was still very drunk and I needed a moment to process this. I looked at the glowing bedside clock that read 3.35 am and for a moment considered leaving her there to sleep it off. Jason had such a bewildered look in his eyes that I had to do something.

I pulled on the shirt I'd been wearing at dinner and calmly

walked around to the other side of the bed. Jason was too scared to move as if he might trigger a grenade. I rushed into Harriet's bedroom to find her lights still on and grabbed a woollen blanket laying on the bed. Back in our room, Jason was now standing by the window in his boxer shorts, hunched and ready to tackle someone. I draped the blanket over Harriet and steadily slid the sheet from underneath her. She stirred.

"Harriet, honey, you've come into our room by mistake, this is our bed tonight." Slowly Harriet raised her head and looked about the room.

"Wha - I don't understand… *Oh, Christ!* I am *so* sorry, *so terribly sorry!*" She noticed she was naked under the blanket and looked utterly mortified as she clutched it tighter around her breasts.

I helped her to her feet and we walked into the adjoining hallway where for a brief moment Harriet paused at the top of the stairs and arched backwards almost toppling down the marble staircase. I protectively caught her bare shoulders as we silently crept past the room where her husband slept.

Back in her bedroom she muttered apologetically and collapsed into bed. I gently closed her bedroom door and made my way back to our room, tip-toeing along the cold marble floor. Jason shut the door after me and proceeded to stack a chair under the door handle.

"Is that really necessary?" I said. "She's asleep now"

"It's not for her, it's to keep *him* out; we don't know who might be next!"

"It's all probably some misunderstanding. Sleepwalking maybe? She wasn't quite with it and she did drink a lot *and* she is on very strong medication as well for her terrible back pain," I said, unsure if even I believed my words. "Anyway, how did you know she was in here?" I asked.

"The light from the hallway woke me when she entered, but I wasn't sure if it was a dream. Then she whispered something in my ear as she climbed in, next minute she was spooning me, *naked.* Can you imagine if Stuart *had* set this up? He might have wanted to join us!"

"What did she whisper?" I asked, wondering if he was missing out some sordid detail.

"I don't know," he said and silence filled the room. "I didn't catch it"

"Well, it's getting late," I said, "let's sleep on it, decide what to do about it in the morning," I said.

"The *morning!*" Jason said with dread. "Oh god, we arranged to have brunch with them!"

"Well, *that's* going to be awkward," I snorted.

We tried to sleep but the night's events rolled around in our sobering minds. Was it all a scandalous plan of theirs to liven up their marriage without discussing it with us first? Perhaps we had given off unconscious signals indicating that we might be into this kind of thing. Didn't I read somewhere that swingers have magnolia trees outside their houses, as a secret symbol? But I could have made that up. I'd have to check out their trees in daylight. It rolled over and over in my mind. Once or twice Jason told me to shut-up as I clutched my stomach in laughing fits, replaying the look on his petrified face. It was a priceless moment.

We had a dilemma though. Do we bring it up in a jokey way? Did we know them well enough to do that yet? Or did it not matter as we had been forced into this predicament? Do we pretend we were so drunk that we don't remember a thing? How would Stuart take the news if he genuinely didn't know what had happened? Or perhaps he did?

It seemed almost too absurd not to mention it. Just the thought of sitting at a breakfast table across from Harriet would be like denying there was an elephant in the room - wearing pearls, with a blanket wrapped around her shoulders. But all the same, I kept thinking if we brought it up, where would it leave the friendship? We didn't want to purposely cause trouble between a married couple. We agreed that we'd try to get out of brunch and see how things went with Harriet in the morning.

Morning arrived almost instantly and for a moment the little sleep I did have had erased the night's memories. That was until we heard the chirpy whistle and hum from Stuart as he washed in the bathroom with the door open. We fretted, stalling our exit. We made the bed and gathered up our belongings into our weekend bag. Jason dressed and crept to the loo, only to be greeted by a grinning Stuart wearing nothing but a tiny pair of tight pants as he scrubbed his teeth and shrilled, "Morr-ning!" at the top of his lungs.

As it turned out, Harriet never emerged from her bedroom that morning. Perhaps she was still sleeping off the wine or painkillers, or maybe she had remembered the incident and couldn't bear to show her face. In any case, we were grateful for her absence and made a quick departure from the perplexed Major.

**

"And you never mentioned it ever again?" asked Alex, thrilled at the story I had just told him.

We had briefly met in the village the next day, at our favourite meeting place - a bar overlooking the mini grand canyon in our village. I had been bursting to tell him the details.

I opened my hands. "We didn't think the timing was right. At what moment is it appropriate to open the, *by the way, thanks for last night but did you know that your wife climbed into bed with us, naked conversation*? He had given up his bedroom for us after all – perhaps Harriet *had* intended to visit her husband. It could have been a perfectly reasonable mistake," I protested.

Alex gave me the 'look', the affectionate one that said, *come on, you don't believe that any more than I do.*

"A very… *convenient* mistake," Alex says slowly smiling back at me as he took a long sip from his ice-cold Amstel.

"All I'm saying is that if someone were to consume a large amount of booze, mixed with morphine-based painkillers, they're bound to make a silly mistake. They might not be aware what they are doing," I said, still defending Harriet.

Alex leaned forward and withdrew a cigarette from its box.

"And how many people get plastered *and* know full well what they're doing? That person might, for example, feel so dreadfully embarrassed the next morning that they're too afraid to show their face," he said and lit his cigarette, pleased that he'd trumped me.

22. A SERIES OF DISASTERS

A few days later we were on our journey to north-west Spain, the spruced-up caravan in tow. We felt like premature retirees tugging the bulky shell across the country, a trail of cars snaking behind us with palpable frustration. I was thankful that we would only make one trip with it, its destination being its final resting place to serve as a home until the old farmhouse was ready to accommodate us.

The long journey was going well, considering the pets had been cooped up for twelve hours in the car and the frequent toilet stops made an already laborious expedition, insufferable. The Land Rover was packed to the hilt with tools on the roof, rolls of extension cables, months of clothes, medicines, tea bags and other necessities tucked into every available space. The caravan tugged and bobbed like a boat in tormented seas.

Just beyond Madrid, away from the shanty towns, we decided to stop for the night in a service station to get some sleep - our safety and sanity depended on it. It was a smelly, overcrowded Repsol station with a constant flow of trucks, caravans and coaches. Speakers perched high in every corner of the car park, blasted loud static white noise and fast tempo tunes of clacking castanets and foot-stomping trumpets. This was followed by passionate flamenco tunes, which was abruptly interrupted by a staff member who wanted to communicate to his pump attendant. Usually, I'd shake my little hips and wobble my head about to such a lively Spanish rhythm but after so long of travelling at a snail's pace I was exhausted. Jason looked utterly wrecked as he guided the car into the far corner of the forecourt.

Leaving the dog in her basket and the cat to roam free in the car, we made up the bed in the caravan and threw our bodies limply into it.

But sleep didn't come easily and for most of the night, we lay there listening to the beeping of reversing trucks, as they positioned themselves for the night. Occasionally the caravan would rock from side to side as the wind battered us. Speakers crackled, interspersed with adverts eerily voiced by adults mimicking high-pitched children's tones. It felt like torture so we miserably got out of bed not having had a moment of sleep and at five o'clock in the morning we got moving no matter how groggy and hungry we felt.

By the time we got to León Province, the car had potentially consumed most of the diesel in Spain. We refuelled, checked our belongings were still tied to the roof and re-joined the motorway, the tarpaulin hummed a tune in the wind as we made our way north-west. The incline increased dramatically as we hooked our way around mountain corners and before long, we joined a popular tourist road, en route to Santiago de Compostela. We passed drenched pilgrims stomping along worn paths with the aid of their staffs. Each burdened with substantial rucksacks, shrink-wrapped in yellow rain ponchos as transparent as tissue paper. I noticed tiny stone cottages dotted the roadside, with their sunbeam shell plaques – a peregrinos hostal, offering salvation for these weary and lonesome travellers.

León is indisputably beautiful with its green mountainous ranges, knee-high wheat fields and modern, 'eco' wind turbines spinning in the distance. A constant spit of warm rain feeds the vegetation which made us feel as if we were driving through a tropical greenhouse and I wondered why we had never visited such a pretty place before. From León, we had estimated that we would reach our ruin within three hours, which would leave enough time to set up the caravan before sundown.

Madonna blared on the radio as the Land Rover strained with the weight of our load, so it was no wonder a short time later that we heard a worrying clunk from the back wheel, sounding like loose change in a washing machine. Jason was immediately concerned and slowed down, desperately searching for a place to pull over. Conveniently we spotted a Shell petrol station up ahead – seeing that familiar symbol was a relief offering us another kind of salvation in our time of need. As we limped into the forecourt the rattling noise grew louder, then momentarily there was silence, followed by an alarming screeching sound. I jotted down where we were so I could inform my parents of our location - Villafranca del Bierzo, an area that is known for producing deliciously sweet, plump cherries.

The place was already busy with cargo trucks when we both hopped out of the car hoping to see a simple fix to the problem. To our surprise, the wheel itself looked intact. While Jason crawled under to get a closer look I noticed a group of lorry drivers on the other side of the car park, sitting on the tarmac eating their lunch. As if they might have been expecting us, they stood in unison and sauntered over. I wasn't sure if they were friendly so I remained cautious and announced to Jason's feet under the car that we had visitors. I smiled at the group as they approached but they didn't reciprocate. *Was there going to be a problem here?* I wondered. I felt intimidated by them as they surrounded the Land Rover, like a pack of wolves. They looked at me with some degree of interest but didn't say a word. Jason slid out from under the car with an oil stripe across his forehead. All at once, the men squatted on the ground. They consulted among themselves and each took turns to inspect the car and report back to the group. I stood back feeling slightly awkward but I was pleased when I realized they were trying to help us.

They spoke in a language that we didn't understand. One of the men pointed to the wheel and made a circle gesture with his finger, the others agreed with a unified hum. Jason automatically understood this, hopped into the Land Rover and drove in a wide circle around the petrol station. The noise from the wheel stirred again, causing the lorry drivers to nod in agreement at their diagnosis. By the time Jason hopped out, the group of men had concluded that the wheel bearings had sheared, rendering the car useless.

It was incredible how body language and hand gestures could unlock the words that divide us. Our only solution would be to get the car to the nearest mechanic as soon as possible. We thanked the lorry drivers, who turned out to be from Turkey, for their helpful assistance.

Within half an hour of Jason's phone call to the insurance company, the Grua - recovery truck had turned up. Jason had managed to explain some of the technical problems over the phone in Spanish, so we hoped the problem would be fixed fairly easily, but we knew full well that things were never that straightforward in Spain. The recovery man seemed offended at the mere sight of the caravan and pulled a distasteful face. He casually dialled a number on his mobile, lit a cigarette and spoke to someone while shaking his head and examining the caravan. He wasn't remotely interested in the problem with the car.

The recovery driver approached us. "You know tomorrow is a national holiday here?" he said in super-fast Spanish.

"Mierda," said Jason, putting his hand to his head remembering that we had been caught out with a Friday bank holiday once before – when we didn't have a scrap of food in the house and had travelled for an hour to a hypermarket, only to find the car park deserted and every shop closed.

"So you know, the mechanic at the garage just told me he won't work on the car until Monday. You will have to wait here for the whole weekend. We were silent with shock.

"If you want, I can take the car now and leave it in our storage depot but I cannot take *that* as well." He thumbed in repulsion at the caravan.

We were horrified at the thought of leaving the caravan alone on a petrol station forecourt, filled with our belongings and pets – it would be so vulnerable without the car.

We both stood there for a while deliberating our problem, feeling the pressure of answering the man who was waiting. *What about all the tools on the car roof and all the other boxes of equipment?* Where does it all fit without the vehicle it came in? I thought to myself.

We decided there was no point in the car going to the depot if they couldn't work on it until Monday, at least we'd have both car and caravan with us for the weekend. It wasn't the best start to our new renovation project but it would give us a chance to explore a little of this beautiful area on foot.

So that was how we ended up living at a petrol station for a few days. We were helpless and there was nothing we could do but sit it out and embrace the situation as part of our extreme life makeover. We piled things up in a corner of the caravan so we could sit on the sofa and put out a table. We explained to the petrol station staff we'd be temporarily camping in their car park from anything up to a week, and hoped they didn't mind. They were very gracious and offered us the use of the facilities and charged our mobiles behind the counter. If there was ever a petrol station to be stranded at it was this one. The staff were a helpful team of young women and over the coming days, we had hot showers, fried egg breakfasts at the petrol station café and lunches in a family-run restaurant next door. I strapped the cat into a small harness so we could take him and Macey for walks by the river. It was a relief for the pets to walk about outside, but the incoming trucks scared the cat and a few times he attempted to escape my grasp. We tied a long rope to a crash barrier so that we could hook Macey's lead to it and she had some freedom to sniff about the car park.

Overnight we had become nomads, stuck between places and making the best out of what we had. We wore the same clothes for days, and bought bottles of wine the lorry drivers watched me sneak into the caravan. We had other comforts as well. Harriet's delicious Thai curry had inspired me to cook a batch of takeaways for the trip. The supply would certainly see us through the weekend, reheated on a camping stove. As we settled down in the caravan, our evenings coasted into entertaining ourselves with jigsaw puzzles and card games. We flicked through tourist information and tested each other's Spanish by randomly selecting words from the dictionary.

In the mornings, I liked to sit by the window and watch the changing weather outside. Heavy rain one minute, hailstones the next that would thump on the flimsy panelling. At times the clouds hung so low, I thought I could have touched them through the caravan sunroof.

With a free weekend on our hands, we tried to sum up enough energy to plan the house renovations, but neither of us was in the right mood. It was hard to imagine what the place might look like now; for all we knew the heavy rain might have washed away the dry mud holding the stone together, and caused the building to collapse.

Previous to our departure, we had sat in astonished silence watching a news report on the television. Animal activists had freed minks from a fur farm near our Galician house. Farmers were searching scrubland and nearby ruins in the hope of finding them before they ravaged any crops and livestock. I was now convinced that we would arrive to find a hundred-thousand beady-eyed mink cohabiting in our barn.

The truckers' community at the petrol station was small and welcoming, and there was always some kind of exotic music filling the air as drivers made tea and played dominoes. Almost daily these men offered to share their small lunches with us, even though every time we declined their kind offer. It was humbling to have such generous strangers offer what little they had.

I speculated how hard their life on the road must be, going for months without seeing their families. It made sense to me, then, how isolated their world must be and how being here, resting for the weekend with the other men, was probably the closest thing they had to a family.

Finally, Monday arrived, and we were awakened by a loud banging on the caravan window. I pushed aside the curtain to see our mechanic impatiently signalling towards a tow truck, his engine still running. We threw on our clothes and raced outside to greet him. The replacement part had arrived from Madrid so he was ready to tow the car away. After a reshuffle of our possessions, Jason hopped in the tow truck as our car was winched up and taken away. I was left alone with the caravan with Jason's instructions to chain it to the crash barrier in case an opportunist tried to steal it.

A short while later Jason arrived back at the petrol station in a taxi. The mechanic had told him that the car should be fixed by the following day so it was looking like our stay here was dragging into a five-day visit.

I walked Macey through a knee-high grassy field where I spotted a woman selling fruit and bought a punnet of dark red cherries. I shared them with the lorry drivers and when Jason returned we sat in the caravan doorway scoffing through the rest of the cherries as the sun began to set. Jason's mobile rang with the news that the Land Rover was ready so he dashed off to the petrol station desk to order a taxi.

As darkness was falling we decided it would be too late in the day to travel on that evening to our stone ruin and would depart early the next morning so we could set up the caravan in daylight. This place I called home for several nights would remain a bizarre but special place in our Galician adventure.

The next morning, after thanking the petrol station staff and leaving them with a gift of chocolates, we got back on the motorway.

Before long the landscape became familiar and I felt a nervous excitement at how close we were to our new adventure. We pulled off the motorway onto a busy single carriageway, on route to our local large town. Up ahead we noticed the army-green uniforms of the Guardia Civil. They were flagging vehicles down for a routine document check and we knew, from our load it was likely we would be stopped. The two officers indicated that we pull into a narrow bay on the edge of the road. But with little notice, Jason hadn't enough time to negotiate the space, causing the caravan to stick out at an awkward angle and hold up the flow of traffic behind. The officers didn't seem bothered we were causing a roadblock, they were more concerned with our caravan from the glares we received. We tried to remain cool.

Jason handed over his car documents to one officer as the second peered into the back of our car, only to find Macey staring right back at him, wagging her tail. He circled the caravan, peeking through the window. He must have been disappointed to see open boxes of camping and cooking supplies, wellies and packs of English tea, rather than a van of illegal immigrants.

"Driver's licence" instructed the first officer in Spanish. Jason handed it over as the second officer joined him. He looked closely at the laminated card.

"Oh shit, they're foreign." The first said to his colleague.

"Really, where from?" said the second officer, intrigued.

"I think they're from the Ukraine."

"Oh, fuck that's all we need!" said the second officer, clearly irritated.

Jason and I exchanged appalled looks.

"Why you here?!" the first Guardia Civil officer bellowed. "What you doing in Galicia? You here to rob us?!" he said directly to Jason, with a smirk on his face.

We were so utterly shocked at such stupidity that for a moment we were speechless. The officers had assumed the 'UK' letters on Jason's driving license was an abbreviation for the Ukraine, not the United Kingdom, and had made racist assumptions based on this. They hadn't realised we could understand what they were saying.

Impatient cars honked from behind the crooked angle of the caravan. The first officer held up his hand for them to wait, then placed both hands on his hips so that the right was resting on his gun. He faced us and my heart began to palpitate.

"So, where you from?" the first officer asked as if he was starting his interrogation all over again.

"London, England," Jason replied.

"Eh?" said the second officer, confused. "Passports!" he barked.

I handed them over and the second policeman jabbed his colleague on his lapelled-shoulder pointing out the mistake cross-referencing the passports with the license.

"Ah, I see, yes, of course, England," the first officer accepted, but he was clearly annoyed.

"What you doing in Galicia?" the second officer asked but this time he seemed a little relaxed.

"Holiday," Jason said. It seemed pointless to explain we were there to work and it would only prolong the hold-up. We had the caravan with us after all.

"Holiday, huh - Who is *she*?" He nodded at me, making me feel about an inch tall. I introduced myself and the policeman visibly relaxed.

"Time to pull out the trump card," Jason said to me from the side of his mouth.

"Mi padrastro es Gallego." I stated.

"*Su padrastro es Gallego?*" the officer repeated. He considered this for a moment and nodded, thinking it through.

Joseph had always told me that if we ever got pulled over and questioned in Galicia we simply had to say, "My stepfather is a Galician."

"It will work," Joseph told me, "trust it."

And the policemen 'trusted it'. We were released from questioning and drove onwards to the ramshackle house that awaited.

But less than fifteen minutes later it appeared we were still running on bad luck as we took a wrong turning towards our little hamlet. It had been a while since we purchased the house so we couldn't quite remember the way. It didn't help that the small lanes all looked identical and weren't signposted.

We pulled off the main highway into a narrow lane, barely wide enough for the caravan to pass without scratching the sides. Right away we knew we had made a mistake but with a caravan, in tow, it was impossible to turn around, or reverse, so we reluctantly pressed forward.

A farmer with his herd of cows walked out in front of us and blocked the lane, causing our frustration to reach boiling point. After a long wait, Jason tried to edge forward but the car wouldn't move and it was then we noticed that the caravan had fallen to the left and was leaning precariously against an old stone wall, – the wall of someone's house to be exact. The left wheel had slipped and was wedged down a rain gully.

We both got out and Jason stormed off to get a jack from the boot of the car. I tried desperately to call my parents and ask for help. But the mobile reception was so bad that when I finally got through, all my mother could hear was, "- problem…caravan crashed…lost!" before the line went dead.

Seething at my phone, I looked up into the craggy face of an old countrywoman. She wore a blue gingham calf-length apron and hefty leather boots with thick brown socks. She looked as if she belonged in another decade. Her arms might have belonged to a burly sailor they were thick and muscular, folded tightly under her conjoined twin breasts.

"Hola," I said to break the ice, my hands now a little shaky. My blonde hair, straggly and smelling of petrol caught her attention as I messed about with it. She knew I wasn't from around here, she frowned her forehead into a Neolithic point. I realised that this must have been the village we could see from the top of the hill, just down the road from our hamlet. We were so close and yet in more trouble.

Without taking her burning eyes off me, the surly woman tilted her head to one side and wiped her muddy hands on her apron as if to clean them before throttling me. She bared her needle-sharp teeth as she shouted over her shoulder. I was aware that Jason was somewhere in the background, swearing and fretting, but he had left me on the front line.

As if summoned, three more unpleasant women popped their heads out from surrounding doorways before clambering outside to ambush me.

The burly woman, clearly the leader of this village had strategically positioned her posse around me. I tried speaking my best Spanish and apologized for the caravan incident. I didn't know what else to say and had no idea if she even understood me. But the woman talked over me in rapid Gallego, and then all the other women in their rusty stained aprons pitched in. It was impossible to listen to all of them at the same time. The noise was deafening, it certainly wasn't helping my already explosive stress levels and all I wanted to do was to run away. Their hand gestures became wildly threatening, pointing at my face and then to the caravan.

Why couldn't they empathize with me? Surely they could tell it was an accident? One of the ladies prodded her chest hard and then pointed to the area of the accident. *It was probably her house we had crashed into, yes, I understood that. I was very sorry, but it wasn't as if the building had collapsed?*

I was convinced that any minute now she would try to grab me and shake some compensation money out of my pockets. She worked herself up so much she had a coughing fit and then slapped the top of her own head which startled me so much I could feel tears bursting behind my eyes. I guess for me, with my British ways, all this shouting was quite uncalled for, given that I could actually feel my hair going white from the stress.

Finally, before I resorted to multiple acts of violence, a helpful young villager the women called Juan, appeared with a log stump and a flat plank. He must have seen what had transpired and come to our rescue. At Juan's presence all of the women retreated inside, I assumed back to their cooking pots from the delicious aromas emitting from the windows. Juan dropped the wooden stump into the gully and used the longer piece of wood to lever the caravan upwards. His enthusiasm was a little overzealous as he thrust the wood under a non-supporting area of the undercarriage causing pieces of plastic to shear-off. Before Jason could protest Juan ordered him to get into the car and drive forward. It worked and the caravan was back on the road. Jason vigorously shook Juan's hand, grateful for the help and we drove on to our village, dragging the wrecked caravan behind us. We felt so relieved that we wouldn't be spending one more moment in this strange place.

The little accident had left the caravan in bad shape. I was surprised to see how little it took to break it; The door hinges were damaged so that the door was slightly crooked, the awning rails had been squashed flat, sidelights and reflectors were cracked and two windows had deep scratches but I didn't care, at least we were on the home-run.

In just the first week of arriving here in Galicia, we had worried our parents by being stranded at a petrol station for five days, questioned by policemen, toppled our caravan in a hostile village and we hadn't even seen our house yet. Things had to get better.

Two minutes later we reached our little hamlet and thankfully all was quiet. We drove past a small cluster of houses and turned right toward our road, which was also fairly narrow. A white-haired old lady stood outside an open door in her apron, clutching a small bloodied knife in one hand, a dead rabbit in the other. She did have a friendly smile though which put me at ease despite the weapon. We jumped out to greet her and she introduced herself as Manola, proudly stating she was 87 years old and was our nearest neighbour. After our brief introductions, and welcoming us to the neighbourhood, the conversation became more difficult. I was used to bending my ear around Castellano Spanish but Old Manola's Galician language was so thickly masked in a regional dialect that it was impossible to understand her. I just smiled and nodded and hoped, for now, that would be enough.

Jason manoeuvred the car and caravan towards the back garden gate and tried to reverse in. But the angle of entry was too tight and no matter how many times he tried, it wouldn't fit. Inevitably the caravan scraped along the stone exterior of our house almost ripping off the last unscathed window.

I pointed out a dip in the ground, which was stopping the caravan from moving forward. The injured caravan – now looking very ropey – sloped on one side and leant against the stone wall as if it had given up the will to live. Jason used a jack to lift the fallen side of the caravan so he could fill the gully but the jack broke and in a moment of fury, he kicked the useless metal object into the road. Old Manola retreated into her house and closed the door.

Exhausted with our cycle of incidents, I felt like going back to Valencia on foot. Defeated, I called my parents for assistance. They were relieved to hear we hadn't been in a major pile-up and agreed come straight over to help.

While we waited for their assistance, we took the first glimpse at our project. It wasn't the best moment to re-introduce ourselves to the enormity of it and we both sat down in the dirt and almost wept with what faced us. What on earth had we done?

Thankfully before despair took hold, my parents showed up and Joseph tackled any problem by firstly rolling a brown liquorice cigarette in his usual calm demeanour.

Old Manola appeared again, no doubt curious about my parent's arrival giving her opportunity to further question about our plans for the old farmhouse.

Jason dismounted the caravan from the car, then the four of us each took a corner position so we could push it through the gates to the garden by hand: my mum and me on a handle each at the back, and Jason and Joseph at the front pulling it over the ditch we had hastily filled with stones. But once through the gate, the caravan took on a momentum of its own. My mother and I couldn't see where to direct it from the back and hadn't realised Joseph and Jason had let go as it rolled with the slope of the land. We began to run with it, screaming and digging our heels into the soft grass and hanging on for dear life as the cemetery wall loomed closer.

Once the caravan had come to a stop, both Mother and I peered out with dread expecting to see coffins and cadaverous arms spilling from a break in the wall. But the caravan had, in fact, come to an abrupt stop thanks to a boggy pit covered in nettles at the foot of an enormous lemon tree. We looked at each other and burst out laughing.

23. IN OVER OUR HEADS

Our small village was tucked deep inside the bowl of a valley, surrounded by grassy mountains. Seen from a distance, the tiny church and our stone house were the most prominent buildings in age and size and would have at one time stood with just two smaller dwellings for many years before it was crowded with other, newer houses.

At the entrance of our village green stood a tall, carved stone crucifix on a platform and behind it an imposing moss-covered concrete house where our communal bins were kept. Up a bank on the right sat a small abandoned pub with a football and tennis court which was so neglected that weeds had claimed the land back.

On the left was a vast grassy field that sloped downwards and gently rose to a forest clustered hill. A donkey stood there, tethered to a fence, grazing in patches of daisies which reminded me of flowers back in Britain. It gave me such pleasure seeing, lush grass and flowers again in the streets and on the side of the roads when in Valencia nothing grew abundantly without irrigation.

It was a shame to see that some of the areas in the village had been spoiled in the time we had been away; an old mattress, a sofa with the stuffing hanging out, a toilet and scrapped cars had been piled into some of the hedges. It was a small example of how rural life had its blemishes. Joseph didn't seem concerned by the wreckage but he did point out that a resident had started to build what looked like an extension onto their existing house without a sniff of planning permission, within the short time it had taken us to purchase our house and return to Galicia. Rubbish was piled high all around the shack, dirty, sun-bleached toys were strewn all over the front yard. But what shocked me most of all were the three hunting dogs, that were confined to a tiny cage under the hórreo – the space no larger than the boot of a car. Those dogs looked more broken than anything else I'd ever seen. Joseph pointed out that he thought they didn't seem like well-educated people and we should stay out of their way as best we could. He thought they were most likely settled gypsies who usually lived in quite large numbers in one house. It seemed ironic then, that we were the ones living in a caravan.

For the first two days, we were pleased to have the caravan as a distraction. While the cat enjoyed shoving his paws into the many mole holes in the garden, hoping to claw a new type of victim. We fiddled with the complexities of caravan dwelling. My mother had given me just the right advice before she left us the previous day

"Don't even look at the house again just yet," she said in all seriousness, "Or you might cry for five days as I did with ours. Don't worry though, it'll pass eventually."

As usual, my mother was right with her advice and we stayed away. I didn't give in to tears despite it being a shock seeing how much money and effort we would have to put into this project. We were pleased the three-hundred-year-old house was still standing and hoped we could carry the project through to the end. It was a huge risk, coupled with the doubt as to why had we mortgaged the Valencia villa for it.

A few days later, and a good catch-up on sleep, we finally did have a good nose around the house separately. My heart sank when I popped my head around the bedroom doors and remembered the extent of the repairs. Rocks that had fallen from unsupported walls lay on the floor next to skeletal bird remains.

There was so much to repair and rip out we didn't know where we would start. It was going to cost a lot more than we had previously thought to renovate, and I was certain that we were well over our heads on this one.

But I learned my first property developing lesson then, overcome anything with ridiculous positivity. My spirits lifted and once again I fell for the charms of the original features, the sun-bleached shutters and natural curves in the beams above my head.

Overall the farmhouse had that look of rustic charm for which we Brits go weak at the knees – as long as you didn't look too closely at the mould and creatures living in the walls. The disorder of the terracotta country roof tiles gave the farmhouse that charismatic charm we associate with romantic, panoramic shots in foreign films. The whimsical moment when shutters are sprung open and the dust is released symbolising a sense of serene freedom and purpose and newfound responsibility. Aside from the old farmhouse, the matching stone barn at the back of the garden was an exciting prospect *and* there wasn't a runaway mink to be found. It housed carefully selected planks and blocks of beautiful chestnut timber. At the very back of the barn, large pieces had been stacked in piles. They would make excellent replacement beams which would help our budget.

The next day over breakfast, fat droplets of rain relentlessly battered down on the caravan's thin roof and it felt as if summer was never going to arrive. As the rain worsened, pouring harder every hour, I wondered if the caravan would be washed away in the night or, even worse, end up sliding into the field next door. Against the battering downpour, Jason rigged a tarp over the top of the caravan so we could have the air vents open and have a porch-like cover under which to take-off our muddy boots.

A few days later after the rain had stopped long enough for us to duck back inside the dark house, we looked in with horror to find it weeping in every corner. A stream had found a new path through the house that trickled its way along the corridors. We discovered the roof leaked where the tiles had broken so we scattered an assortment of pots and pans, buckets, bowls and jugs across the floors to catch the drips. We formulated a break-down-plan, roughly sketching down how we would achieve drying out the house, starting with the roof. There were three separate roof sections which thankfully, were not all were ruined but varied in some degree of repair. From broken tiles or collapsed beams to more serious woodworm rot. Access to the roof was tricky, complicated by the three different roof levels and a curve in the building. We hatched a plan as to how Jason would access the awkward parts of the roof and chimney by breaking a hole in the roof. Once the work was done the hole would eventually become a Velux window. Only one roof needed to be completely replaced and Jason was going to undertake the project with advice from Joseph and the guidance of a DIY book.

The rain worsened as it hurtled at horizontal angles and hindered our progress outside. We had to find other gutting and clearing jobs to keep us busy. In the following days, Jason and Joseph talked endlessly about the pressure involved with such a huge renovation. Joseph offered whatever support we needed to get through it and warned that working with stone was a delicate process that had the potential danger of collapsing should we not get it right from the beginning. I was starting to regret not buying a standard brick house.

The following week we drove around building supply companies, pricing up basic materials of sand, cement, and wood. We got lost in industrial parks, asked locals where we could buy things and used every contact we had to guide us to the right places. We marched to our nearest garden centre and bought ten young conifer trees to screen off the back of the grave compartments. In comparison to Valencia, the selection of building merchants was limited to just a handful of places. Even though I had always admired how non-commercial La Coruña city was, there simply wasn't enough choice which meant we ended up spending more on materials than we had previously budgeted – but we had to take what we could find.

We got to know the husband and wife team who owned a local ferreteria hardware store in town who were always pleased to see us. It was nice doing things the old-fashioned way, hunting down small family-run wood yards to hand-pick joists for slicing on the flatbed machines. When we greeted the carpenter we had to scuttle through wood shavings so thick you couldn't see the floor underneath. The proprietor, an elderly gentleman dressed in denim dungarees and a baseball cap often chatted with Jason in great lengths to find out the purpose of our requirements. Jason noticed the man's right index finger was missing, leaving a purple stump. No doubt he had lost it on the very flatbed he was about to use to cut our wood – A thought that made my knees go weak. He scribbled incomprehensible figures in pencil on the rough piece of wood to make sure there were no misunderstandings before he made the cuts, and waved our money away, saying that we could pay whenever we liked – like all his good customers he trusted us to come back and pay when we could.

We found many friendly plumbing merchants, electrical shops and paint shops, down cobbled alleyways. The downside to sourcing all of these unique, individual shops was that it could be so time-consuming. More often than not when we had driven out especially for some woodworm treatment, or to hire machinery, the shop was unexpectedly closed.

On these occasions, we learned about patience like never before and headed straight for the nearest coffee bar. A delicious almond cake in a pastry cup washed down with strong coffee would always make up for it.

24. INDISCREET DELIVERY

With the help of Joseph's negotiating skills at the town hall, we got the go-ahead from the planning office to start our reform. It would take months for an official Obras works certificate to be approved but with a wink and firm, mutual understanding of the word 'discretion' we could go ahead.

As we were about to walk out of the town hall the planning officer stopped Joseph and whispered to him,

"If a neighbour happens to denounce you for starting the build before the permit has been issued, we will deny any involvement of this conversation and you will be fined." Joseph nodded and thanked him before ushering us to a nearby bar to explain as if this was all some covert operation. It seemed standard practice to do things with a tap of the nose here - but with the prospect of the works permit taking anything up to six months to arrive, had no choice but to make a start as soon as we could.

The following Friday afternoon a delivery truck arrived with large quantities of building materials. Despite our numerous warnings that our access road was so narrow, it would only accommodate a small delivery truck, the building company had sent their standard bulging lorry anyway. It had turned up packed full of pallets, with a hydraulic arm bent at the back and ready for action. Unfortunately, the driver managed to wedge the truck between a small stone house on the corner and the ancient churchyard wall. We cringed as the driver struggled to move the lorry forward, narrowly scraping the moss-mottled stone leaving the religious villagers to stare disapprovingly at the driver.

Smoke poured from the engine, the young driver hopped out and declared that the truck was now broken, and he needed to phone his father to come and fix it. It would be hours before they could unload the materials so we hung about outside, sweeping the road and trying to look as casual as possible.

With all the commotion over the delivery it wasn't surprising that we were drawing unwanted attention to ourselves – and our restoration project. The older residents of the village wandered out of their homes in slippers and dressing gowns and stood around whispering and asking questions.

Most of the village population – except for Old Manola, ambled into our private garden that morning. As curious as children they crept over to our battered caravan and pushed their faces to the Perspex windows – cupping their eyes from the sunlight with their mucky hands, unknowingly depositing a breathy fog on the plastic windows.

In some ways, although I know it shouldn't have, it disgusted me. I have never been one to be over-clinical but strangers were invading our personal living space and it made me anxious. After all, I didn't invite them over, they had wondered over as if some village announcement had compelled them to it. I hopped inside the caravan and pulled the blinds down, hoping the villagers would go away. I realised then, though, that this was just another cultural adjustment for me to make. This was a normal attitude for around here, *Su caravana, es mi caravana.*

I will try to adapt, I thought to myself. Inevitably the questions would come and I knew that the locals were just curious about us. I stepped back outside and came face to face with another local woman who took no time to ask, "Do you have children, I don't see any? Is there something *wrong* with you?" Her direct bluntness silenced me, and even though I was sure she meant no harm in it, the question was still intrusive.

Joseph had advised me that it was best to answer such questions as vaguely as possible. But I was beginning to think there might be a flaw in this method - my evasion only made them ask again more forcefully. I wondered if they would accept that we were still young and kids weren't on our agenda yet.

"Why do you need a washing machine when you can wash the clothes in the fountain over there?" another one asked. Then I realized they were just old-fashioned and unused to modern ways. For now, it was best to pretend I didn't understand all of their questions than to respond and risk offending them.

Like a group of unsatisfied journalists, the locals pounced on Jason as they noticed him clearing space for the delivery supplies.

Doing away with introductions, the villagers' bombarded him with questions about our house renovations, it felt very hostile, and my mouth was growing sore from forced grinning.

Suddenly I heard a thunderous voice from the apron-clad crowd and out stepped a wandering vagabond. He stood over six feet tall, his cumbersome head supported by a solid neck and wide shoulders. The white of his eyes were tinged nicotine yellow, his puffy, tanned face suggested an outdoor lifestyle that made him look older – I guessed his real age to be anything between forty-five and fifty but he could easily, have been sixty.

He had few teeth, which seemed quite a common look around here. His moustache and unkempt beard matched his yellowed hair. He wore a blue checked shirt that was filthy and gaped in places where he had misaligned the buttons. Only one half of the shirt was tucked into his ripped jeans and bagged to one side as if someone had just dragged him by his collar. It exposed his bare shoulder and a worrisome lump the size of an egg on his neck. His military-style black boots were not laced up fully and had been crudely cut open at the front to allow room for his giant toes to peek through. His blackened feet, reminded me of Dirty Janet.

He stumbled from side to side and I caught a whiff of alcohol. Here, was a man with a strong character and a heavy drinking problem. But something else struck me too, just how much of a likeness he was to the late Oliver Reed. Unlike the other villagers, he had a softness about him and I felt a strange, albeit repulsive, warmth towards him. He shook our hands enthusiastically and introduced himself as Oscar. He immediately offered his assistance to help Jason clear the area as the others watched on.

Oscar's drunkenness gave us an advantage; his speech was slow, deliberate and repetitive which gave us time to absorb bits of Castellano he used instead of the local language. While Oscar pointed to the brick debris that Jason was already scraping away, the truck driver took long strides towards us and announced the news that his father had fixed the truck.

The driver manoeuvred the lorry with the guidance of his father so that it was in place, ready to crane the materials over into our garden. Most of the crowd had finally dispersed for lunch leaving us, the driver, the driver's father and Oscar, who was accompanied by his young daughter Maria. Once in position, the driver wasted no time unloading the materials with the use of a hydraulic arm to lower the heavy pallets down. Jason guided them over and checked off the items as they landed. Oscar shifted about, desperately hoping to be of some use. *Let me help,* he insisted, even though he could barely stand in his state of drunkenness.

After two crates of breeze blocks, a ton of sand and a pallet of cement had been lowered to safety the delivery truck groaned as the mechanical grabber was kicked into more demanding use. Jason unhooked the claw ready for it to be reloaded for one last drop. The metal claw rose up in the air but at that moment the electrics in the truck begin to malfunction, causing the claw to sway uncontrollably in jerky movements while Oscar stood directly underneath, completely unaware of the danger above. We all shouted at him to watch out, but he stood there, hands in pockets, wide-eyed and planted to the spot, confusion dawning on his brow.

As the truck driver struggled to cope with the faulty electrics of the mechanical arm, black smoke pumped into the air. The old truck shuddered as the driver's father instructed Jason to hop aboard and pump the accelerator to get the power to the grabber while he and his son tried to gain control with the failing electrics. Oscar, still unaware of the claw above, beckoned for his daughter, Maria, to join him. Maria, a large girl for the age of twelve, bounced in from the side-lines to join her dad in the danger zone. The driver screamed,

"Move, you drunk idiot! Someone get them out the way!" Young Maria looked up then and realised what the fuss was about. She tried to pull her drunken father away to safety but it was no use, Oscar was rooted to the spot so she gave up trying. And then, right on cue, the metal hook took a giant leap into the air. Our eyes followed as the claw gained momentum and sliced through the air, coming back down with its weight like an anvil that landed squarely on Oscar's head with a thud.

Everyone groaned, then fell silent waiting for Oscars head to split open. We searched for Oscar's reaction, waiting for the fury of pain to arrive, but it never came. He scratched his rubbery purple nose and Maria cupped her hand to her mouth to stifle her laughter. Oscar must have been so drunk he was numb to the pain, which in this case was a good thing.

It was at this point that I realised our 'discreet' delivery had turned into a full-blown circus – including the clown.

The driver managed to unload the last of the supplies safely but it took a further hour and a half for him to exit the road when the truck got wedged on another house as he backed out. The residents looked at Jason as if it were his fault, probably gauging whether they could claim for damages. The driver looked furious – his whole afternoon had been a complete disaster – so finally he sped off without leaving us the bill.

That mild evening, while seated under the grapevine on a bench constructed from bricks and a long plank, Oscar joined us as we drank some well-earned beers to celebrate the start of our daunting renovation. Oscar talked about his past jobs as a road labourer and how he came to take over his parent's sheep flock when they both had died. As Jason handed Oscar a fresh beer, Maria joined us which I was pleased about as she seemed like a shy and lonely girl. I handed her a soft drink which delighted her, and she beamed a smile to her feet. Being alone with Maria allowed me to ask her some questions of my own when I felt that she was relaxed in my company.

"Where is your mother?" I asked tentatively.

"Dead, since when I was a baby," she replied without hesitation as if she had been expecting the question.

"Oh no, I'm so sorry," I said, feeling remorseful for bringing it up. She thanked me for being sorry and bent her head as if there was nothing more to be said.

Oscar felt the need to ask Jason more questions about the house renovations, now that we were away from the crowd. "Why do you need all these building materials? Why can't you live in the house as it is?" he asked.

We explained that the house needed new floors, starting with new beams to hold up the new floors as the house was in a dangerous condition. Oscar looked utterly perplexed at this answer. "You could always use another part of the house?" he suggested. Oscar got up and wandered into the downstairs area of the ruin to see for himself. We followed after him. He looked from one bare stone room to the next. While I still considered that some parts of the ground floor looked no better than the muddied remains of an archaeological excavation, Oscar shrugged, indicating that it was perfectly liveable – clearly, he didn't see things the same way we did.

Long-standing resident Old Manola, was the village elder and the nosiest neighbour we had ever met. Within those first few weeks I learnt that she had eyes everywhere, an old-fashioned spy disguised as a sweet elderly lady.

We had first met her when we came crashing into the village

with our battered caravan. At that time Old Manola had stood there, dazed, with her freshly deceased rabbit, as we descended on her village. We must have seemed a strange bunch and only one of us, my stepfather, who could speak her language. Since that initial meeting, we had come to know Old Manola a little better and she seemed kind and forgiving of our lack of Galician language.

As part of her expert cover, Old Manola seemed to remain on neutral territory and never took sides in a conflict. She remained cool and indifferent, and I admired her for her self-sufficient, independent lifestyle. She masqueraded as an eighty-seven-year-old, 'butter wouldn't melt' super-granny dressed in poorly-fitting outfits, plastic clogs with thick socks, a quilted jacket with an apron over the top, her sleeves always rolled up to the elbows. She told us she had *ten* children, a fact that almost made me fall over; the thought of so much childbirth! Her children, now grown up with families of their own, were scattered around the globe and she was lucky if she saw three of them a year. She lived with her second-born son, aptly nicknamed *Segundo*. Segundo wore glasses with lenses so thick they magnified his eyes to epic proportions. He kept himself, very much to himself, avoiding contact with almost everyone and busied himself with fixing farming equipment on Old Manola's separate farming land, behind our garden wall.

But Old Manola's sweetness by all appearances didn't fool me. She was one of the quickest curtain-twitcher's I'd ever seen; she would also hide behind pillars and doors left open just a crack so she could eavesdrop and relay the smallest detail to the community. All the while she kept busy, pushing wheelbarrows, or digging up potatoes on her land as if she were forty years younger.

Old Manola had quickly spread the word that we did not speak any Gallego, and more importantly that we did not have any children yet. In this community, with a population of approximately fourteen people, news spread almost instantly. The other villagers had no shame. I became blasé to the pretence of mourners visiting graves just so they could peek over the adjoining wall into our garden. They were neither convincing in their grief nor subtle in their mischief so I could not help but smile when I listened to them whispering and clambering up behind the graveyard wall to get a better view of us. In most cases, they seemed to end up hurting themselves in the process which I considered their penance for being so nosy.

It seemed that even the most gruesome job of emptying our cassette chemical toilet gave them something to talk about – they watched curiously from the cemetery wall as Jason poured waste down the sewage pipe into our cess pit. We were baffled and, in an odd way, flattered at the interest in us – and, apparently, our daily routine.

A few days on, finally weary from being spied on, we took a trip to the local garden centre and bought two rolls of bamboo cane fencing. We tied the screen to the back gate and added a hefty unlocked padlock to the chain.

Later that day, Joseph came over and we held a village conference. After having listened to me whine-on about the intrusiveness of the villagers, Joseph thought it would be a good idea to mediate so that the villagers could take the opportunity to ask us questions and he would help translate. The problem was, however, that not only did Joseph have the ability to exaggerate small details in a humble way - making everything seem believable, but he sometimes got so carried away with the attention he tended to, on occasion, makeup stories that could spin wildly out of control, so that even he couldn't stop them. By the time he and my mother tootled off in their Volvo back to their remote village, our neighbours had scattered to their houses and frantically started mopping their steps. They brought gifts over to the house: home-grown broccoli and spinach leaves for Caldo soup with complementary caterpillars and a bag of muddy potatoes that they left hanging on the brass fist of our door knocker.

Curious to understand why the villagers were suddenly behaving so nicely, I called Joseph from the one place in the nearby field where we could get a decent phone signal to ask him what he had said during the villagers' conference.

"Oh, not much, not much. I just mentioned Jason was a policeman back in London."

"What? Why on earth would you tell them that? They're going to hate us now!"

"No they won't, they're scared of authority. Besides, I couldn't remember what the word for 'Prison Officer' was, and anyway they might leave you alone now," he said.

"But I don't want them to avoid us completely! What did you tell them about me?" I asked.

"Oh – can't remember. Publishing assistant or something."

"Well, at least that's true," I added

Joseph paused as if there was something else.

"Oh, and if they ask, I'm an architect and your mother's a lawyer," he said.

"For crying out loud, Joseph! What's got into you?" I said.

I heard my mother shout in the background, "I have the perfect leather briefcase so that I have all my papers for court!"

Was she collaborating with Joseph now?

We ended our conversation and I wondered if I was the only sane one in my family.

25. THE SPIRITUAL LIFE OF DOS RIOS

The church next door was tiny but I liked it because of its simplicity. It was unpretentiously filled with a few hand-carved pews and the small stained glass windows brought colour to the granite walls. There were no ostentatious amounts of gold paint, no chalices or religious oil paintings depicting biblical scenes. Iglesia Santa Maria seemed so calm and holy I felt the need to light one of the candles on the rack by the altar. I did not know who it was for but it felt like the right thing to do. I was disappointed however to find the candles weren't real; you had to put a coin in a slot and a fake red candle would light up for you, provided the unit was plugged in.

I had made peace with the cemetery next door. Having death stare at us from such a short distance made me realise that our whole life cycle was undeniable. It was almost irrelevant to me by now, the cemetery had become such a large part of our rural landscape that days would go by with me hardly noticing it.

It was only when the wind stirred and strange noises arose from the cemetery that I remembered the coffins were there. When I heard rhythmic scratching from the back of the graves, I was convinced someone had mistakenly been buried alive and listened for moaning sounds. But I was always fooled when I found the source of the noise to be a black crow scuttling on the granite roofs of the monuments.

At the weekends there was a certain amount of church activity that gave the village a bit of an uplift. For the residents who were stranded in the village without a car, it gave them a reason to get up in the morning. Priests arrived and floated about in their fine robes on the freshly cut church lawn, it was lovely to see how happy it made Old Manola, she grew very animated as if God himself had arrived!

Funerals were far more frequent than weddings at the church which seemed to be in constant succession and were welcomed with as much interest. It was only Oscar who seemed uninterested, sneaking off during these times in the direction of the woods.

It is important to mention why there was such a frequency of funerals here. At first, I could not understand why, for example, two mourning sisters became so familiar to me. I thought how unlucky these women were to attend so many family funerals, assuming their family members were dropping like flies. But I was soon told about Cabo de año – meaning, 'end of year anniversary or mass'.

On the anniversary of a person's death, the Spanish celebrate the end of the grieving process, they are released from the intense loss that they have endured during the last twelve months after the person's death and this is marked by a second funeral. If that cannot be arranged, a family meal is made to remember the dead.

In the case of the two old sisters, they must have frequently been visiting all deceased family members. I would see them arrive with bundles of pink and yellow plastic flowers and dedicate their time to a ritual of cleaning, praying, chatting and flower arranging at their family's graves. They paid particular attention to the grave of their mother, over which they fought endlessly. Sometimes one sister's flower arrangement wasn't quite up to the standards of the other sister, which prompted a furious amount of shoulder shoving, teeth sucking and vase wrestling. From the upstairs window of the old schoolroom, I watched the sisters sit for hours at their mother's resting place. It seemed their old mother still couldn't rest in peace, with them fighting on her grave.

Aside from the Cabo de año, masses were also held for the deceased throughout the year. These were not necessarily held on any specific date of a funeral or anniversary but brought families together to pay their respect when they could all make the time.

These memorial days were important to devout Catholics, although generations had diluted the dress code, to make the memorials a less sombre affair.

With all these funerals, anniversaries of death and masses, not forgetting the first communions and weddings, it was an active church to live next door to.

It was during one of these Cabo de año memorials that our greedy rescue dog Macey decided there might be something to eat in the churchyard bin. A chorus of hymns made its ascent through the slits of the narrow stone windows, and while one over-enthusiastic man drowned out his fellow churchgoing friends, I grappled to get the dog back as she clambered over the fallen stone wall, heading fast towards the outside waste bin. Racing back through the house I squeezed through the priests' secret passageway and into the garden behind the church. I called for the dog but she had disappeared. About to give up, I turned to walk home but then the back door to the church opened and a small number of people congregated into the tiny churchyard as I stood trapped with my back against the graves. They stared at me, unsure if I was someone they might know – a gatecrasher with a dog's lead in her hand. I apologised, blushed, and ran off in search of the dog where I found her outside the gypsy's house sniffing some bones that had been thrown out into the street. I put Macey on her lead and dragged her away from the scraps and just as I did, three mangy strays I hadn't seen before crept in from nowhere and snatched the bones away. It was a reminder that from the very day we arrived in Galicia there was something undomesticated about the place. I stood there for a moment as the evening drew in and felt a spiritual shift in the breeze. I hoped this wasn't due to our dead neighbours waking up for the night but from the Celtic history, the place was shrouded in. I heard a low howl echo through the distant forest and knew instantly it was the lobos the locals had talked about. It was known that wolves still roamed these parts and it added to the excitement that one day I might be lucky enough to spot one.

After that meeting with the scavenging dogs, it seemed they felt encouraged to follow us into the forest occasionally. They would cautiously trail some distance behind us and it was on one of these walks that we had met Abuela the Grandmother of the Gypsy family. Abuela was short and plump with grey curly hair and had a smile that reached her kind eyes but unlike Manola she didn't go out of her way to welcome us. It was evident too, that when her family were home - she disassociated herself from us. Perhaps they disapproved of us in their village but nevertheless, Abuela remained pleasant. Whenever I saw her she was cheerful and chuckled continuously, especially finding it odd that we walked our dog. I supposed she thought it unnatural that we dedicated time to walk Macey, when she kept hers cooped-up in a cage.

According to Oscar, Abuela's family had illegally extended her small house a little at a time over the years to cope with four generations under one roof. Oscar, whispered this news with alcohol-infused enthusiasm one late morning; adding, that to ease this housing crisis Abuela's family had managed to claim little pieces of land, poco a poco - gradually. Oscar suggested that land was being stolen from him and his family as they were all in one way or another distantly related. It was a bad line to cross and could lead to bitter, drawn-out disputes that could last forever. We were not sure how true this was coming from Oscar but he was their neighbour after all. We had been so wrapped up in our renovations that we hadn't noticed how huge Abuela's entirely new extension had progressed in just two weeks. Her house had doubled in size, precariously tall but at least it had improved the shack-like appearance of the existing dwelling.

Living in Dos Rios was far more interactive than we were used to in Chulilla. Every day a produce van whizzed through the village, nearly killing dozens of chickens and lazy stray cats basking on the tarmac. The bread van was like a ghost train - we hardly ever saw it but heard it screaming and rattling through the village leaving bread parcels swinging on every door knocker as it passed through. Monday came the fish man, Tuesday the meat man, Wednesday came the general groceries man and every so often on a Friday, a clothes man would show up – when I heard this I had to take a closer look. Sure enough, the driver was selling every kind of farming-related clothing gear you could think of from the back of his van, down to wellies and aprons and funny little sun hats. It now made sense why there seemed to be a countryside uniform. The villagers never needed to leave their village for anything, unless they preferred high street fashion of course.

A few times a week a postwoman delivered letters from her silver Ford Fiesta. She handed us batches of unpaid electric bills addressed to the previous owner of our house and sometimes the odd postcard arrived from our friends on holiday. Our English friends thought it was amusing to address the postcard "To the English" along with the name of our village, which was all they could remember while they were on a beach somewhere without their address books. Amazingly enough, the postcards still managed to reach us even without a postcode or our real names.

"Jason" was a name that some people found tricky to pronounce. It amused me when Jason repeated his name slowly many times to teach the pronunciation of it and in the end relented, agreeing to accept a something similar, Yaysone or Señor Jackson - only our new friend Oscar could pronounce it properly.

As the weeks flew by we muddled through, speaking Spanish every day with Oscar and young Maria and they were not shy to correct our mistakes. Old Manola discreetly hung vegetables on our front door and we returned the favour by leaving sacks of wooden off-cuts from our restoration projects to fuel the old fashioned iron stove she cooked on. It was an arrangement that none of us had spoken about, and although I had thanked her many times for the vegetables, it was as if she didn't want to hear it. For the time being, our neighbourly trade made me feel that we were contributing fairly.

There was an odd rivalry between Old Manola and Abuela that I hadn't quite witnessed until one morning when the yellow bread van screeched to a halt to speak to Abuela. While she was distracted, Old Manola dashed over to me and quickly pushed a cauliflower into my hands, all the while glancing over her shoulder to see if Abuela had noticed her perform this act of kindness. Old Manola held her finger to her lips - gesturing for me to remain silent, then raced off into her house before I had the chance to thank her.

Feeling both privileged and confused, I hid the cauliflower behind my back to keep the secret safe. I'll never figure out why giving me an extra vegetable was such a big deal. Unless of course, the cauliflower was one of Abuela's - or perhaps it was customary to share the produce with old friends before offering it to new neighbours? I had read somewhere that Galician country folk have been known to pass around second-hand animal bones for their cooking pots until they are grey and lacking any sort of nutritional goodness so I hoped I wouldn't find a bag of old bones hanging on my door knocker one morning.

26. AN UNINVITED GUEST

A hard day's graft in the ruin was filthy work. We demolished a badly-built brick partition wall that fell with almost no effort. We each used an electric chisel to pry-off, three-inch-thick blown plaster from the walls and Jason made a start dismantling the broken roof tiles. When evening arrived I couldn't wait to strip off my damp working clothes in the caravan and shake the loose plaster from my bra cups.

One of these nights I was particularly tired. I stripped off in the tiny shower cubicle that housed the toilet, washed in the pathetic dribble of the shower and indulged myself in some fond and distant memories of our clean Valencian home. I thought of fresh-smelling clothes and reading by the pool. Of internet access and the warmth of the pool deck beneath my feet. I smiled to myself with the irony of it. How funny that human nature dictates how we only truly appreciate things when we don't have them.

With little time left before my shower water ran dry, I stepped out and wrapped myself in a towel that smelt of a damp attic. In the fading sunlight, I took a deckchair, sat in the middle of the garden lawn with both feet soaking in a washing up bowl and proceeded to shave my legs. I didn't care if Old Manola saw me over her allotment wall or not, I needed the space and light to get these things done. Back inside the caravan and dressed, I started preparing dinner with military organisation to cope with the limited kitchen space. The only preparation area I had was the glass top that folded down over the gas hob, so I balanced pots and pans on the sofa that was waiting to go on the stove. It was a tiring process, especially after such a physically demanding day but I hoped the curry I was making from scratch would make up for the lack of takeaway that Saturday night.

Jason refilled the water barrel and jumped into the shower where I could hear his elbows banging on the thin walls as he washed. I grabbed an onion from the larder box and began to chop it. The fumes made my eyes sting as I blindly reached for the kitchen roll to wipe them with. It was then I noticed Oscar's big, round bloodshot eyes staring at me through the window and I screamed – partly because I was not expecting him and also because his purple drinker's nose looked like a slab of salami pressed up against the little plastic window. Jason flew out of the shower to see what had happened, a tiny towel covering his modesty. He found me rubbing my watery eyes and pointing at Oscar, fuming mad at this new intrusion.

"He scared me, he ought to know his boundaries by now!" I shouted at Jason. I leapt out of the caravan door, pointing half an onion at Oscar

"This is no good!" I shouted at him in English. He looked utterly confused – as if I was angry about the onion. Jason, also frustrated at the lack of privacy, hurriedly threw on some shorts and took Oscar away to the entrance of the garden for a disciplinary chat.

I felt bad then – poor Oscar. He looked mortified and hunched his giant shoulders as he plodded towards the gate with Jason. I watched from the caravan window and hoped Jason wasn't being too harsh. I could see much arm-waving back towards me, and then Jason checking the padlock on the gate. Oscar demonstrated how he breached our lock by sticking his Hulk-like arm through the bamboo fence, breaking pieces off in the process, unlatching the bolt to let himself through. Camping onsite had its plus points but having little privacy wasn't something I had considered when it was inside the walls of our garden.

As far as Oscar was concerned we were his friends and therefore he didn't need an invitation to come over whenever he liked.

Two cultures had collided. I could see Jason carefully piecing his Spanish words together to get his point across. He was being kind but firm and eventually, Oscar seemed to accept the privacy rules of the friendship. Before he walked away he asked Jason if we were all still friends, "Of course we are friends," said Jason with a slap on Oscar's heavy shoulder. Oscar beamed and said he'd be back the next day.

Jason padlocked the gate after him and a moment later we heard Oscar bursting into his cousin's house.

***

Every day I noticed how Galicia was so very different from Valencia. There was a detachment from the rest of Spain that I hadn't felt before now but that was the truth of how it felt to me. It was as if there was a reluctance to progress into a modern world, which I don't suppose is such a bad thing if you want to experience the traditions as they would have been hundreds of years ago. But being so stuck in the past meant there were moments of such utter frustration for us; trying to pay utility bills manually at a counter that was hardly ever open and then having your electricity cut off because the old contract was still in debt from a previous resident. We found it particularly frustrating when we received letters from the council written only in Gallego, without a hope of us understanding it. It was impossible to investigate how three hundred and seventy euros had disappeared from our bank account without a trace. Even with the help of Joseph translating the vague letter.

Despite these moments of insanity, we began to use our time in more fruitful ways. We choose Sundays as our exploration time and travelled to coastal areas. We drove to Ferrol's fishing port and the town of Pontedeume, which I loved for its quaint little cobbled streets and colourful fishing boats. I fell in love with the Jurassic coastline of Plaja La Vaca in Arteixo with its giant jagged rocks protruding from the smooth, clean, butter-coloured sand. Its wild choppy waters and shallow caves had me captivated from the moment I stepped out of my shoes. I had found my favourite beach in the world and there was not a soul on it.

I was surprised to hear that some Gallegos had never been outside of Galicia, let alone outside Spain making me wonder how important it is to have a comparison to other places. Gallegos would assure you that there is no place you will find better seafood and meat produce - and I certainly could not disagree with that. But I considered if this might not make foreigners seem more alien, with little or no chance of ever fitting in?

In the days when we popped into town, I played a silly game of trying to make people smile. But it was proving to be quite a challenge and I ended up feeling resentful. In the supermarket, money was snatched from my hand and change dropped down on the counter as if I were a despicable human being. It was disappointing. I was not sure if everyone was this miserable towards foreigners or just miserable in general? I hoped someone might surprise me and be friendly in return one day.

27. PIGS IN PEASANT CLOTHING

Our morning hadn't started well. We had a long list of tasks to complete and both of us were in terrible moods knowing we would waste another day driving around to find the things we needed. We had been in four queues that morning but hadn't got anywhere and I was frustrated that simple things such as buying a few postage stamps seemed so complicated.

"We don't have stamps," the woman at the post office told me. "You have to go to a tobacconist." *Of course, I thought.* We pounded the cobbled streets off in search of a tobacconist which we found but was closed. We queued for over an hour to pay an electric bill in a shop that sold light-bulbs that had hundreds hanging from the ceiling, yet the store was so dimly lit we stood in near-darkness. As each customer shuffled forward to the desk, they seemed to share a common complaint of their extortionate bill. The girl dealing with these inquiries obviously had no training in customer service as her reaction was to scream at them in response. By noon, the time most Gallegos' take their mid-morning snack, I was so fed up all I wanted to do was to go home but instead, Jason took me to the nearest café to refuel.

After a terrific cup of coffee and a delicious almond cake, I felt relaxed and ready to tackle the rest of our errands. We headed to the nearest internet portal in town so I could handle some Valencian rental bookings. Internet cafés weren't commonplace in this area so computers were housed inside a noisy video-gaming arcade. It was where most of the local teens hung out, drinking Fanta limón and smoking cigarettes in the doorway.

Twelve ancient and boxy computers sat in cubicles wired up to slot machines. A euro gave you around thirty minutes but my euros tended to get swallowed up before I could even sign into my email account. We shared and swapped computers with the African and South American girls, who came in on rotation. They were always smiley, kind and helpful. They dressed in synthetic, provocative clubwear and trotted around in towering transparent plastic heels. They seemed outgoing and I liked the way their presence balanced up the macho clientele; the "doorway" boys behaved themselves when they were around.

I had no idea at first that these girls were 'working girls'. Being nosy (a trait I learned from Old Manola) I sneaked a peek at the girls' computers one day. I didn't put two and two together until I noticed they were all using the same web page, their names on a booking form that showed their commitments in hourly slots. They did not need to write anything down as they checked in so regularly. It was interesting to know that not everything was done the old-fashioned way, perhaps things were moving on here after all.

Or so I thought.

A quick visit to the supermarket changed all that and plummeted us back into the wheelbarrow of rural life. I could not quite believe my eyes when I saw a grotesque supermarket display, depicting a farmer and his wife, in the refrigerated meats section. Only, the farmer's head wasn't an artistically carved melon or pumpkin or anything cute like that, it was the severed head of a pig on the shoulders of a human form. It was *Pigman*. This was someone's cheap attempt at livening up the Jamón and cheese section by inventing a scene other Campesino's – country folk could identify with. It was brilliantly disgusting! Something you might see in an Italian Mafia film.

I squeezed the newspaper-filled arm of the life-sized farmer. Standing at about five foot tall, Pigman was dressed in dark trousers, a blue gingham checked shirt and an ill-fitting beige body warmer. A straw hat and a thick winter scarf finished off the provincial look.

The farmer's wife, standing by his side, wore a black calf-length mourning dress with an oversized blue knitted cardigan, fastened at the neck with a ribbon bow. On her head was a scarf with holes cut on both sides so the piggy ears could poke out.

Both 'pig-farmers' had been painstakingly stuffed with straw and paper to pad out the clothing to realistic form. The cuffs had been tied with string to keep the hands – or pig's trotters in this case – from falling off onto the floor.

The smell was disgusting. The skin of the pig's faces had the pinky, yellowy marbled effect one might see on a corpse. To make it look even creeper, the pig's faces had no eyes. The eye socket's shrunk just enough to give the appearance of a pigs mask.

The setting around these pigs in peasant clothing wasn't that inviting either. A picnic table held a bizarre arrangement in front of them; a bottle of vodka and two glasses, disposable plates, a basket of dried pigs' ears (in case they were peckish) a wooden barrel containing a bouquet of flaccid spinach, a string of black sausages and a pig's trotter, which I was guessing had been thrown in as it was going spare.

If anything, this whole scene put me off pork instantly. We took our mobiles from our pockets and took a series of photos to show our friends back home. I could imagine the uproar it would cause back in Britain if this had been a display in any popular supermarket.

That night I had a horrible dream of Pigmen police knocking on all the neighbours' doors in our village, demanding to see their residential papers. Instead of police badges, they wore discount stickers and transported themselves on ramshackle skateboards. They barged into houses making horrible screaming noises to flush out the residents and when I woke with a jolt I could still hear the awful squealing.

It was dawn and my sleepy eyes adjusted to the familiar mould spot on the caravan ceiling. Jason was still asleep and most of the village dogs had started their familiar, lonely howl. I could hear muffled noises coming from our barn. I got up, threw on a dressing gown and wellies and walked across the damp grass. On the other side of our adjoining barn wall, I could hear Old Manola talking softly to herself. She sounded like a little girl playing with her dolls and then I remembered she kept rabbits in her barn in a locked cage so I guessed she was talking to those. - Not long ago Old Manola had dragged us inside her shed to proudly show us her crops and animals, I hesitated, worried about seeing anything kept in horrible conditions for this would surely have added to the anguish I went through every day with animals that needed saving. But not wanting to appear rude, I went over and by all standards, I was relieved to discover Old Manola took some pride in taking care of her animals; after all, she would be the one eating them.

There was a flurry of activity from the barn, followed by an awful high-pitched scream. Old Manola then made her way back through the allotment with two floppy grey rabbits in her hand. This was rural life as I was learning to live in it, the unchanged tempo of existence.

Our friends Alex and Kazimir drove up from Valencia to see how we were progressing with the build and to explore the northwest for a few days. It was a welcome surprise and although I had been keeping Alex updated there was still a lot we wanted to show them. They had booked a room in town, a dark dingy place situated above a chocolate shop which sounded more appealing than it was in reality.

We took a couple of days off the renovation and enjoyed hitting the tourist sites of La Coruña with them. We hopped aboard an old wooden tram, which took us on a delightfully breezy tour - starting at the city's seafront through the port and towards the famous Tower of Hercules lighthouse. Kazimir, Jason and I climbed over a hundred steps to the top of the lighthouse where we took photos of Alex standing below on a giant blue compass mosaic. Its arrow pointing north to its Celtic brother lands beyond the choppy Atlantic sea. Against the wind, I pointed out to Kazimir that further west on the Galician coastline there is a place called Costa da Morte.

Its name meaning the 'Coast of Death' derives from the many ships that have tried to enter the port and were smashed into the rocks. A legend is told that the wind on this exposed coast can cause a deadly wave to rise from calm seas in an instant.

We walked along the coastline, our cheeks turning pink from the battering wind. We stopped for lunch and drank cold beers in the cobbled Plaza Major. It was just the break we needed, in the company of good friends.

Back at the little hamlet, in the fading light, we walked around our dilapidated farmhouse, explaining the grand plans we had for the place. Alex and Kazimir were both stunned at the amount of work we were taking on, but like all good friends, they praised us on the little we had achieved so far and spurred us on with buckets of positivity for the remaining hard slog.

Old Manola took a moment away from her allotment to meet our guests, greeting Alex and Kazimir with her usual warm smile. Alex looked utterly perplexed when he tried to converse with her in Spanish and didn't understand her reply. It was good to know it wasn't just us that had trouble understanding her.

On our last night together the four of us decided to enjoy a home-cooked meal rather than eat out at a restaurant. Under the canopy of darkness, enveloped in our humble caravan, we sat around the small candlelit table having shaken off our shoes to warm our toes by the oven. Jason opened a bottle of red as I made up a salad and shoved a lasagne in the little oven. Kazimir smiled fondly at me and shook his head, he said it was funny to see me dancing around the tiny kitchen preparing a two-course meal in such an uncompromising space. We drank and ate, laughed, told stories and in that most bizarre place to have a dinner party, it was a better atmosphere than any restaurant could have offered. We talked endlessly about the locals and the pigs in peasant clothing and it ended up being possibly one of the best evenings we had ever had together.

28. A HEATED MOMENT

Our visitors had distracted us for the right amount of time, allowing us to feel refreshed and also see the restoration with fresh eyes after they had gone.

Despite being dry outside, inside the house was bleak and chilly, the stone walls saturated to the touch. Joseph had told us that apart from airing the house regularly, it was important to have frequent fires to dry out the stone thoroughly, otherwise, it would always remain damp and encourage wood-eating bugs. After hammer-drilling more plaster off the walls that morning, I planned to give my arms a rest and make a fire in the old kitchen fireplace downstairs. This would be a good way to clear the mounting pile of wood and warm up the house at the same time.

The lareira was an integral part of the farmhouse's structure, the beating heart that pumped heat through the floors and into the bedrooms. Having already sorted through a heap of rotten beams that couldn't be reclaimed, I had enough of a woodpile to keep me busy for a few hours.

I stepped up onto the knee-high platform inside the lareira and crouched to build a small heap of sticks and paper ready to light. I looked up inside the chimney and scanned the blackened bricks until my eyes caught the brightness of the sky. I marvelled at its carefully balanced slate and wooden structure. How had it stood all this time? Perhaps decades of soot had kept the stone cemented together. As my eyes adjusted, something caught my attention. A small, red leather bible, the size of a pocket dictionary, had been tucked inside a gap, perhaps for safekeeping. I extracted it as well as other trinkets; old Spanish coins, a glass drinking flask, a broken hand-carved crucifix. I ran my hand over the carved wooden post. The craftsmanship was beautiful, a testament to the history of the property and all that sat under it. I hoped in every way we could restore it to its former glory.

I lit the fire, it briefly took but only for a few seconds before dying out.

After a few more pathetic attempts, it still wouldn't light. Perhaps the kindling was damp? I was determined to do it myself without the help of Jason. Finally, after using up half the matches in the box, the fire caught and so I began feeding it with old cereal boxes and rotten Galician newspapers, of which there were numerous crates. I was careful not to overload the lazy flames but then realised, by the volume of smoke that some newspapers were damp and the fire went out. Feeling defeated, I dragged Jason away from his work duties and asked him to get the fire going for me.

One simple match strike later and a little fire was crackling away. He left me to my burning while he carried on working upstairs on the roof. Impatient over the time I had wasted already, and wanting to get the room cleared of all the wood, I added long pieces of old timber at a time, pushing them further into the fire as they burned. I broke some rotten chairs into pieces, added those. Half an hour later the pile of wood had halved and I felt like I was making a good practical contribution to a day's work. The fire started looking a little short and needed more fuel so I decided to have a quick look around the house to see if there was anything else I could burn.

I found a bulky wooden treasure chest in a bedroom and dragged it downstairs. It was the kind of pirate's trunk that as a child I might have spent hours hiding inside. I lifted it by its curved lid, riddled with woodworm and without breaking it up I dumped the entire thing on the fire. A minute later and it was ablaze. The metal strips around it popped and sprung, I stepped back from the heat and waited till it died down so I could move it with a broomstick I was using as a prodding tool.

Then out of pure stupidity, I made a really bad decision. I thought that it might improve the fire if I flipped the chest up on its end. At that moment it never occurred to me that putting a tinder-dry, air-filled box on the fire this way might encourage the flames to an unimaginable height. Positioned upright the flames engulfed the box, boosting the fire to a full-blown, uncontrollable blaze. I dropped the broomstick and backed into the wall behind me as if waiting for an explosion. The whole room with its low ceilings gradually filled with smoke and I could no longer see the tops of the flames as they were drawn into the blackness of the chimney.

A hot sweat of panic flushed over me – it was a monster out of control and I couldn't get near it. Smoke choked my eyes and throat so that I had to run outside. Meanwhile, Jason was upstairs, whistling a happy tune while cementing the roof beams into place. I tried not to panic him when I shouted up in a voice as calm as I could muster,

"Er, Jay, can you give me a hand down here?!"

Straight away he knew I was in trouble.

By the time Jason raced down the ladder and a flight of rickety stairs the fire looked formidable. Seeing his alarmed face only confirmed that we were in a lot of trouble. He stood motionless for a moment trying to figure out how this had happened, as I sank further away from the heat and into my own shameful corner. I pathetically prodded the box with the broomstick again, hoping the chest would disintegrate to ashes. Fear gripped at my chest and crushed my lungs; I found it hard to breathe in my panic. I noticed with horror that the precious chestnut shelves had caught fire and were turning black before my eyes. A cluster of disconnected electrical wires had broken off and was burning like dynamite fuses. Everything nearby began to burn and I remembered the conversation we had the previous night, about how house insurance was a pointless safeguard, justifying that we'd be saving the cash because it was already a wreck, so what more could happen to it?

Jason calmly demanded I run and get the hose; this was one fight we were going to have to take on ourselves. As I scrambled out to the garden I prayed I had reconnected the hose to the trigger and not left it connected to the washing machine as I had to do every time to use it. I hoped we hadn't had a water cut and that the hose would reach far enough through the house. As I handed over the length of pipe to Jason, he was busy moving objects out of the way. A laundry bag of his best clothes had been drying out by the fire, but the plastic was melting into the fabrics. I ran back out to the garden and lunged at the tap, pulling it on full blast as Jason went to work fighting the flames. He noticed that halfway up the chimney stack, rocks were beginning to fall out. The fire had loosened the mud that cemented them into place so that ember chunks flew down, landing at our feet. I grabbed my heavy-duty dust mask and put it on, added my blue hard hat and stepped out the way.

The heat was unbearable so I ran around the house opening windows and doors to release the smoke. Strangely enough, no nosy neighbours came round to see if things were all right. It was siesta time so our little community was probably all tucked up in bed with no idea that we were battling a raging fire. I was about to run out to a neighbour's house and ask them to call the fire services but I had a feeling it would be a waste of time and Oscar would most likely hold up the fire truck by standing in front of it and ask too many questions. Plus I seriously doubted a fire truck would ever find this tiny village that was so off the map.

On a positive note, the inferno was contained within one area. The main risk was to the wooden chimney structure, if this was to collapse it would bring down the meticulously constructed chimney stack made entirely of hand-cut slate. There was a possibility that some of the floor above or even the roof tiles that Jason had been working on might follow suit and cave in but there was no point in worrying about that before it happened.

Jason worked on the fire, skilfully avoiding the core and cooling off the surrounding areas. By this stage the timber frame inside the chimney flume was so burnt it had started to crumble, falling in on itself. It seemed ridiculous to us then why someone had used wood to construct the interior of a chimney in the first place – but then a talented craftsman wouldn't have known that a few hundred years later a clumsy English girl was to buy that house, and attempt to build a giant bonfire inside it.

Sweaty but still amazingly calm, Jason proceeded to rain the flames down. It seemed an eternity watching the raging fire being tackled, and it didn't burn out without a fight. The blackened internal structure kept reigniting from the heat alone despite the amount of water hitting it. Eventually after an hour of fire-fighting, and every inch of Jason was covered in soot, we relaxed with a well-earned beer now our ordeal was over. It took a further hour of hosing down the stone walls around the fireplace before the remaining wood stopped smouldering. Once the smoke cleared we noticed that unbelievably the slate structure hadn't moved even though the wood structure supporting it had been damaged. The surround however was a different story, the fire had rolled under the mantle and scorched the beautifully carved shelf into a lump of charcoal. I winced at my idiotic mistake and the damage it had also done to my pride.

We banned access to the old kitchen in case there were instability issues, but I think the only unstable one was me after that. Jason resumed work upstairs, knowing I wasn't getting into any more trouble and I kept meekly out of the way, sweeping and mopping up the gallons of black, sooty water that had flooded the front part of the house.

I swore to myself that I would never light another fire again.

An hour or so later, Oscar made an appearance. He slumped in, leaning on the open door with sleepy eyes and hair flattened on one side of his head. I pointed out the fire damage but he thought the disaster was an improvement and smiled at how much wood I had cleared from the pile.

In the weeks that followed, we focused on dismantling the old roof - taking away buckets of tiles and termite-ridden cross-sections and thus exposing the antique skeletal frame to the elements. We battled against the wind to secure transparent plastic sheeting to temporary battens on the main beams, which would hopefully keep the rain out and shield the floors below.

There were many times when Jason fell into silence and I worried that he hadn't forgiven me about nearly burning the house down when actually he was harbouring the burden of the labour yet to do. It was hard going for him, and he blurted out during an argument one afternoon that he felt as if the house was falling down faster than he could build it up. Which I guess it was in a way – *if I had anything to do with it.*

"It has to get worse before it can get better," I kept repeating to him, hoping to convince us both, but my mantra was wearing as thin as the gloves on my hands.

When I wasn't wheelbarrowing broken tiles to our new secret dumping ground – the mud floor of the garden barn outbuilding, or neatly stacking the reclaimed tiles in rows on our overgrown lawn, I was at Jason's disposal. He was tirelessly banging away on the roof and made fast progress considering he was up there by himself. I handed him tools up the ladder and he passed down broken tiles or clumps of moss in buckets. When he didn't need me I pottered about lifting bags of rubble, clearing the area for the next job.

We planned, plotted and marked-out areas that would eventually become hallways, bedrooms and bathrooms. Big changes were happening, even if it felt like the progress was taking forever.

We worked constantly from morning to night to achieve our daily goal and had accidents with chisels, drills, saws and hidden nails. We shed blood, and tweezed gravel, cement, and wood chippings from each other's eyeballs. Jason fought wasps on the roof and banged and scuffed his head on low beams at such regular intervals, it was surprising he had any skin left on his head at all.

And despite a visit to A&E after a bad reaction from a mosquito bite to my left eyelid that left me looking like I'd been beaten, life couldn't have been better.

When we were in good spirits, we would call out to each other, "Hey, honey! Living the dream?"

"Yup, living the dream!" would be the corny reply.

And we were. We were doing exactly what we had dreamt we would be doing. Maybe we had underestimated how exhausting the work would be, but the moment I recalled leaving my resignation on my boss's desk, I knew it was worth it. Every day of our new life abroad brought bursts of unpredictable - and sometimes scary, freedom.

29. A SUMMER FULL OF FIESTAS

There were so many Galician fiestas in the summer it was hard to resist them all. We enjoyed watching the boating fiesta Os Caneiros, where groups of local people, mostly in their twenties and thirties would hire boats and travel down the river to a vast picnic area to eat. The picnic would evolve into a rowdy all-night party that would eventually end up in the water.

In Betanzos, we stood, submerged in the massive crowd at the San Roque -El Globo fiesta where we waited until midnight when a huge paper hot-air balloon, decorated with political cartoons, was lit and released into the sky.

Another favourite was the Dia de Santiago - St James' Day fiesta in Santiago de Compostela. A historical light show that is projected onto the cathedral façade followed by a magnificent fireworks display. Being present in one of Spain's most religious cities was unlike anything I had ever seen and such attractions brought enormous crowds where you could be trapped, shoulder to shoulder for three hours straight.

During the second weekend of July, the Feria Franca Medieval fiesta in Betanzos is held. We decided it was an ideal place to meet up with my stepsister and her boyfriend while they were on holiday and we could all enjoy the beautiful weather. The town is famously known for its Roman and medieval history – a perfect backdrop for such a fiesta! And on this occasion, every effort had been made for an authentic experience. Locals performed wonderfully disgusting roles; drunken and diseased scavengers –

gruesome flesh falling from their faces as they were dragged around streets by tethered wrists. Crowds had already filled the town centre, giving us no choice but to shuffle and pause as we made our way towards the many stalls. It was strange to hear English and American accents after being away from home for so long.

Dedicated Peregrinos, en route to Santiago, paused on the pathway to marvel at such a spectacle and stop for tapas. As we entered the main square we saw men professionally sword-fighting, clashing metal was observed by small, wide-eyed children as they perched on parent's shoulders. A pyramid of young, loved-up couples sat on the steps of the town hall so they could get a better view of an archery arena scattered with straw and bales of hay. Costumed men wearing black and red robes sat poised on horseback, waiting for the games to start as their horses grew agitated.

The four of us pushed through the crowd and made our way towards a row of cafés under impressive stone arches. We had arranged to meet a Galician couple who were friends of my parents; they were our age and were also undertaking a stone house restoration project of their own. As we passed under an ancient stone doorway, to the oldest part of the town we walked deeper into the street-party atmosphere, the crowd of mostly young men clinking their cider tankards and singing to serenade their girlfriends.

Stalls selling old-style crafts and potions, hand-carved wooden spoons, and leather bracelets lined the streets on either side, making passing through a slow process. The vendors themselves dressed in regal costumes: red, green or black velvet low-cut dresses exposing beautiful cream corsets with ribbons. Some vendors were dressed authentically poor, in green wrinkled tights, a sack tied at the waist covered in stains.

I was impressed just how much detail had gone into creating an authentic medieval atmosphere. Event organisers had covered street signs, and traffic lights with woven sacks to disguise all modern-day equipment. Green wheelie bins and bottle banks had been hidden behind hay bales and broken wooden pallets. The streets we had got to know, now seemed unrecognisable.

I noticed people in the crowd were drinking from rustic terracotta cider mugs and wanted to be part of it. We asked our friends and she explained; you buy a mug for two euros; one euro for the mug and one euro for the cider refill. We were all hooked on the idea, so set off in search for a cider stall. Every fifty metres or so our new friends bumped into acquaintances, old school friends, work friends, and shop owners. It seemed that there wasn't anyone they didn't know. Soon we grew hungry and requested to stop off for a drink and tapas to refuel. We were introduced to another friend, a blonde girl called Camilla, who insisted we join her for chocolate liqueur shots, served in a cork sized pot made of dark chocolate. Camilla held out a tray loaded with liqueurs and we all threw back the sweet liquid and gorged on the chocolate vessels – We loved them, and requested another before heading off in search of our cider mugs.

A group of children ran past us dressed in adorable peasant tunics and felt hats and I couldn't help but feel ridiculously clucky over how cute they looked. They played wooden flutes and pulled handmade toys along the ground – It was a refreshing sight from plastic ones. They threw their heads back and belly laughed as they pointed at a fibreglass cow a farmer was pulling around on square wheels behind him. It bobbed up and down, much to the amusement of two little boys who screamed in delight bravely tugging at the cow's tail, then jumping back in case it took revenge.

At the town hall, a stage had been erected for the evening's medieval play. Our friends told us it was a gruesome show, embellished with dark humour, screaming wenches, men beating women and promiscuous witches. One of which, ends up being burnt alive on a bonfire.

We walked up a steep cobbled passage, pausing at a meat and cheese tapas stall to try cubed samples. And then finally we found our rustic cider tankards at a cart on the side of the road. The best two euros ever spent!

As early evening slipped in, the atmosphere shifted into a wind-chime-twinkling calmness. Voices hushed as children grew tired and slept in their buggies while their parents picked at delicious pieces of slow-roasted pulled pork stuffed into floury baps. The food smelled so delicious we ordered some for ourselves before heading off again. We reached a church at the highest point of the town and sat in its adjoining square to rest our aching legs and devour our food.

The crowd that had trickled upwards were young; perhaps the uphill climb had filtered-out the more unambitious folk. By a fountain, under a brown canopy stood a cider bar crowded with revellers. We joined them to refill our goblets, tossing a euro into the basket. The bar wenches took on their roles with relish, with fake facial warts and busty outfits that distracted many young boys' eyes. A muscular falconer sat at the bar with his wingman – an enormous eagle that majestically perched on the gauntleted forearm of his master. I was curious to how heavy the bird might feel as I eyed its deadly looking talons. The man couldn't have looked more masculine if he tried.

Nearby to us, under a black marquee three magnificent birds of prey perched on high posts. A big Tawny owl, a White owl and a Golden eagle blinked in the fading light. Their presence in this environment only made the theme of the fiesta more convincing.

The evening drew to a close and the four of us, along with the couple we had met at the fiesta moved on for one last drink before heading home. My parents had told them about our renovations so they wanted to show us something to give us inspiration for our project as well as theirs.

We were ushered into a white-painted stone building, which from the outside didn't look very inspiring. Originally used for horse and cart deliveries, the high arched entrance was tall enough for a rider to bring the cart in without having to dismount. The ceilings were high vaulted with wonderful curves. Long, grey and red tapestries hung from sturdy cast-iron fixtures on the walls which gave the room a sense of grandeur. It had been simply furnished with a bar constructed of bamboo and oak and upright beer barrels as high-tables - no chairs, no fuss. I was amazed at the gigantic size of the stone boulders that formed parts of the walls. We drank-in the smallest of details: the chunky studs on the curved door, the narrow windows, simple lighting that illuminated the ceiling and the beautiful dark oak floor.

We ordered some drinks and I was handed a small terracotta bowl of cool white wine. We thanked our friends for bringing us to such an inspirational place. A place, we all agreed that would have been in a rough condition, to begin with. We left feeling slightly drunk and dizzy with ideas for our house and it was the inspiration we needed to keep going with our renovation.

30. OUR FIRST GOODBYE

After the fiesta weekend was over and my hung-over stepsister and her boyfriend begrudgingly returned home, we threw ourselves back into the restoration for the rest of the month. The following weekend my mother and Joseph popped round for lunch to see how we were getting on. They were impressed with our progress but I wished we had more to show them.

I felt lucky to have such creative parents who could see a pile of rubble and imagine a castle, visualising something grand from nothing. They guided our ideas, either by shattering them and pointing out something we hadn't foreseen or by encouraging us to push ahead with the good ones. They suggested converting small, awkward windows into large doorways, facilitating light and space contributing to a greater flow of the layout. They had done it all before themselves, so it was incredibly important to us to have their input – whether we took the advice or not. In turn - every fortnight or so, we would go to their house and see what renovations they had been doing, what Scandinavian colours my mother had been mixing or to see how Joseph was getting on with his latest project - an old stone ruin that had completely crumbled to the floor and would, eventually, become a cottage.

Every day he could be found in his workshop, a tiny sharpened pencil nestling behind his right ear as he planned and scribbled his ideas in an old notebook.

Keen to hand down his carpentry skills to Jason, Joseph gave him few lessons in routing corners to achieve a more professional finish to an edge. Jason soon learned how to create linear details on doors, cupboards and shelf edgings *and* as it was impossible to find a kitchen to suit our budget and style, he was prepared to make one with the help of these new valuable carpentry skills.

Rural life was busy and we had settled comfortably around the rhythm of our neighbours' lives. We had kept up our scrap-wood offerings for Old Manola, leaving sacks by her door when we knew she would be passing by. Consciously we turned-off power tools during lunchtime to respect the all-important siesta, funerals and weddings. We stalled our evening dog walks so that Oscar could shepherd his sheep along the route we used, without having to worry that Macey might frighten them.

During our first short summer in Galicia, we had learned a little more about Oscar too, under the watchful eye of Old Manola. She had seen that we were forming a friendship with the man and he was comfortable coming and going to our house. She strongly disapproved of his drinking habits, disappointed when he spent his welfare on drink, rather than clothes and supplies for himself and daughter Maria. She told us that Oscar, as a single parent, barely held any responsibility for his daughter and quite often aunts and cousins had to step in. We knew he had his problems, he told us often enough but it was hard to not be affected by the aching sadness in his eyes and give him a friendship that others could not. Over time we would learn more about him but for now, he had proved himself to be a worthy friend. Old Manola was one of those distant relatives that had grown tired of picking up the pieces and as such had resigned herself from the responsibility. No one could deny that he would drink if money or opportunity allowed it. The addiction so acute that when his dole money arrived, he fell into the same pattern – disappearing into the woods or his house for days until the booze ran dry. During this time the normally placid gentle giant became an intolerable man - his voice boomed through stone walls and repeated the same words - how life always dealt him an unfair hand.

Oscar and Maria occupied just a small part of their large concrete dwelling leaving the rest of the space for the livestock they owned. Unlike the other villagers, they never appeared to have any visitors but perhaps this was because they were embarrassed – when their front door was open you could see why - The concrete floor was littered in rubbish, ankle-high; tin cans, plastic wine bottles, eggshells and food wrappers. Cats and their kittens scavenged for food on the dining table, twitching with lice as they licked the crockery clean. It was a shocking environment and made me realise what little they had.

For her thirteen birthday Oscar fetched Maria a puppy who she named Trampas – the name meant 'to trap' or 'trip over' – as the puppy was always under her feet. She loved her new friend, an adorable German Shepard cross, with floppy ears and a marbled coat of greys. It was nice to see her happy and have a companion when her father was sometimes absent.

Occasionally I saw her crying as she ran off into the woods. It broke my heart as I wondered what kind of future lay ahead for her. Maria was aware that her life with her dad was different from that of most girls her age and tried her best to endure the simple life her father was able to provide.

As autumn approached, weeks that normally flew by began to drag as our energy took a dip. I woke up feeling groggy, and began to long for Valencia, just to feel the dry heat on my skin. We had a few more weeks left before we could return to our villa, the holiday rental period would soon be over. And although I would miss my parents, I longed for simple luxuries like a hot bath and our decent bed.

I staggered into the caravan's tiny bathroom and stared into the cracked mirror. I felt and looked disgusting. My eyes, bloodshot and dry, made me look antique. I pinched the skin on my cheeks to release colour but they flopped back reluctantly into a rubbery mask that I hardly recognised as myself. The renovation wasn't doing my skin any favours, perhaps a downside of living our dream. The sun finally began to show itself and it boosted me a little. I slapped on some high-factor sun lotion, pulled on my paint-crusted jeans, and threw on a promotional DIY t-shirt that had come with a delivery - I was set for another day. I sighed and picked up my tools and got on with the jobs on my list. We both pushed hard, working relentlessly until another full week was done when we stood back and scrutinised the work. We had spent three months working in Galicia but by looking at it you'd hardly of imagined we'd touched the place. It was a depressing thought to be abandoning the house now with half the roof exposed to the elements, with only plastic to protect it from the harsh winter that would soon follow.

September arrived briskly, our departure imminent. The plan was to leave for Valencia early the following morning. I imagined myself already there, happy to have a break from the restoration.

After stopping at my parent's for lunch, we packed up the caravan, double-wrapping everything in plastic to shield it from the impending dampness. What a delight it was to be leaving the caravan and not have to tow it anywhere, averting any potential disasters.

Oscar seemed at a loss when we told him we were heading back to Valencia for the winter. He had known for some time that this day would arrive but I think he had got used to our presence. Perhaps being ostracized from the other villagers was something that connected him to us - a kinship over both being viewed as outsiders - although for very different reasons.

We said our goodbyes to him and Maria as the car stood idle outside Oscar's house. But Oscar seemed hesitant to let us go, his eyes brimmed with tears as he awkwardly held his head inside the car window just centimetres from Jason's face. With his habitual boozy breath, he asked copious times when we would return. We shook hands, and still, Oscar held on, stalling our departure until we convinced him it wouldn't be long before our return. Just so we could leave, Jason had to ease the Jeep forward slowly so Oscar had to remove his head from it. I imaged him as a stowaway, hanging onto the ladder at the back of the Land Rover - frozen stiff as we made our descent through Lugo and Madrid only to be discovered back in Valencia fifteen hours later.

We had grown fond of our village drunk and it seemed he felt the same about us. As we drove away, Oscar's shrinking reflection in my side mirror looked sallow; a lumbering figure and his sidekick daughter stood alone and abandoned. My heart sank a little as they both refused to return my farewell wave.

31. TEDDY

Moistness evaporated from every pore as we encroached the road south-east. The journey back had been effortless, with the landscape turning back to a more agreeable temperature as if we had driven back through the seasons. Being back in Valencia was immediately uplifting and we appreciated everything.

We were once again living our 'other' lives, away from the damp stone building and cramped living. The wide-screen TV came out of storage, the nice, homely photographs and soft furnishings made their way out of packed boxes in the shed. Just a few of our things made the house seem ours again. For the first two months, we regained contact with Jason's friend, Christopher in Valencia and met up with the neighbours in the village square for coffee.

As November arrived, I flew to the UK to catch up with family and old friends whom I hadn't seen in years. I was dumbstruck with the change of technology on public transport and the soaring cost of a simple cup of coffee. All technology had advanced and I hadn't even noticed until my friends pointed out how old my mobile phone was; I shamefully admitted it was brand new. These differences were small but to me seemed like I was from another planet. I walked around London in a daze, slow and observant. It felt like I'd just woken up from a ten-year coma and had discharged myself too early without the mental preparation. London was super fashionable making me realise I needed to go shopping to update myself before I too became comfortable in slippers and a gingham apron.

Christmas came and went in Valencia and the UK break was just what I – and my wardrobe – needed. Jason had his turn for a UK visit while it was my turn to stay at home alone and look after the pets.

Jason had only been back in Valencia for a week when a beautiful but very grumpy rust-coloured American Cocker Spaniel came temporarily into our lives. One of our neighbours Jorge owned a secluded white villa at the pinnacle of our mountain that looked over the cluster of houses. The house was Jorge's second home, a weekend retreat that remained unoccupied apart from Thursdays' when he would drive in from the city to tend to his land and throw a bucket of food to his ferocious guard dog.

It was Jorge who had found the male Spaniel trapped in his house. The little stray had sneaked into the property when Jorge left the front door open and had survived the week by drinking out of the toilet. Jorge assumed the dog was ours and brought the little Spaniel down in his car. When we told him we had never seen the dog before, he was unsure what to do. Unexpectedly, Jorge got back into his car and drove off leaving the dog chasing after his car in a heart-wrenching scene. We didn't think we'd see the dog after that, we presumed it would have followed Jorge to the road and trotted off towards the village, possibly back to its owner. But soon enough the dog came back and waited just as Macey once had, at our gate.

Heartbroken for the little dog, we brought him into our garden and gave him food and water. His eyes sagged, his coat was filthy, his rust-coloured fur far too long – it had probably been years since it had been clipped. He wasn't easy to approach, he growled and retreated into a corner when I tried to touch him. A short length of metal chain hung off his collar, suggesting perhaps he had been neglected and broken away from his home. He had a handsome face with a short snout, a real heartbreaker - so it was hard to imagine that someone wasn't missing him unless something had happened to the owner.

We photographed the Spaniel and made some posters, which we taped to some trees in the area. But just a few days later someone had torn the posters down. I couldn't believe how anyone wouldn't want to be reunited with him or at least be so against us finding his owners. Someone didn't want anyone knowing he was out there. We fostered the little dog, which we named Teddy, and over the following weeks grew to understand him a little better. I tried my best not to get too attached to him. We discussed the dog's future with Jorge - which one of us could give him a better home? As we were soon to return to Galicia, we were concerned about how he would handle long car journeys or get under our feet during the renovation. But, Jorge had an idea, his daughter in the city might take Teddy if she was willing. So we were happy with the new arrangement and hoped Teddy would be well-loved in his new home.

The following weekend Jorge came to collect Teddy. It was hard to let him go and a part of me didn't want to, but we knew it would be unfair to drag the dog around the country when Jorge had promised the dog would have a good home with his daughter.

We returned to Galicia refreshed and ready to continue working. The house had fared well in our absence and for the next three months, we made better progress than ever before on the roof and walls. When our time was up and we needed a break once again, we made our way back to Valencia for another rest.

One afternoon, just days after our return to Valencia, we heard the unmistakable howl from Teddy coming from the direction of Jorge's house. We realised Jorge must have taken the dog in himself. Perhaps Teddy hadn't got on well with the daughter and he had been removed. I felt furious we hadn't been informed and from the sound of it, the dog sounded as if he was suffering.

In the heat of the sun, Jason hiked into the vastness of Jorge's land to investigate. I listened for voices but it was clear that Jason was up there alone.

A short while later Jason stormed back, furiously shaking

his head as he hurriedly explained the dire situation. Once in the garden, Jason had located the spacious dog pen where he knew Jorge's ferocious guard dog was kept. He pulled himself up a wall and peered into the pen to assess the situation. It was then he noticed Teddy cowering in a corner, blood everywhere, as the guard dog dominated most of the caged space. Jason couldn't believe that Jorge had been so thoughtless as to place the two dogs together with only one bowl of food, that was to last a week. We had been so naïve – poor Teddy had been suffering daily attacks, in desperate hunger to reach the food. If we had known the dog wasn't living with Jorge's daughter we would have taken him without hesitation.

We decided to act immediately, with or without Jorge's permission. Jason grabbed a ladder and marched back up to the white house. Once in the dog pen, he noticed right away that the Spaniel had terrible wounds. Some were recent, some were not. His fur was so long it was hard to tell the extent of his injuries without a proper examination. Jason shouted at the guard dog to stay back and held a stick at arm's length just in case the dog was prone to attack. As if Teddy knew he was being rescued, he ran forward into Jason's arms and they quickly exited the pen.

When Jason got home carrying Teddy in his arms I burst into tears at the sight of him. The little dog's injuries looked so bad we didn't think he would survive the night. His small scalp had been torn open in a horseshoe-shaped flap exposing the bloody skull. He had older dried puncture wounds to his neck and muzzle and heavy bruising where areas of fur were missing on his back. His eyes were crusted, his skin dry and flaky, suffering from overexposure to the summer sun. The problem, for now, was that he didn't want to be touched at all and we didn't blame him for being cautious. I wondered how the poor dog would ever trust anyone again.

We phoned Jorge and asked him to explain why Teddy had ended up in his kennel when we understood that the Spaniel was to be placed with his daughter in the city. He muttered a weak excuse that Teddy had snapped at his daughter's boyfriend so Jorge had decided to keep him as an extra guard dog. I told him we were disgusted at how the animal had ended up in this condition due to his neglect. I emailed horrific images of Teddy's injuries as proof and Jorge promised to pay for the vet bills although he didn't utter a word of remorse of the injuries Teddy had sustained.

We rushed the Spaniel straight to the vet's where they patched him up without using any anaesthetic. We were sickened when they poured hydrogen peroxide onto his bloody scalp, which made him whimper and cry as the peroxide fizzed burning all the blackened bits of scalp clean. I thought I might explode with rage. Why would a vet want to worsen this poor dog's trauma? The vet argued that as the dog was micro-chipped in Jorge's daughter's name, they couldn't be liable for any bad reaction an anaesthetic might cause. The vet smiled at me and reassured us Teddy would be fine.

He shook some aluminium powder on the scalp, which would act as a natural scab and aid quick healing. Teddy seemed to relax with relief that it was all finally over. All we wanted to do from that moment on was to love and protect him from any further harm and vowed that we would keep him no matter what. I placed my finger on Teddy's crusty black button nose and he looked up at me.

"You're one of us now," I said, and we left for home.

32. LOCAL HERO

While our little furry adopted family was growing, three sets of our friends fell pregnant at the same time and life, it seemed, was moving on so fast we felt we were being left behind. We realised with all the travelling back and forth between Galicia and Valencia we had almost forgotten why we had moved to Spain in the first place - to have a better life together.

We were engaged, Jason had proposed a month before we emigrated and the last six years had flown by without giving a thought to planning a wedding. It was as if everything else always took priority and we realised we needed to do something about it.

So we made an exciting decision to put the renovation aside for a moment and plan a simple wedding. We sat under the marquee by the pool, shading ourselves from the Valencia sun, with two content dogs at our feet and a table top covered with bridal magazines, holiday brochures and a lengthy to-do list. Jason poured himself some more coffee as we considered where to do the nuptials.

"Let's get married on a tropical island!" I suggested on a whim. At that moment, the house telephone rang and I charged around the pool to answer it.

"¿Hola?" I said to silence on the other end of the phone.

"It's your mother, turn on your TV right now, Spanish news channel!" She sounded so excited I wondered if Joseph had finally won the village syndicate lottery. "Why, what have you been up to now?" I asked, half worried about the answer.

"It's Oscar – he's on the bloody TV!"

Out of all the people in this world, Oscar was the last person I expected to see standing in front of a news camera. If I had thought about it, the only reason Oscar might have been on television would be because he had died in his highly infectious kitchen and his cats had half-eaten him. But there he was, alive, red-faced and having undergone a makeover that transformed him so drastically I barely recognised him from our hobo friend. His lanky straw-like hair had been scrubbed to a bright crop of gleaming white and styled in a flat-top cut closely resembling an American war veteran from the Sixties. He appeared to have been freshly shaved and bathed and wore a blue checked shirt and clean pair of jeans. But it was the same old Oscar, with the same sad full moon eyes and kind, gappy, idiotic smile.

A small gathering of apron-clad locals stood passively in the background unable to move in the camera's presence. Oscar was being interviewed by a pretty young girl no older than twenty. He was enchanted by her attention but this didn't last long as it seemed Oscar wasn't making himself understood. As the camera panned left, Oscar went out of shot and we saw Abuela fussing over her youngest great-granddaughter, Zara, as they stood outside their aluminium door in our village. The presenter was hailing the little two-year-old, calling her a local hero!

The news report went something like this,

"Zara, a child of two years old, has always been close to her neighbour Oscar. When she isn't sitting on her grandmother's porch step singing and playing with her dolls, she likes to walk with Oscar accompanying him on his daily shepherding duties, to a nearby field. Zara idolises him as if he were her grandfather and even calls him Grandpa despite the two not being related. But one morning last week after dropping off Oscar's sheep in the field there was an event that strengthened their friendship.

As Oscar and Zara walked along the road back towards the village Oscar got too close to the edge of the bank and slipped. He plummeted far down a ridge, into thick blackberry bushes and disappeared. Zara, stunned by the disappearance of her grandfather, ran back home and repeatedly called his name to her grandmother while pointing to the embankment where he fell. The alarm was raised and the fire services called. After some time searching they found Oscar unable to move from his injuries. He had fallen ten feet down, into the depths of thorny brambles where he had to be carefully winched out and taken to hospital. Thankfully he only sustained minor cuts and bruises along with a bad sprain to his wrist. If it hadn't been for the love and friendship of this little girl, it is unlikely that Oscar would have been able to get out of that situation, which could have turned grave. This village now has a new hero in the form of a two-year-old child."

The reporter nodded back to the studio, as Zara was being fussed over in the background, wearing a brand new white and red dress and shiny red plimsolls.

I switched off the television. *So* that *explains his makeover,* I thought. The nurses must have washed and trimmed him at the hospital. *Where had Maria been during all of this?* I wondered. The little girl, Zara, who had never had any early schooling or kindergarten, and who was deprived of parental attention, was an incredibly bright child and I was pleased she hadn't got hurt in the incident. Surprisingly I missed them all. I missed that crazy little village with its shiny black graves and sneaky, curious locals, and now heroic babies.

***

Our free time in Valencia planning the wedding went far too quickly and before we knew it, we were making our way back to the north-west peninsula at six in the morning with our new addition, Teddy, in the crowded car. He took to travelling quite well apart from when we stopped at traffic lights, where he would bark furiously at other cars, we guessed it was all new to him. The journey took us a good fifteen hours in the slow but sturdy Land Rover – the blessing of not having to tow a caravan eased the stress.

For the last part of the journey, Jason consumed as many

caffeine-fuelled drinks as was humanly possible to get us there while I navigated with the badly ripped and mangled map.

Eventually, just before the last of the sunlight disappeared behind the mountains, we arrived in our cosy, quiet, little village, and our home.

After nervously turning the giant antique key and pushing open the heavy stable door, I blinked into the darkness until my eyes adjusted to see a thoroughly wet and mud-filled hallway.

I dreaded returning to the house after months away, there was always some horrible surprise that put a damper on it – quite literally this time.

The natural spring that normally flowed gently alongside the exterior of the farmhouse had unfortunately found a new route, through our house. It had trickled through the back walls and worked its way along the corridor to the front door before joining its old route back outside, continuing towards the church.

We were so exhausted from the journey we barely felt bothered by it. Jason checked that the roof hadn't leaked and apart from some loose plastic on the roof – overall it was fine. I stood in my wellies and wondered if we could go through all this again.

We took a three-day rest before tackling the house again. The neighbours kindly granted us some space, in which to settle back in and we were grateful for the solitude.

Oddly, Oscar was nowhere to be seen for those first few days either. We never dared to knock on his door. Oscar had his routine and wanted to be seen on his terms. Jason expected he might wander over when he saw our car, but for a while, we wondered if something had happened to him with all the silence of the place.

Jason scraped mud and gravel in the road to redirect the water flow back to its usual route, while I looked for Oscar in the sheep fields and took a stroll to the bins, passing his front door. It was locked and his cats sat outside, hungry and skinny. Was it possible he had left the village for once in his life? I hoped for his sake he had. Perhaps the accident had left him humiliated – after all, he was most likely drunk when he fell down the embankment. Nevertheless, I hoped he was all right.

I wiped away the persistent green and black mould from the caravan walls and inside the cupboards. The caravan had degraded substantially in the short time we had been away, largely due to the dampness penetrating from the ground. As I turned on plastic taps and readjusted pipes they crumbled to the touch, at this rate I hoped our accommodation would last us to the end of the build.

By the end of the afternoon, we had worked around the problem of the degrading parts by inventing something functional we could use instead. It may not have looked great but the hose sticking through the tiny kitchen window with a spray gun on the end worked perfectly well instead of the tap and pump. A kettle of boiling water poured into a washing-up bowl and mixed with cold water, thrown over us, had to do for a shower. We soon got used to it and when we fancied a soak, Jason rigged up the rusty iron bath that had been abandoned in the garden. He created a screen by draping dust sheets over ladders and beams which went some way to protecting his modesty. Jason enjoyed those al fresco baths. I, on the other hand, felt too self-conscious to expose my naked self to the graves and the neighbours. You never knew who might be about or what wind might bring. Whenever Jason had a bath outside, I could have sworn Old Manola she was pushing her wheelbarrow past extra slowly.

We had only been away for a few months but even our spare clothes were smelly and damp, despite having taken prudent steps to protect them in storage. Nevertheless, after a quick spruce-up of our dwelling, we were revived and it did feel good to be in Galicia again. This time we knew what to expect, and once we had unpacked and rearranged our living space, we could pick up the tools where they lay abandoned, and get back to work.

As we waited for a heavy downpour to stop, we sat in the caravan and planned our new to-do-list. Easter week was approaching and many of the shops we needed building materials from, would be closed over that period.

Just before Easter Sunday, as the village was becoming lively with the priests preparing the church for the festivities, Oscar finally made his grand reappearance along with his daughter. They stood in the field by the hórreo hollering for us to come over, Oscar smiley and reasonably sober.

"How are you?" I asked Oscar as we warmly shook hands. And the answer was always the same

"We're getting by, surviving," he said, with sadness.

It was good to see his face again, but although he looked clean and respectable after his recent makeover, the grooming had unveiled the seriousness of his troubling health and exposed the gruesome tumours on his neck. I tried to ignore the angry egg-sized ball below his right ear lobe. He was wearing the same checked shirt he wore on the day of his news interview and I was certain it hadn't been washed in the months since. It gaped at the top to show another sizable lump by his collar bone and I feared for his health and Maria's welfare if he were to deteriorate.

Maria had grown in height and width in just a few months. She stood almost as tall as Oscar and had inherited his large hands and feet. Apart from her long glossy hair that she wore down, she was devoid of any femininity, looking more tomboyish than her female cousins. It was extraordinary how at thirteen she had physically matured into an adult so quickly yet she still lacked a mental maturity, causing me to wonder how Oscar would handle her teenage angst as she grew older. His guidance was lacking so much that most of Maria's lessons into adulthood had to come from someone else - teachers, Old Manola, Maria's auntie and very occasionally, from me.

We stood on the wet grass and caught up with Oscar's news. He wasted no time in whispering village gossip, which he delighted in. We told them about our upcoming wedding plans and the moment when we had seen him on television. He remained quiet about his brief fame so we showed them our new addition - Teddy, and Maria seemed to delight in laughing at the silver crust on his head, which, she pointed out, made him look like an astronaut-dog. Maria whistled for Trampas to join us.

The young Alsatian limped around our legs in an excited frenzy and immediately we noticed a gruesome V-shaped gash halfway up his front leg which was open to infection if nothing were to be done about it. Maria was concerned but Oscar had other things to worry about and shrugged it off with a laugh. The dog had most likely snagged his leg jumping the barbed wire fence. There wasn't much blood - Jason pointed out - and suspected that a tendon might have been damaged as the dog would not put any weight down on it. It seemed unlikely that Oscar would get the dog to the vet, so using the medical kit we had for our own dogs and with Maria's assistance, Jason set about, sterilising, folding the flap back, and bandaging the dog's wound.

Oscar laughed at his veterinary attempt.

"No good, the dog will bite off the bandage," Oscar said shaking his head. And he was right. Moments later the dog was trotting around the village with the bandage and the tape hanging off. There was nothing more we could do.

A week later the dog's leg had healed quite well – it could have looked better but the flap had sealed itself and Jason was pleased with the dog's recovery. Oscar was so grateful he turned up at our door and gave us a dozen rotten eggs in a dish covered in chicken faeces as a thank you. I didn't know what to say but just smiled instead. Gratitude doesn't have to come in pretty packages.

33. IF YOU SPEAK IT, TEACH IT

Little Zara, the heroic two-year-old child whose only stimulating conversation was between her and her loving great-grandmother, played on her porch step with a tatty pink plastic doll.

As usual, her young mother and delinquent boyfriend were nowhere to be seen. I was in the front of our house, bent forward, tugging at the insistent weeds that had attached themselves to the mossy stone.

"Hola Zara, ¿cómo estás hoy?" I asked, and wiggled my fingers in a childish wave, the way only people without kids know-how.

She stared, her mouth open as if my presence scared her. I turned back to my gardening chores and carried on pulling the weeds.

"Hello Georgina." said a small, chilling voice behind me, not only in perfect English but precisely mimicking my Surrey accent. I turned to face little Zara, *had she said that?* Astounded, I wanted to hear her talk again. She was shy at first, but then she smiled, before screaming at me, "Hello, hello, hello!" as if her voice had been freed and she wanted the world to hear her.

"How. Are. You. Say it, Zara. *How are you?*"

"How. Are. You." She repeated, exactly in my tone, sounding like a tape recording of me. I laughed, I felt jubilant. I wanted to teach her more.

"What is your name?" I asked, and prompted,

"*My name is Zara -*"

Zara thought about this for a moment and opened her mouth

to speak. But just as I felt I could teach her every English word and sentence in the world, Abuela came out and waved her inside. Zara's smile faded, and she started to cry. I was sad for her, she had very little interaction with anyone and when she did she was deprived of it.

All those times when she had been sitting on her porch playing with her doll, she had been absorbing little snippets of our conversations, listening to how we pronounced our words. This fascinated me and awakened me to the idea of pursuing it further one day so that I might make a valuable contribution to the community. If I were to teach this child my language and she was to soak it up like a sponge and speak it, imagine how different her future might become?

But I could only presume that her parents wouldn't like it. They would most likely feel that I was imposing on what they felt was already a perfectly acceptable environment for the child. They considered us outsiders and were our most reluctant friends in the village. We were polite to each other, but it was rare that we had the opportunity to talk - although I was sure they knew a lot about us through the grapevine.

I considered what it would take to become an English teacher as I turned back to pulling weeds from the rocks. From inside her house, I heard Zara yell at Abuela in the few English words she had learned. Her rebellion had started and she wasn't about to let up.

After this very brief encounter, rumours began to circulate in our micro-village that I was an English teacher. It was a ridiculous thing to presume if they knew me. Until that moment with Zara, I had never seriously considered teaching as a profession and even then I had dismissed it as just another one of my fruitless career ideas. I had no formal training, no clue about grammar and verbs and all those tricky little rules that comes with teaching a language intimately.

Although growing up in a household with a Norwegian mother and a Spanish stepfather gave me plenty of correctional grammar practice – as well as correcting their letters and invoices – I had never been academically gifted. In my experience, English teachers were naturally smart, they remembered important details and found clever ways to make learning fun. Most of the time I forgot what day of the week it was!

That week, somewhere between Tuesday and Friday, when our stable door had been propped open to let the sawdust escape, I found Maria and Oscar hovering awkwardly in the doorway. Oscar had been listening to the rumours and wanted to get in on the schooling action before anyone else. I had to admire his opportunistic ways. He begged and pleaded for me to teach his daughter English.

"No, Oscar, I can't. I'm not an English teacher, it is not true," I tried to explain. Oscar was a man who didn't give in easily. He muttered a few incomprehensible words to Maria and she ran off in the direction of their house. I felt bad then as if I had let her down. I wondered if I should run after her to see if she was OK.

But in a flash, she was back again, with a pile of thin English textbooks. Just like her dad, she wasn't going to take no for an answer either.

"I am not qualified," I repeated

"But you speak it?"

"Yes, but —" Oscar held up his hand to stop me speaking

"I can pay, I don't have much but a little something," Oscar said, digging in his filthy jeans for loose change. He didn't have a decent roof or shoes, let alone extra money for private tuition. I hated being put on the spot like this. But Oscar and Maria pulled their best 'abandoned puppy' faces and somehow, although both of them looked mildly deranged, they cracked my sensibilities and I gave in.

"OK, OK, a one-hour class, Saturday mornings, 10 am. For free, OK? No money" I said in my worst Spanish. I certainly didn't want any rotten eggs as payment. *What was I doing?*

Both of them beamed and exchanged looks. Oscar shook my

arm but I moved back in case he was going to move in for a grateful kiss. Maria could hardly contain her excitement but Oscar soon told her to keep it quiet – he didn't want anyone else getting free lessons but him.

I wondered what I had got myself into. I might be a terrible teacher, Maria might be an unwilling student? As a first test-dummy student, I hoped that she would be patient and forgiving of my floundering ways. If she resented me for ramming a baffling language down her throat at least she couldn't complain and ask for her money back.

As they both trotted off, my doubts subsided and I considered how the lessons would help us both. All of a sudden I wanted nothing more than to teach. I wanted this for her, what I wanted for Zara – a chance – and the lessons were a start.

34. THE VILLAGE FIGHT

I threw open the bedroom shutters and flooded the upper floor with light so that particles of dust danced at my feet. I planned to make a start on cementing the wonderfully curved walls, leaving some areas of stone exposed around the windows.

I looked up and got the shock of my life when I saw Old Manola's face pressed to her upstairs window across the street – a ghostly white complexion through netted curtains, lilac rollers in her hair. I stepped back from the window, assuming that it was me she was spying on but something else had caught her attention.

I followed her gaze down to street level to a middle-aged couple in the street, smartly dressed, taking photographs of a little stone house that had been up for sale. They stepped delicately around the overgrown garden and wrestled the front gate open, stamping down prickly blackberry branches as they went. The man opened the door using a giant key, just like the one we had for our property.

The stone cottage was minuscule, having every bit of character as that of a gingerbread house with its tiny window panes and barn door painted in a traditional Verde Galicia green. Like ours, the house had been neglected for decades and would need substantial effort to make it a liveable dwelling. Old Manola's block building next door towered over it which only made the cottage more diminutive, cowering in its shadow.

I realised the couple must be the new buyer's Oscar had mentioned last week. We had almost bought the little house once, it had been advertised in the local paper but when we peered inside, the cottage dimensions were far too small to divide up into further rooms and it didn't come with a scrap land. I was pleased to see someone else had bought it and even more pleased that we were no longer the new people in town.

Out of curiosity, I watched Old Manola's curtains shift as she spied on the people below, other residents in the street casually pretended to go about their chores so they might be the first to get the gossip. It was rather satisfying to see that this couple were just as startled at the attention as I once had been. I chuckled as I watched the apron-clad housewife from number eight approach them and bombard them with questions.

We threw down our gloves and made our way outside to greet them - *it would have been rude not to*. The aproned lady from number eight rambled on in her incomprehensible dialect and then scuttled off into her house, leaving us to make our introductions.

The new arrivals were a smart professional couple, Maria Carmen and Miguel from La Coruña city, who owned an estate agents' and had snatched up the property at a cheap price after it had been stagnant on the market for years. They were an attractive couple with sweaters thrown around their shoulders, beautiful suede loafers and freshly showered scented hair. They told us they had aspirations to restore the stone house at the weekends and we explained that's exactly what we had been doing too. They spoke in a mix of English and Spanish and seemed pleased to meet us but they couldn't believe such a young British couple were living out here in the middle of rural Galicia when we weren't even from the area.

My stepfather is a Galician, I told them.

"Ah, that explains it!" they said, and let the matter drop. We invited them into our place, so they could see our restoration so far - much to the outraged glares of the other neighbours.

We talked for a little while as we sat under our grapevine on the makeshift bench drinking coffee. Maria Carmen and Miguel were pleasant people but seemed to be an unlikely couple to take on such a big project; they were hesitant about the work, almost as if they regretted the purchase so we tried to persuade them that the overwhelming feeling would eventually subside. After a little while, they seemed more positive and took us across the road to their ruin and explained their ambitious plans. The stone walls were meticulously constructed but I wondered how they would cram the amount of desired rooms into such an uncompromising space.

As lunchtime approached we left Maria Carmen and Miguel to explore the village while we settled into the caravan for a cooked lunch.

We were halfway through our food when we heard shouting coming from outside. We ignored it, assuming the row was just a normal village conversation at high volume.

Voices rose again in the wind, just as the rain had started to spatter on the caravan roof at intervals. As the yelling became louder we recognised it was Oscar's angry, thunderous tone so abandoned our lunch to see what was occurring.

We snuck upstairs into the old school room so we could gain a better view through the windows. From above, I spotted a young woman screaming in the street, around the age of twenty. She was extremely skinny, had gaunt cheeks and wore flared jeans with a loose-fitting t-shirt.

I then realised she was the granddaughter of Abuela, who was usually so absent from village life that it seemed she avoided daylight altogether. Her dark hair reached past her hips and swayed as she gestured angrily with her long, thin arms. Having only seen her once or twice before, I had nicknamed her Spider-girl because of her spindly limbs and dark beady eyes. On those occasions, she retreated into Abuela's ramshackle den, where the smell of marijuana seeped out of the chimney-pipe. Spider-girl made so few appearances in the village that an introduction this late on would be a pointless formality for either of us, although we both had an awareness of each other's existence.

From my position, I could not see to whom she was venting

her anger but knew Oscar was part of it. Despite being obscured by the neglected cottage his voice thundered through the village like an enraged lunatic.

A moment later, Spider-girl's menacing boyfriend, Rico, made an appearance and stood crookedly by his girlfriend's side. He too had made so few outings in the village that it was only the second time I had laid eyes on him. The first time was when he had returned from months in hospital and Abuela had helped him out of an ambulance onto crutches. I remembered Oscar telling us that Rico, together with some friends had stolen a car and gone joy-riding. But the car had crashed and flipped onto its roof crushing Rico's lower body with devastating impact. Seeing him again now, wasn't pleasant.

Rico leaned heavily on a hospital crutch, one leg of his tracksuit had been rolled up, exposing a cylindrical wireframe with complex pins that had been inserted through his bruised thigh.

We tried hard to listen to the onslaught but the language was so heavy with its regional dialect that I could barely separate the words. Spider-girl shouted back to Oscar and I managed to make out something about abandoned cars in the area.

Curtains twitched from inside Old Manola's house, just as Oscar came into view.

Maria looked upset as she trailed behind him, hanging onto the back of his shirt. I had never seen Oscar so angry, his face was contorted, his cheeks wet with tears. All four of them now stood directly below us outside our front door and I worried where this was heading.

Maria shouted at her dad to stop arguing, pleading within an inch of his face. But Oscar was too angry to listen – his voice boomed with overbearing force as he held Maria to the side and she bounced back, coming between himself and Spider-girl.

Whatever Oscar had yelled it made Spider-girl turn to walk back to her house, abruptly she changed her mind and flew back at Oscar, pointing her finger and yelling in his face. Rico stood a little behind Spider-girl and joined in on the verbal abuse. We watched as all three were bellowing moving closer to each other. Maria implored them to stop. My heart raced as we ran down the stairwell, unbolted the heavy barn door and burst outside to break it up. In the few seconds it had taken to get the door unlocked, the row had already diffused. Young Maria had eventually managed to force her father back towards their house and Spider-girl and Rico hadn't stuck around long enough to notice that we had come outside.

We walked around the corner towards Oscar's place to see Maria trying to push her dad through the doorway, his arms comically locked on either side of the door frame, resisting movement.

Spider-girl came running out of Abela's house once more and shouted

"¡Borracho, sucio!" calling him a dirty drunk. She retreated inside her cave once more, the situation diffused.

We walked back home and as we reached our front door, our new, smart neighbours Miguel and Maria Carmen, stood in their overgrown doorway in open-mouthed shock, unimpressed at the scene that had unfolded. I expected they now regretted buying in this village. Miguel put his index finger to his temple and circled it while rolling his eyes. Without saying a word, I nodded and smiled.

Back inside the caravan, we cleaned up our lunch things. Calm had been restored and we were sure that Oscar would be sleeping off the episode, by this evening the whole thing would most likely be forgotten.

But then we heard a terrible scream, and my stomach tightened with the harrowing noise. The argument had started up again, so Jason and I raced outside to see that Oscar had Spider-girl in a headlock, seemingly to protect himself against her wild swinging punches. She was in a pretty dire position considering Oscar probably hadn't had a bath in months, let alone a daily spray with deodorant. With any luck, she would pass out and Rico could drag her back to their den.

Just as I was thinking about him, Rico staggered towards his girlfriend, dragging his metal-framed leg behind him. He had abandoned his crutches in the middle of the road and held a rock the size of a coconut in his left hand.

Once again Maria's instinct was to protect her father and she threw herself on her knees at Rico's feet, wailing and screaming at him to leave her Papa alone. I eyed Rico and the rock in his hand. He noticed me and my scrutinising eyes upon him and my presence made him a little hesitant. Little Zara stood on the steps and bawled as she watched Oscar wrestle and whip Spider-girl around in the road, clumsily hanging onto her neck, which I thought could break at any moment. It was awful to see Maria on her knees begging for Rico to not hit her father with the rock. I wondered why nobody had stopped her. Rico looked unsure as he raised the rock towards Oscar once again and my biggest fear was that he might hurt Maria instead.

But Jason had enough of standing on the side-lines and in one swift motion lunged forward and tore Spider-girl away from Oscar, throwing her into a spin on her heels, her hair lashing in circles. New arrival Miguel stepped in holding an arm like a barrier to Rico's chest and everything cooled off within seconds.

Rico snarled his lips like a crazed wolf, exposing beastly stained teeth. His lanky hair plastered to his pale face, the rock still firmly clenched in his hand.

"Look at the children!" I blurted-out to Spider-girl in English. "Look what you are doing to them!" I hoped Spider-girl would feel some remorse for her little daughter. Zara stood alone on the porch in her usual filthy day dress and gulped lungful's of air between sobs, her nose runny and bubbly with snot. Spider-girl looked up at me and for the first time, our eyes met. I thought she wouldn't have understood but then she surprised me and said in English,

"He no good, he drunk! He lie!" She pointed to Oscar who staggered backwards, exhausted from the fight. The argument was over for now and I doubted anyone would apologise for their behaviour.

And then for no reason at all, I let out a high-pitched, nervous laugh which made everyone including Jason stare at me in confusion, as if I had lost *my* mind. I am not sure why I laughed. Though perhaps I thought they were all as bad as each other and I had never seen people act in such an undemocratic way. There was so much I wanted to say but I didn't understand these villagers as much as I thought I did, nor did I have the right vocabulary to express my disgust at them. It seemed, though that no one else did either.

We each stood in silence for a moment, until one by one everyone retreated like Neanderthals back to our caves. Rico tossed the rock to the side of the road and dragged his leg behind him. As he entered Abuela's house, he called for Zara to follow.

It was irritating to be part of this community where you threw punches first and asked questions later. Where a thirteen-year-old girl was forced to defend her father and take the brunt of his loose words. *Who would protect her?* I wondered.

"What do you want to be when you grow up?" I asked Maria.

Maria stared up at the caravan ceiling where flies were mating on the plastic surface.

"Maria, do you understand my question?" I asked. She nodded but seemed devoid of energy.

"So?" I urged softly.

"Architect," she replied, "I building like."

"I like buildings," I corrected, as I checked my watch. "OK, let's call it a day. I think you're probably tired and we've covered a lot for our first lesson. Everything alright with your father at home?" I asked.

"Hmm, yes," she said meekly. "Thank you."

It was our first Saturday lesson, and after the fight, I wasn't sure if Maria would even turn up. She seemed passive and looked tired but it wasn't surprising after the stress she had been through.

For the first twenty minutes of the lesson she was so distracted by sitting inside the caravan itself it was hard to get her to concentrate on the books. She was like a child from a third-world country standing in a grand hotel for the first time. And our caravan wasn't exactly the Dorchester.

I asked questions to engage her; what actors she admired, places she had visited, what music she liked. But her interests weren't the same as an average teenage girl's. She was an underprivileged country girl who had never been out of Galicia, let alone abroad. Her clothes were hand-me-downs and she didn't own a single item of technology. I realised with embarrassment that these were silly, materialistic questions she could not answer.

She sat on her hands and scanned the awkward space until she came across something that interested her, *food*. Cookbooks in fact. I made her a cup of English tea. She sniffed at the milky beige drink and scrunched her nose but I encouraged her to try it anyway. We had sat there, flicking through recipes, speaking in both English and Spanish while dunking biscuits, she relaxed and I think it was the first time I saw her smile a genuinely happy smile.

As Maria left the caravan after our lesson that cloudy morning, I cleared the table of teaching material, recipe clippings and pages from fashion magazines. The class had been a little awkward to start with. I had used her school books to gauge what level she was at with her English and then repeated the parts she had difficulties with during the class. In truth, I had no idea what I was doing but I hoped I was on the right track somewhere. Private tuition was new to us both, so at least we had that in common.

May arrived and in between the restoration, we talked over our wedding plans during our tea breaks in the caravan. We took a day trip to Santiago de Compostela where we enjoyed a stroll around the old cobbled tourist lanes and bridal shops before stopping at a quaint café for a menu del dia lunch. The weather had forecasted rain so we thought we might as well get out and explore if we couldn't risk taking the plastic roof off at home.

Finally, that day arrived when the clouds gracefully parted to allow a bucket of sunlight to pour over our village. We crawled out of the caravan, peeled back the plastic sheeting and inspected the roof supports. We hoped we could work fast enough before the next downpour.

By the end of the week Jason had half the roof on and the reward felt amazing. It was always good to have another focus apart from the build - and our plans for our lo-key wedding was becoming an exciting reality. In six months we'd be getting married on a beach in Mauritius and it would be wonderful.

35. NEVER THE SAME AGAIN

At the end of May, my mother treated me to a trip for a girls shopping weekend in London with her. We stayed with her friends and ate Indian take away and relaxed in the madness of so many people rushing around. I hopped on buses to bridal shops and gawked at the ridiculous prices. Eventually, after two days of exhaustive shopping that I wasn't quite used to, I managed to find the perfect wedding dress at a fraction of the cost, a romantic triple-layered bandeau dress from a charity shop. The only problem was that it was too big for me but my mother agreed to alter it for me when we got back to Galicia.

The next day we flew back to Northern Spain ready to make adjustments to the dress and plan the wedding party we had decided to have in Valencia. But something wasn't right on our arrival back at the airport. Joseph, stood slightly crooked at the arrival lounge; he seemed dazed, confused and slightly weak, as he clutched a soft toy in his hands. As we dragged our suitcases closer my heart sank into my stomach, my mother looked at me to confirm what she saw. His face was wrecked with the characteristics of a stroke.

As we approached Joseph in the airport lounge, passengers rushed past to hug their families and kiss excited babies. We hadn't expected this, how had this happened after such a short time away? We didn't know what to do with the fear that engulfed both of us. We both stood either side of him and soothed him - almost expecting him to fall. We talked to him as he tried to roll a cigarette but every time he tried he failed, frowning as the loose tobacco fell silently to the floor. We quickly realised that he was unsuspecting of his condition, appearing to act almost normal despite his lopsided face and the slowness in his speech. My mother's hands trembled as she tried to conceal her concern, fussing over him, stroking his hair. We headed in the direction of the car park and both my mother and I managed to grab each other's attention while we put the luggage in the boot.

We couldn't let him drive, he wasn't in any fit condition. But at the same time, we didn't want to alarm him. All we knew was that we needed to get him help. It was an impossible situation. Our attempt at persuading him failed and he argued that he was the only one insured to drive the car. We had no choice but to let him. He drove us away from the airport through the city and out towards our rural town. We were thankful that the traffic that day was quiet as he zigzagged from left to right, only just keeping within his lane on the motorway.

My mother clung to the passenger's handle above the door, her knuckles white with the strain as she delicately questioned him about his health. He lost his temper and snapped aggressively when we pushed too much. I suspected that his memory was failing but at that point had no idea what we were dealing with.

As I sat in the back of my parents Volvo and recalled past moments with Joseph that now seemed blindingly obvious. At first, there had been small things. Things that, at the time, hadn't alerted us into thinking that anything was wrong. His memory had started to slow and he took twice as long to finish a project in his workshop, preferring to read and watch television or be alone.

Sometimes he seemed confused with simple things, the time and what day of the week it was but like all children of parents who are getting older, I just put it down to ageing and the impending role reversal that would take on its own momentum. I could see he had lost something inside, but I had dismissed it thinking it was nothing. How wrong I was.

He battled to find love and enjoyment in things that used to make him happy. And I remembered once, a long time ago, he had taught me a beautiful piece of flamenco music on his classical guitar and had promised me that when I had mastered it perfectly he would teach me the next part, for all its torturous, finger-picking consequences. Months later when I had learned the piece as best as I could, he seemed pleased, but I still hadn't mastered holding the guitar with my thumb on the back of the neck. My long fingers wrapped around it tightly, instead of holding it with any grace. But, although he didn't say so, I knew the offer of teaching me the second part of the tune had been withdrawn. I couldn't understand why after so long his patience had run out and his interest in something he loved had been lost. We had had a short argument about it and he dismissed me curtly, saying that that was *the end of the conversation.* I argued back, hoping to persuade him to pick it up again, that it was a shame to abandon a hobby that had once given him such pleasure. It was not what he wanted to hear and he cast the guitar aside as if there was something inadequate about it. He placed it in its hard case and slid the once-beloved instrument under his bed, forbidding anyone to touch it.

Many months later, after much consideration, he changed his mind and told me to practise on the piece. I was allowed to use his guitar again, but the love he had for the instrument was still lost on him and I hoped that he would come round to teach me the rest of the complicated piece one day.

Worry churned my stomach with those memories. As the car trundled on, I searched my mind for further clues. He was an eccentric man by nature, and at times difficult and jealous – *normal* wasn't part of his character. He was intelligent and affectionate and often he could be the butt of a joke without knowing how funny he was. A real-life *Manuel* of *Fawlty Towers.*

Another memory popped up, this one more concerning as it was more recent - just three months back.

Early one evening, he and my mother had gone shopping together in a large complex in the middle of the city. They had enjoyed a nice lunch together and then decided to explore some shops separately and meet back at the car park an hour later. But Joseph never turned up, leaving my mum waiting for hours, desperate and confused as to his whereabouts. Joseph had the one set of car keys on him. He didn't have a mobile phone, hated the idea of them. Eventually, as darkness fell she got a taxi home. My mother called me, repeating the words *I've lost him, I've lost him* in a daze.

Jason and I had driven over to my parent's house in a panic, unsure at what she meant by *lost* – had he died in an accident? What had happened?

We arrived to find my mother's Galician friend Lourdes standing in the hallway, pale-faced, speaking on her mobile phone. My mother sat at the kitchen table chain-smoking, her hands shaking as she warmed them on a cup of coffee. They had spent hours calling police stations, Joseph's close family and hospitals hoping for an answer to his disappearance.

Finally, at midnight, Joseph strolled in with a Chinese takeaway under his arm, wondering what we were all staring at and why had my mother been crying. We were all dumbfounded at his lack of empathy. Despite this seemingly odd behaviour, this was not completely unusual for him. He would get caught up for hours talking to someone on the street, at the local DIY store or out getting a bottle of wine. Only, never quite as long as this time. Over the following days, my mother was convinced he was having an affair. It was the only reasonable explanation that made any sense to her. He seemed wounded at the accusation and convinced us that he lost track of time; in truth, he himself had no idea where he had got to.

Seated behind him now I was worried his dangerous driving was going to get us all killed. After an agonising ride, we met Jason outside a parade of shops at our halfway point in town. We all tried to convince Joseph he needed to let us take him to hospital but it must have felt like the three of us were bullying him and he point-blank refused. Bad timing meant it was the weekend and we knew that Joseph wouldn't receive any kind of assessment until the doctors were back on their Monday morning rounds. It was likely that he would discharge himself if there was no one telling him to stay put. As I distracted Joseph, my mother and Jason hatched a plan to convince Joseph to see a local doctor. We hoped that the more gentle approach would keep him calm and comply. But by the time we reached my mother's house and a plan was in place, he had become a little fearful and his aggression and denial grew. We felt trapped in a part of the world where we couldn't explain the situation adequately enough that would convince a doctor - who didn't know Joseph - to see that he wasn't himself. Up until that point we had always relied on Joseph, the one full Spanish speaker to help us out in difficult situations.

The next day we returned to their house to take Joseph to the local doctors but he refused again. His stubbornness was infuriating. Our gentle approach wasn't working and even though we didn't want to scare him, to tell him our suspicions of a stroke, brain tumour, or blood clot. We had no choice but to be brutally honest.

After a serious lecture, my mother managed to convince him to see the emergency doctor at the local clinic in town. It was a start but there was still the problem of explaining to the doctor all the symptoms we knew Joseph would hide. So just before he walked into the doctor's office we had a Spanish friend call the doctor and explain the facts. The doctor took one look at Joseph and referred him straight to the hospital in the city where they would start a bombardment of blood tests and CAT scans immediately. Joseph found the urgency hard to absorb but we were just relieved we were finally getting somewhere.

A few hours later we arrived at a white marble fronted hospital campus that overlooked the city's beach. The hospital resembled a sterile art gallery inside with glass walls, artwork and a sleek white marble lobby that led way to a series of elevators'.

A long afternoon and evening followed as Joseph was pushed from different rooms in a wheelchair looking small in his hospital gown, one test followed by another as we waited nervously and hoped for the best.

We didn't have to wait too long before the first results came back. We held our sickened stomachs and listened to the doctor explain that the tests revealed a large tumour in the right side of the brain, the part that holds all sorts of important data such as our memories, body functions, emotions and awareness. The mass in his head, whatever it was, was pressed up against the frontal-lobe and was the cause of the brain misfiring signals.

My mother was devastated but the doctor's hadn't confirmed it was cancer, nor did it have the characteristics of a blood clot. According to one doctor, the tumour could have even been there for a long time following an injury in the past. The neurosurgeons seemed to take particular interest when we told them that Joseph had been involved in a hit and run motorcycle accident when he was just nineteen, resulting in him being in a coma for two days. With this information, there was some hope that perhaps the tumour in his brain was a growth of damaged cells and had been there causing no harm until it had grown too big. I had heard of people recovering from brain tumours all the time. We hoped that he might be one of these cases.

Joseph was transferred to a private room and given medication to put balance back into his brain. In his hospital room, there were two beds and a couple of plastic covered lounge chairs with enough surrounding space to accommodate many family members. Joseph told us that the usual protocol was that spouses' would keep a bedside vigil day and night for when the patient needed you, we weren't entirely sure if he was joking or not.

Aside from when the doctor does his patient examinations,

there are no restrictions on hospital visiting hours. And to take the pressure off nurses' duties, it is the families' responsibility to get the patient what he needs.

I asked the nurse for some water and was promptly shown a closet halfway down the corridor filled with towels, hospital-monogrammed bed linen, cardboard kidney trays and film-wrapped batches of bottled water. She pointed inside the cupboard and instructed us to take what we need.

The next day we dropped into the hospital again. As we rounded the corner into Joseph's room we felt a wash of relief at seeing him comfortably upright in bed. It was hard to not be impressed with the national healthcare and little luxuries made all the difference; a patient wash kit, a sparkling clean en-suite with an Italian marble sink and shower, a television and nice views out to the sea. It was better than most hotels I had stayed in and a far cry from the hospitals back in the UK.

In front of Joseph sat a steak lunch on a bulky beige hospital tray; his appetite had clearly returned, as he chomped his way through his main course followed by fruit, coffee and yoghurt. A menu hung from a clip on the tray, with a list of choices for tomorrow's meals.

"What shall I order for tomorrow? Ha! They have Dorada!" he chuckled. His head had been shaved in preparation for the surgery that afternoon, a sight at which I saw my mother swallow hard to hide her immediate shock. She had always admired his black and silver-streaked hair – she said it gave him his distinguished, Latin appeal that complimented his dark olive skin.

That afternoon Joseph was taken into surgery and instead of taking just a biopsy, the entire tumour was removed. The five-hour operation had been a success but it would be a wait before the results would come back and we would know exactly what we were facing. Joseph took two full days to recover in intensive care before he was moved back up to his room. Thankfully the surgery had instantly changed him back to the man we all knew and he seemed brighter and happier than he had been in weeks.

Over the course of the week, the doctors themselves were more of an enigma. They did their hospital rounds at ten in the morning and then disappeared. Their white coats floating briefly into view at the far end of the corridor, causing us and other desperate families give chase, only for the doctor to vanish into thin air. Although the hospital and quality of care was impressive, I was disheartened by the lack of communication when we needed answers. The doctors avoided our questions and in our despair, it seemed as if someone was playing a cruel game. I cursed the unforgiving bedside manner that was so lacking and yet so desperately needed.

Eventually, by the end of the week, we had worked out the confusing system - devised by someone who clearly had never had a relative in dire circumstances. Feedback was offered on a limited basis, on Tuesdays and Fridays. Relatives were expected to wait outside the doctor's office where they were individually summoned to write down the patient's name and room number. The doctor would add this room number to his list and in return hand a ticket with the same number on it back to the relative. The relative is then sent back outside to wait with the crowd until called. The whole process could take an entire afternoon - an agonizingly long time to hear a prognosis.

It seemed an arduous, heartless way to gain such vital information. In my mother's frustration for answers, she lost patience and caught a young doctor creeping out of a side door. She charged up to him and pinned him to the wall, her arms locked either side demanding answers for her husband's condition. He looked furious as he muttered something about waiting for more test results before managing to escape from my mother's grip, and in his haste got swallowed up into a crowd of other relatives who wanted immediate answers too.

Jason and I desperately wanted some good news as we took my mother back to the hospital every day. Wrecked with emotion, she looked smaller and frailer through lack of food and sleep. Close friends and family flew over to help, and their support gave us hope in such unknown circumstances.

When we weren't with my mother at the hospital, we were back on the restoration but it was hard to concentrate on any little job. Every time the phone rang my stomach would churn with anticipation of bad news. At weekends we tried to distract ourselves by restoring old furniture but it felt like our hearts weren't in it any more.

After fourteen agonising days, we finally got confirmation from the doctor. The removed tumour had been grade-four cancer of the most advanced type. The news bludgeoned us, especially as we had thought we had been through the worst of it. And although they had removed the surrounding tissue cleanly, it was possible that cancer still might reappear, due to the nature of it. As a result of the surgery, the oncologist warned us that Joseph might have seizures, and so he'd never be able to be completely independent or drive again. It was all too much for my mother to take in, and she entered into a state of such utter despair that we had to get her doctor to prescribe sedatives to calm her nerves. I wished there had been some kind of support group to help her but the reality was that we were in Rural Galicia and didn't have access to such things. We were as alone to fight with it as much as Joseph was.

With little time to prepare, my mother had to make new changes to her life. She would have to make key decisions and learn to drive in Spain, something she had assumed Joseph would always do. She didn't quite realise how much she had been depending on her husband for such things.

The doctors put a positive spin on things and told us, if all went well, Joseph could make a full recovery following chemo and radiotherapy.

We remained positive and before long a new kind of relief washed over us. Two days later we were in my mother's kitchen drinking tea and smiling for the first time in ages. Joseph would come out of hospital soon. We hoped that this was the end of his, and our, nightmare.

We had discussed the changes my mother would need to implement to care for Joseph, in co-ordination with his treatment plan and to take charge of his vital brain steadying medication. On the practical side, my mother swiftly got rid of the old British Volvo and bought a reliable car. Jason took her out on quiet country roads and under the dark canopy of the eucalyptus trees, she relearned how to drive under his instruction. Although she was a perfectly competent driver it was her confidence that needed to be encouraged, a confidence that was in tatters along with her nerves. It was a brave challenge for her to undertake at sixty-three years old considering she had only ever been a passenger in her ten years in Spain.

After just a few lessons she took to driving in a foreign land beautifully. We were incredibly proud of her courage, giving her a new lease of life. She was surprised how much freedom she had gained, and Joseph seemed pleased with the change too although I think he found it hard to admit that he would miss driving. We kept him buoyed, saying that it was hopefully only a temporary precaution and soon he could drive again. For my mother at least, being independent in the things she could control, kept her head above water during those dark times.

36. A HELPING HAND

It was May and another rainy week lay ahead. Jason had managed to get the roof watertight so we were able to rip out the floor and construct a new one over the level joists. This was an exciting phase and we were keen to get working double time. But with just the two of us, it became apparent we needed paid help. We asked the other villagers if they knew of a good builder and hoped word would soon spread. We had plans that once the floor was in we could finally move out of the wretched caravan and gain back some spacious living.

Oscar had heard our appeal and found just the man for the job - an old friend of his called José María, who was not only experienced in stone renovations but was currently available for work.

José was short, slim and rugged. He was around forty-five years old, although my guess could have been grossly overestimated. A combination of heavy smoking and outside elements had visibly destroyed his facial skin, sagging at the eyes and cheeks. He had short black hair that he combed back with his fingers, and wore baggy jeans that needed regularly hitching up. He drove a black, rusty motorcycle with balding tyres and kept his modest tool collection wrapped in a brown jumper strapped to the back of the bike.

To put his capabilities to the test we started him on the mammoth task of chipping away the old cement off the stone on the front of the house, where we had erected some scaffolding.

Most of the tough cement was around the upper floor windows. It was a horrible job as it had adhered so solidly to the stone and could only be removed by a machine, flakes at a time. We had estimated it would have taken us a week of hard-slog, but José completed the task within just a day, barely stopping for lunch as he hammered off shards and chunks into the road – the man was a machine. We were thrilled when we noticed how much he had transformed the frontage already. He was certainly living up to his reputation of being fast, affordable and very capable.

Oscar was extremely pleased with himself for introducing us to the builder and decided that he would, from now on, act as José's manager. He didn't lift a finger to help, instead he stood in doorways and distracted the builder as much as he could in order to feel he was part of the effort.

We felt extremely lucky to have José as part of our team, good builders were hard to find and my parents could vouch for that. They were in the unfortunate situation of taking their cowboy builder to court for shoddy workmanship. It was a hassle they could do without, let alone the added misfortune of their builder then counter-suing them because they refused to pay the remaining invoice for his appalling work.

A few weeks later the house build had come on vastly thanks to José who was a constant, enthusiastic and reliable workman. We praised him to our new Galician friends we had met at the medieval fiesta and before long they had put in a request to employ him once we were done. While our builder continued cleaning up the stone on the exterior, we concentrated on jobs inside. José was happy to do the jobs we hated and once he had accomplished a task he would beam a huge smile - equally impressed with himself as much as we were.

Even, when he had the task of jet-washing the packed mud between the old stone in the pouring rain - he still seemed content. Only one incident had deterred him, the disturbance of a baby viper nest, causing the builder to jump off the scaffolding and run screaming *"Mierda! mierda!* Jackson!" as he ran, terrified into the house.

The renovations moved on smoothly but we quickly noticed how fast our cash was disappearing having an extra man on board. Jason dished out José's wages every Friday and the builder was thrilled to announce he would spend it at a nightclub in the city with his friends.

His enthusiasm, however, wasn't to last long.

One Monday afternoon – a month into his employment, we found an unusually subdued José slumped in our doorway.

He was four hours late for work and visibly hung-over as he stood picking at his dirty fingernails like a stroppy teenager. This was a change from the energetic man we had started off with.

With new instructions we left him to it, hoping he would snap out of his mood and concentrate on a new task of rebuilding a fallen stone wall at the back of the house. It was an area where eventually we would put in a Galleria – a Galician version of a conservatory with expansive glass panes which would give us panoramic views of the garden.

From upstairs I heard Oscar burst into our house, causing his usual havoc among the dogs whom he had startled. We calmed the mayhem, coaxing Teddy out from under a chair while my parent's dog, Coco - who we were babysitting - went wild with her over-protective barking defending us from the giant figure. For some reason, she instinctively didn't like the man and at just a foot away, on her hind legs, she bared her teeth right into Oscar's face. If it hadn't been for the chain around her collar holding her back she might have gone for Oscar's throat, not that he would have noticed. Undeterred by Coco, Oscar ignored the vicious growling and took a wide step towards the builder to see his latest work but in doing so crushed José toes. The builder yelled to be left alone, Oscar obliged much to everyone's relief.

By the end of the long day, Jason handed José a well-earned beer as we all stood to admire the reconstructed stone wall. At least his mood had lightened a little, and he had done a great job.

Over the following days, Oscar didn't resurface and productivity on the build increased so that we all felt animated with its evolving progress. Together with José, we finished one job to the next, saving the fulfilment of admiring our work until the end of the day. We couldn't remember a time when we had worked so physically hard, pushing our bodies to the point where we had used our last morsel of energy until there was nothing left. All we could do at the end of each day was to eat a hearty meal and collapse into bed.

One midweek morning when Jason and José had popped out to collect more materials, I carried on mixing cement in the old kitchen. By now, evidence of my fire accident had almost been erased. The low ceiling had been freshly painted white, the beams cleaned of soot and the chestnut fireplace gleamed with its thick coats of varnish. Light bounced around the room and into the hallway making it look remarkably different from the primitive kitchen it had once been.

I climbed inside the stone pig trough with a trowel and a board piled with cement. My task was to work the mixture onto the walls before the mix went off. As I smoothed the cement I felt a puff of breath behind me, I turned reluctantly to face Oscar.

As usual, his manners didn't stretch far enough to put any space between us. He swayed gently, emitting an alcoholic haze that filled the room with toxic gas. He must have pushed the front door open, *the cheeky sod*. I felt irritation rise in me. *I don't have time for this.* I wished he could see my thoughts.

"What are you doing, girl?" he asked simply.

"I'm very busy Oscar." I answered hoping he would leave before my cement dried out.

"Ha!" Oscar exclaimed and poked the area of soft render I had neatly applied five seconds before. I felt like poking him in the eye with my trowel.

"But you're a woman?" he cried out as if pointing out my

gender might make me take a really good look at myself and think, *Bloody hell, he's right, you know. A woman shouldn't be doing this kind of work, I should throw down my pallet and be thankful for his wisdom.*

I tried my best to ignore Oscar and his sexist comment. He shuffled his boots closer, scrutinizing my work until he had me boxed me into a corner. I turned from him and expertly flicked my wrist, catapulting a lump of sticky cement into the muddy cracks, then smoothed it over just as I had seen the experts do it. I hoped my professionalism might convince him to leave me alone.

"Why you doing that?" asked Oscar with a stupid grin. I took a deep breath through my nose. No answer I could give would satisfy him. He motioned for me to come even closer as if there were some big secret he wanted me to hear. I noticed he had an eye infection that was making his left eye weep until there was a single glassy tear on his cheek that didn't seem to fall. His purple cheeks moved up and down as he struggled to find the words in Castellano Spanish that would be easier for me to understand. He brought his nicotine-stained finger up to his large bloodshot eyeball,

"I see everything," he said mystically as I stood there bent over staring into his eyes with no idea what he was talking about.

Just as the situation couldn't get any more uncomfortable, Maria's dog Trampas, burst through our barn door, chasing a black and white cat through the house like a scene from a cartoon. This gave me the small window of opportunity to jump from the trough and squeeze past Oscar to pretend to chase the dog. Oscar, clearly thinking this was a game, ran after me like a bumbling giant. Eventually, I managed to lose him outside by ducking behind a parked car and slipping through the secret priests' passageway into the sanctum of the graveyard still holding my trowel. When I got back into the house I dead-locked the door and carried on cementing.

When Jason and José returned from the builders' yard an hour later, Oscar stumbled back into the house behind them, dragging José with him to point out my handiwork in the old kitchen.

"Ha!" exclaimed José - just as Oscar had. "Its good work, I suppose – for a woman!" They both laughed together, two toothless village idiots.

Jason gave me a sympathetic look, knowing the comment had irritated me. I was very proud of my walls and didn't seek or need approval from these two.

Feeling undermined, I carried on cementing with twice the effort until it was completed. Then a feminist force took over me and I continued to push myself, smashing stubborn old cement and tiles from the wall with a pickaxe. *I'll show these pesky locals how a woman does things around here.*

That night, during my deep slumber, a surge of pain shot through my right shoulder blade at such intensity, I presumed that I must have been shot by a stray bullet. The pain was deep and burning, causing me to sit bolt upright in the caravan bed and growl through gritted teeth. I grasped at the agony in my shoulder that took my breath away and checked for evidence of blood on the sheets or my bedtime T-shirt in the dull moonlight. I broke out in an instant sweat and twisted the quilt in my hands as I wondered what to do next. Jason, still asleep and exhausted, stirred next to me as I sat bewildered in the darkness, thinking, irrationally, of all the scenarios that might have led to this.

I then realised that perhaps in my wild 'Jane of the Jungle' moment trying to prove my worth to José and Oscar I must have injured myself. Had I dislocated my shoulder using the pickaxe? Was that even possible?

Thinking about the two toothless villagers laughing at me, it appeared that perhaps I had been the idiot. In trying to prove my strength to them, I had ruined myself. Broken a part that couldn't be easily fixed, and there was still so much to do. I flopped back down to try to sleep, the pain eased and somehow I managed to get a few hours' sleep after lying awake for what seemed like an eternity.

37. EVER THE OPTIMIST

The next morning, while my mother was taking Joseph to another appointment, I was being seen in the emergency department of our local hospital. The doctor, who looked too old and weary to continue practising medicine, squinted through filthy round lenses as I struggled to hold the weight of my arm out in front of him. He stood small, swamped by his oversized white coat.

"Nothing wrong with you, young lady," he said making me feel as if I were making up the pain and the total lack of strength as my arm flopped back down beside me. I gathered all my energy and lifted my arm again as I peered sideways into the mirror on the doctor's wall. The right shoulder blade was clearly sticking out at an alarming angle. Unfortunately, the doctor couldn't see what I could and prescribed some painkillers instead.

By the time Joseph had started his six-week radiotherapy sessions, a new chemo trial had become available, making it easier to take by tablet at home. We agreed we would take turns in driving him to his short radiotherapy sessions at the hospital to give my mother a respite from her duties.

Our first experience of this was disturbing. So many dreadfully sick people on the conveyer belt of treatment, waiting their turn. We talked in hushed tones as I tried to distract Joseph from worrying about his first exposure and he, in turn, remained upbeat and almost too accepting to be there. I knew he was just putting on a brave face for us, protecting us from the fear of the disease.

Patients sat in wheelchairs wearing tight-fitting scarves on bald, pale skin. Joseph quickly made friends with other patients and they appreciated his positive wishes and warmth towards them, although some seemed disturbed at how well he took his own diagnosis as if he wasn't affected by this malicious disease that had resulted in deep surgical scars and metal staples crowning his scalp. He took to the sessions with confidence that everything would be all right and we admired his positivity even when at times things looked bleak.

With my arm in a sling made from an old strip of muslin my mum had donated from her fabric collection, I continued to take Maria's Saturday morning English classes. With all the hospital and parental visits over the past weeks, my English classes with Maria had been intermittent. But the absence had seemed to revive Maria's appetite for learning.

For me, it was a comfort knowing that my mother was adjusting to Joseph's needs while in my spare time, I had the distraction of teaching Maria.

When it was sunny outside we could afford the luxury of enjoying the warmth on our backs, sitting on the makeshift benches as the church bells rang behind us.

My friend Alex had advised me to swat up a little on practical grammar terminology but he had also told me that I would gain a better understanding of English grammar as I continued to delve into it. It wasn't something I could learn in a month like I had hoped he might say. With the help of a few books I'd bought online, I spent the evenings sitting up in bed studying the fundamental principles of the English language. Who knew there was such a depth to my own language? The terminology alone was enough to make me throw the books to the caravan floor and launch my face into a pillow – *preposition words, passive verbs, modal verbs and verb forms, present and past participles?* Simply speaking the language wasn't enough of a basis to teach it, unless I understood how each word performed on its own.

And then, one afternoon, when I wasn't sure if my efforts were making a difference, Oscar staggered into our doorway bursting with pride. Maria's English grades had rocketed from a low to a high grade in just a few months. Oscar embarrassed me by thanking me endlessly from the bottom of his heart, cocking his head to the side, exaggeratedly clasping both hands over his heart, and performing a little bow towards me in honour. He had already been drinking in celebration that morning, I was certain of that but I was pleased he was happy.

The news was as much of a surprise to me, as it had been to him. I really had no idea how much English Maria had absorbed during our lessons. Sometimes she had behaved like a stroppy teenager and had hidden from me behind trees. Other times, she had beamed when she successfully translated a few of her father's words.

After that, I would often find a bag of stinking rotten eggs hanging on the door knocker left by Oscar. This was his way of thanking me for Maria's lessons, encouraging me to use the eggs for traditional Spanish omelettes but the only thing I could do with them was to run with the bag through the house holding my nose and bury the putrid eggs under the compost heap.

Maria's tuition had caused a ripple in the village, just wide enough for the other residents to comment to me about it.

"So her grades have improved, eh? Would you believe it?"

I was unsure if they were implying my teaching capabilities weren't good enough or Maria was an unlikely bright student. The gypsies remained cautious of my influences, but I did notice they gave little Zara a book one day, the first time I had ever seen her with one. I made a silent promise to her that I would fetch a colourful book from my collection in Valencia, and bring it back to Galicia with me, a gift her parents wouldn't be able to refuse.

Three weeks into June, the weather had improved to a very

agreeable twenty-five degrees. The landscape was blooming with colour, brooks bubbled underfoot and tall eucalyptus trees popped their seed capsules as they warmed in the sunlight.

I had followed my mother's advice and managed to get a second opinion on my shoulder injury from another doctor. Finally, I had the diagnosis that I had suspected all along; a torn tendon that held the shoulder blade in place, hence why it was protruding. The doctors offered nothing but drugs and rest and I knew that I would have to fight long and hard to gain a place on the physiotherapy list. Still, it was nothing compared to Joseph's problems. I strapped up my shoulder and limited the things I could do around the house.

In the coming weeks, Joseph's health remained steady, and for my parents, their life was getting into a new routine. Although his mobility was slow and frustrating for him, all he felt he needed was sleep. The realisation of his illness had hit home too. He was still feeling hopeful, but had now, over time, managed to grasp the full seriousness of what he had been through and was yet to conquer. We made regular visits to their house, which gave us all a chance to share stories of village life.

When he was strong enough my mother drove Joseph out to our village one Sunday afternoon. We took a short walk into the forest behind our house, the change of scenery seemed to lighten his mood. He inhaled deep breaths of eucalyptus air and I hoped he would momentarily break away from his troubled thoughts, if not but for a few hours. Between the shadows of the stone houses the sun deliciously warmed our stressed necks and just then, as we turned to head back inside our house, we heard Oscar's familiar drunken growl coming from his barn. The cry of a man so deep inside his own despair, it was as if he were drowning. We all knew it would take a miracle for him to tackle his addiction and become the man we hoped he could be.

38. RUSE FOR A BOOZE CRUISE

Much to our disappointment, our builder's enthusiasm had plummeted to an all-time low. He either turned up late, took prolonged lunch breaks or sometimes didn't show up at all. It was frustrating, especially when we were good to him, paid him well- over the average rate and paid in advance if he requested it. But it seemed José was taking advantage of our kindness, so one day while in conversation, Jason was able to use the valuable phrases in Gallego, Joseph had taught us to whip the builder into shape.

Am I paying you to stand and smoke? Do you need something to help you work today? Jason echoed through the hallway in his best Galician, and it worked – to a degree. But we could tell there was resentment for telling him what to do.

The builder stomped and threw tools around, screaming, cursing, shouting at Teddy for getting under his feet until his mood was so intolerable I thought Jason might sack him on the spot.

We left him to work it out himself but at the end of the shift, Jason took him aside out to the garden with a can of beer as a peace offering and had a heart to heart with him to see what was really going on.

José confided that he had fallen out with his father because he had refused to join the family building firm. He was happy being independent with his stonemason craft which he took great pride in but the firm wanted José to work on less-skilled projects to help out. His father had given him an ultimatum that if he were to pursue his own path rather than continuing the family trade, he wanted nothing more to do with him.

But our builder's problems didn't stop there. His wife had kicked him out of the house, leaving him homeless. His vintage motorbike needed repairs that he couldn't afford. He had no spare money for travel expenses as he had spent it on a girl he had met at a nightclub. He felt the world was against him.

With nowhere to live, he had moved into Oscar's squalid house - an offer that had at first seemed like the ideal arrangement but only if José could somehow manage to turn a blind eye to the nastiness of the dwelling.

Hoping to make these living conditions more bearable he had tried to convince Oscar to clean up but Oscar took great offence and the two had a falling out. Oscar argued that he should not have to change the way he lived for an ungrateful, so-called *friend*.

But as always, Oscar, as cunning as an old Galician fox, did not do badly out of the deal. He had convinced José to pay for his keep by supplying him with cigarettes and a few litres of wine a day.

José vehemently stated his reasons why he was appalled by Oscar's house. "He lives like an animal, but he cannot see it."

Jason couldn't offer much to console him and by early evening José had packed up his one bag and moved out of Oscar's. He told us he had arranged an alternative place to stay locally so he would be back the following day.

Unfortunately, José didn't appear for the rest of the week, so we continued to work without him. Throughout the weekend our disappointment deepened, especially as he had started off so well.

He reappeared late on Monday afternoon when he staggered in unwell, sweaty, stinking and broke. Without explanation or apology for his absence he demanded his wages for the days he had worked and declared he wasn't going to continue until he felt better. We were annoyed with his unreliability, he was getting worse and we couldn't continue going like this when we had deadlines. We paid him for the little work he had done and Jason told him that if he wanted to keep his job he had better turn up the next day or he was out.

To our surprise, he did show up and we outlined what we wanted from him - bluffing that we could replace him if he let us down again. I hoped it wouldn't come to that because despite his moments of childish behaviour and long absences, he was a great worker with many skills and it was unlikely we would find someone to replace him. Our pep-talk seemed to work and he ploughed on for a few more days, our faith somewhat restored.

Then late one morning he stumbled in looking rosy-faced and set to work reconstructing a wall in the new area of the kitchen that the farm animals had once been tied to. An hour later we noticed a quietness that implied we had been deserted once again.

After a brief search, we found José flat on his back under a tree in the grassy village square. His excuse was that he had eaten a dodgy burger and he was suffering from food poisoning.

I immediately jumped to the conclusion that Oscar had cooked it. But he said he had bought it from a café that had a disgraceful reputation and he should have known better. Jason knew otherwise and wasn't convinced of his lies. "He's had a skin-full." He stated as José tanned complexion turned grey. We left him to it, but he soon found his feet and trotted after us.

Back in the house, the builder immediately convulsed in pain and dry-retched into his hand. We stood motionless, as we watched him theatrically embark on a strange regurgitation process on all fours - the same way a cat might summon a fur-ball from the throat. Once satisfied and suitably watery-eyed, José ended this performance by spitting phlegm onto the dusty kitchen floor, as proof of his discomfort.

Jason offered to drive him to the local pharmacy, which José gratefully accepted. Twenty minutes later they returned and it seemed all had not gone too well. Jason had watched José run off towards the pharmacy but instead of going inside, it looked as if the builder had darted into a bar next door instead. When he returned to the car empty-handed it was obvious which choice of medicine he had settled on. This was not good for us. We already had one town drunk to contend with, and it seemed we were in the company of another.

Back at the house, Oscar strutted in with an air of superiority about him. He didn't have much loyalty towards José after the criticism he had received over his dirty house. He leaned in towards us, whispering in his loud, boozy way that José hadn't had food poisoning at all that afternoon. He paused for our reaction which we dutifully gave him.

"In truth," he said, his finger touching his nose,

"*That* man has a bad drinking problem." He tutted as if he never touched the stuff in his life.

The next morning Oscar returned to our house with an urgent request.

"Jason, you take me to next village?" he asked hurriedly, in almost incomprehensible Galician that it took both of us a moment to decipher.

Oscar had been banging loudly on our front door all morning, which we had tried for the best part of an hour to ignore. We gave in but only because Macey and Teddy both looked so anxious from all the noise. Jason had been connecting a series of copper pipes in the new bathroom upstairs and it wasn't the right time to be distracted. We were hoping if all went well that morning by the afternoon we would have the luxury of using a real ceramic toilet, and even better, turning on a real tap – it was a crucial development and Oscar, as usual, was ruining our plans.

"Give me a ride?" he asked again with more force, oblivious to his obvious intrusion.

"Not right now. I'm working," Jason responded, waggling some soldering wire in front of him to make a point.

"No?" Oscar said, stunned by Jason's refusal. "But it's important, I have no food, no food at all for my sheep and they are hungry." He turned his mouth downwards to emphasise the sheep's unhappiness. I was surprised he didn't bleat.

"Don't they graze in the grassy field out there?" I muttered to Jason in English. Oscar frowned at me, he must have sensed that I was interfering with his plans. Desperate to win me over, he put on his best-begging face.

"Ten minutes to the house of my cousin. He will give me food, ten minutes please!"

Jason and I looked at each other. Since when did Oscar ever go to such trouble for his sheep? We had seen him leaving them in woodland where the wolves were known to have lurked. Oscar's request had the smell of deceit all over it.

"I don't have much time today, tomorrow maybe?" suggested Jason and turned to walk back upstairs.

"*Tomorrow*? Impossible! No, no, no!" Oscar shook his mop of greasy hair. And then he seemed to change tactics, his massive head looming closer in a slightly threatening manner.

"Am I not your *friend*?" He cocked his head to the side and gently placed his giant hand on his heart to show the depth of our friendship from his perspective.

"And *friends* help *friends* do they not? Oh, I thought we had *AN UNDERSTANDING*!" he boomed with the look of utter contempt.

We both felt a flush of shame. How did he turn this around so expertly?

"Oh Christ, fine! Ten minutes, all right, no more!" said Jason, giving in and throwing his gloves to the floor, much to Oscar's delight.

And so, off they went, hopping into the Land Rover as if they were old buddies, through the country lanes in search of the elusive sheep food.

"I cannot believe that manipulative conman," Jason said as he walked back into the house almost two hours later. I grabbed the kettle and filled it from the long garden hose that was hanging through the window, covering my waist in freezing water from the spray, yet again.

"I take it, he took you for a ride, rather than the other way round?" I asked, smiling, knowing there was a story coming my way.

"You could say that. He had no intention of getting animal feed, it was all a ruse for a booze cruise," Jason pulled off his muddy boots and plonked himself down on a chair before continuing with his story.

They had stopped at a house in a deserted village around ten minutes into the drive. There was no answer at the house - most likely the occupants saw Oscar coming and hid under the kitchen table. They drove on, Oscar directing to an alternative place where they were ushered in for coffee by some nice old ladies, all called Maria. Oscar asked for brandy in his little coffee cup and poured himself a triple shot but Jason didn't think much of it at the time. He thought they were discussing where to collect the animal feed but couldn't be sure because everyone was talking at once. More brandy in coffee was consumed until they moved onto the next house while Jason waited in the car, hoping Oscar would hurry up. Thirty minutes later and Oscar still wasn't back, Jason's fury was mounting. He felt like abandoning him there altogether, but how could he? If he had an accident and ended up down an embankment again it would be Jason's fault. Eventually, Oscar arrived back at the car, drunk but still insisting to go onto the last house where he was sure they'd be some sheep feed.

Jason refused, telling Oscar they were going back to the village, he had had enough of being used as a chauffeur just for him to get plastered.

I handed Jason a steaming hot cup of tea.

"There was no sheep's feed in the end then?" I asked, "he must have been desperate for a drink to make all that up".

"Not as desperate as I am to get this bathroom done upstairs," said Jason and disappeared with his tea upstairs to continue his work.

39. FROM A STONE TO A CASTLE

Sunday was supposed to be a day of rest but even though we intended to take a break from the renovation we found our commitment to the house addictive. We were already pushing our work schedule to six days a week, and sometimes late into the evenings. By now we were permanently out of the caravan, our motivation was spurred on to make the house comfortable.

In the expanse upstairs we had slightly redesigned the layout within the parameters of the old structure so one half of the house kept its original staircase, the steps having been restored from reclaimed chestnut. This staircase led to the former classroom and a new bathroom. The other side of the old house had a brand-new pine staircase that Jason had handmade, leading upstairs to the most finished part of the house which was a clean, liveable area meaning goodbye to cramped caravan living and *hello* to a real flushing toilet and a hot shower. New pine flooring had been laid and stud walls divided the space into three rooms, a bedroom at either end with a small bathroom, corridor and stairs in the middle. We had stuffed foam insulation in between the roof beams, and plasterboard was starting to go up on the walls.

Our view from our new bedroom was of the old hórreo grain store that I had painted in a cornflower blue, the warped slats looked wonderful set against the spectacular forest green backdrop of the mountains behind.

I loved how the sunset would softly illuminate the bedroom through the square cottage windows and filter-in through the skylights in the ceiling. When night fell and we flopped into bed, we were rewarded with a canopy of stars. Here, the bedroom wall had once looked as if it were falling outwards - it was the one structural worry I had when we first viewed the house. But now after bracing the roof and replacing some of the stone - the wall was securely tied into the house. In short - it was a huge transformation. The chestnut beams in this section of the house showed their true structural beauty. Once stripped of rot, they showed their elegant curves, resembling a carcass of an upside-down boat, more slender than the bold trunks used in other rooms. Their colour was lighter as they hadn't been exposed to centuries of smoke and Joseph's tip - to add a little chunky structural nodule to the middle section of the beam - had completed the look perfectly.

The heavy gong of the church bells rang out from next door, indicating another Cabo de año was taking place. A slow procession of people wearing shiny black shoes marched around the churchyard, exchanging faded plastic flowers for brighter ones. When the anniversary funeral had finished the church became quiet again and the crowd split off to their cars or to nearby neighbouring houses for coffee and cakes. Old Manola seemed to have most of the churchgoers at her house that day, and she had dressed smartly for the occasion in a suit. It was somewhat strange to see her wearing anything other than clogs and woollen attire. Her hair looked as soft as bath bubbles piled on her head which I thought made her look radiant, an elegant lady half her age and I wanted to compliment her on it. But this was the first time I had seen her in town clothes and she appeared to be embarrassed by it as if wearing anything else in the campo was being untrue to her roots. She bent forward to chat to a couple who were sitting in a car and never took her eyes from the road. When she saw me, in my shabby denim work clothes, smiling at her, she looked right through me and quickly ended her conversation to disappear inside her house.

The build took us into a new month and every day as our builder José helped us transform the house, its own identity emerged. The old stone walls blossomed as they were embellished with new fixtures to complete the room. Finally, the uneven ground in the former cattle pit was ready for a layer of concrete to be poured over wire mesh.

It was a good job we still had José with us. He seemed happier now that he was living apart from Oscar and with a renewed enthusiasm for the renovation, he had made an effort to patch things up with us and even more importantly fixed the relationship with his father. They had reached a compromise, agreeing that José would help his father on building projects when he wasn't working elsewhere, which seemed to be a decent strategy.

I was grateful for the extra hand now that my arm was still useless from the shoulder injury. I had started my physiotherapy sessions at the local hospital every evening and the nurse had told me that the 'up and down' painting movement would help it heal as long as I didn't over-do it. With plenty of walls to paint I wasn't going to be short of excuses. José was thoughtful and carried rubble sacks for me when he could see I was struggling. But his greatest accomplishment was all the stonework on our restoration. He nodded proudly as he paced into every room, his soul as well as ours had gone into this build, and it was a permanent statement of all our achievements.

40. "YOU'RE NOT MARRIED YET!"

August arrived, along with an unwanted cold blast. I felt envious of our rental guests in our Valencian villa, sunning themselves and swimming in our pool when it looked like we might be in for another wet summer in Galicia.

Stuart and his wife drove up from Valencia to see us for a one-day visit. They had always shown great interest in the region so had added us into their packed itinerary at the last minute, hoping to catch sight of our project.

Our friends had spent the morning driving around the mountainous region and, like us, seemed astounded how different it was from the rest of Spain. They stopped by our house to get recommendations on where to go next and to duck their heads into the renovation. They seemed genuinely impressed with our achievements so far and we felt grateful for their continuing enthusiasm just as we were pushing ourselves to the limit.

While we finished up work with José for the day, we urged Stuart and Harriet to look around the medieval town of Betanzos, before meeting up with them over dinner where we could continue our catch-up. I was looking forward to an evening out of the village, to wear nice clothes and break away from the dust, the bells and crazy village life.

On the way to the restaurant, we briefly popped into Stuart's hotel to update our laptop, utilising the free hotel Wi-Fi that we didn't have at home. Stuart kindly recommended we leave it in their room so we could collect it later after dinner, by which time it should be fully functional.

The evening was enjoyable, despite Stuart's flirtations with the owner of the family-run restaurant in his usual jovial manner, putting a smile on diners' faces as they peered round to see who this extraordinary, animated man was.

After dinner, the four of us took a stroll over an arched stone bridge and along the river to a parade of bars. We showed them our favourite places to eat and stopped for an after-dinner drink at a swish bar next to the hotel. We soaked up the atmosphere and compared it to Santander and other parts of Spain we had all briefly visited. Before we headed back to our remote hamlet we popped upstairs to their hotel room to pick up the laptop.

The hotel was a clash of classical and contemporary design, a good choice with its mock Art Deco pillars and ochre-yellow façade that was sure to impress Harriet who liked to travel in style.

Stuart was desperate to impress us with their choice of bedroom, causing him to rush around in excitement, dashing up the hotel corridor as he couldn't wait to show us the view of the town from the balcony.

Inside the room, the décor was sleek and appealing with its refreshing contemporary colours; dark greys and yellows, silver lampshades and colourful circular rugs on the carpeted floor - a stark contrast to the rustic farmhouse style I was used to with the build. We poked our noses in the granite bathroom and mooched onto the balcony to take in the view of the old town. I felt aware that Stuart was hoping to get me on his own again so in my unease I pointed out the letterbox-style window above the desk that framed the town in the distance and hoped the conversation would keep on neutral terms. Meanwhile, Harriet had engaged Jason in a lengthy conversation on the other side of the small room, which left me with Stuart by the bed. He looked at me mischievously.

"Georgina, you're not married just yet!" he declared and playfully pushed me backwards onto the bed, in a move that was so expertly executed I lay there wondering how my perspective of the room had changed so suddenly. I was acutely aware of the position I had found myself in and before I could speak I felt a body plonk down beside me.

"There's still time!" Stuart offered.

My hair had fanned out behind me and I wondered if he might be leaning on it by accident. My earlier convictions about the couple rose to the surface once again and despite his playful manner, Stuart had crossed the boundaries of our friendship in a way that I wasn't comfortable with.

I scanned the room for Jason whom I had half expected to be standing at the foot of the bed, hands-on-hips, red-faced in a psychotic jealous rage.

But Jason had his back turned to me as Harriet held him in a deliberately prolonged embrace that I could tell he found awkward.

We needed to get out of the room.

Was their game plan to divide and conquer? Or was it all just some harmless, jovial fun that had, once again, been taken that step too far? I swiftly got to my feet. Stuart sensed my unease and looked crestfallen.

"OK?" he said to me, slightly peeved at my rebuff.

"Perhaps not then," and then he loudly laughed it all off as Jason peeled himself away from Harriet and we quickly gathered our things.

I should have opened up the conversation then. I should have asked why we kept ending up in the same situation, what did they expect from us? But it was so difficult and embarrassing to start that discussion. We said our goodbyes, grabbed the laptop and charged down the stairs to the hotel lobby where we pulled on our jackets and caught our breaths. Outside in the street, the air was crisp enough to clear our heads and discuss the night's events as we headed back to our primitive little hamlet in the darkness.

"What were they thinking?" mumbled my mother the next day as she pinned around the hem of my charity shop wedding dress.

Her lips locked and loaded with dressmaking pins. She shook her head in wide-eyed disbelief as we digested the last encounter.

It was strange to think a pattern was emerging every time we had seen the couple and more worrying we were less surprised when it did. *Were they making it the norm?* It was no use trying to make any sense of it. We had enough on our minds with Joseph and the endless restoration, with only a month left before returning to Valencia.

The next day, in our hamlet at five in the morning, we were woken by a loud *WHOOSH!* And an even louder *BANG!* My heart palpitated for a minute and then settled when I realised war hadn't broken out. This was the unmistakable signal of a new fiesta week, induced by the first rocket launch at an ungodly hour. As we both groaned and buried our heads further under the duvet we knew what would come in a few hours' time. The church bells would ring followed by firecrackers and a flurry of activity from the village.

As the kitchen in the house was still a work in progress, we munched on our breakfast in the caravan that morning. The random popping of fiesta banger's had terrified the dog as she had patrolled the garden so Macey launched herself in through the open caravan window, almost breaking my neck and causing cups of tea, toast and jam to fly everywhere as she scuttled for safety.

The loudness and unpredictability of these fireworks captured the essence of the country that we were growing accustomed to and by the afternoon a huge stage had magically appeared in the village square.

A dedicated crew had peeled back the side of a truck, revealing a large platform surrounded by metal rigging. Bulky spotlights and sound equipment adorned the stage fit for a responsive audience. It seemed hardly worth the effort considering the poor turnout of spectators later that evening.

In full support, we had turned up at midnight to watch the band blast out relentless foot-stomping songs - tunes we had heard repetitively on the radio all summer.

Throughout the evening, we caught glimpses of Oscar staggering between bar tents before vanishing into the night. And just when I was feeling sorry for the sequined musicians and the effort they were putting in, heavy showers caused what little audience there was to take shelter in the beer tents or retreat home.

We stood alone under an umbrella on the soggy village green, content with our Jack Daniel's as we watched a lone saxophonist play at the corner of the stage bathed in a single spotlight. Velvety tones escaped into the open-aired darkness and echoed off the mountain walls capturing the romance of our isolation.

41. GRAVE DECISIONS

The fiesta celebrations continued into the week and the church next door became active again with a wedding followed by a funeral. We were surrounded by passers-by who were either bursting with happiness or deeply saddened, with not much in-between. The foot traffic in the cemetery was still frequent, allowing curious strangers to falter mid-stride at our boundary.

Over the fiesta period, we had noticed a tall, skinny man wearing a little green cap, hanging around the churchyard. Now here he was again, taking particular interest in our caravan and garden.

"I wonder if there's a reason why that guy is standing on our wall."

I said to Jason as I cleaned out my pink cement bucket.

"I noticed him earlier. Perhaps he's exhuming one of the graves?"

"No, I don't think so. Maybe he's interested in buying the caravan – he's been looking at it. That would save us having to find a buyer and we're almost done with it," I was desperate to get rid of it, the more it fell apart, the more of a burden it was becoming.

We watched as the man took carefully balanced strides across the stone wall, clinging to the grapevine to steady himself. Jason dropped his tools and we both casually strolled outside to investigate. Looking panicked, the man hopped down into the churchyard and hid, forgetting that his little green hat, would give him away.

Jason introduced himself, but the man did not offer his name in return instead he launched into a baffling diatribe in Galician, at an incomprehensible speed. He pointed to the black granite graves and drew a box in the air with his finger. He took a measuring tape out from his pocket, placed a rock on one end to weigh it down and stretched the tape over a two-meter distance along the wall. Jason and I exchanged baffled looks. Exasperated, we gave the man Joseph's number so he could call and explain.

I worried all the time about situations like this. Apprehensive that local people might try to argue over land on which they thought they had a claim on through old family connections. I had heard the term *rural terrorism* too many times in Galicia and it was something my parents had experienced with their own neighbour. But my worries, in this case, had been for nothing, as Joseph called that evening to explain.

"From what I gather - and he has a thick country dialect that even I found hard to understand, he wants to buy a piece of land from you so he can build his own grave," said Joseph, matter-of-factly.

Silence filled the gap as I struggled to find my words.

"But our land isn't for sale?" I stuttered.

"Yes I know my love, but he wanted to ask you if it is possible to buy some – the land where the caravan currently stands. He told me he was measuring up space for about six coffins," said Joseph.

"Can he do that, a member of the public? No. Wait." I paused and shook my head. "I can't believe we're having this bizarre conversation."

"Look, I'm just repeating what the man told me, I have no idea what rules there are about this kind of thing. All I know is that he wants to build graves" Joseph said.

"Is he planning some mass family murder?"

"I don't know, Georgie, just passing on the message"

As if there wasn't enough to think about already, now I had the added problem of Grave Man hassling us so he could buy land that I had no doubt he wanted for pennies. Even if we had been interested in his proposal, it was a complicated and costly matter to split and sell land. You had to arrange for an authorised land surveyor to come and draw up new boundary plans separating the part that was for sale, have those papers readjusted on your own title deeds and the land registry office. The separated block of land would then need its own title papers made up.

It also occurred to me that surely there must be some kind of church committee that would need to have some input considering the graves would have to be accessible from the church garden and an increase in deceased residents? I knew overcrowding was an issue in the churchyard and we had heard that after a certain period had passed, graves were reopened, scraped out and reused. But we hadn't seen anyone from the church since the last funeral so it was unlikely that an official had been approached about it.

Just a few days after his conversation with Joseph, Grave Man reappeared frequently, hoping for an answer.

He hovered about, pestering us and stomping below the grave columns, brushing away soggy leaves on the ground as if the deal had been done. I tried to imagine the concrete and granite block he wanted to build and I doubted more graves would be a selling point if we decided to sell the house once it was finished. We declined his offer but he insisted we think about it. He would be back – I was sure of that.

During the renovation, Jason had been keeping a close eye on our expenses and he realised that with most of the major work now completed, we were dangerously leaning into the red. Even with the rental income from the Valencian villa we were only just scraping by and still, we had a lot of materials to buy to finish it. We were faced with the very real risk the property business came with; cut your expenses or sink.

As luck would have it, José's tasks were coming to an end. We were incredibly impressed with his stonework and his working attitude had remained stable without further problems.

He had one final task of manually scrubbing the stone with a highly corrosive solution called Agua Fuerte - Hydrochloric acid, that when mixed with water, would disintegrate cement and dirt from the stone's surface, bringing out the stone's colour and mineral qualities. Although I had worked with the solution myself I didn't like to use it. It was toxic, burnt skin and was almost impossible to avoid splashing. Once mixed and wearing two layers of thick rubber gloves you have to submerge your scrubbing brush into the solution and as quickly as possible transfer the solution onto the stone. The stone would then be left "fizzing" away for a period of time after which you hose it off with water and repeat the process if necessary.

Jason equipped José with all the safety equipment needed for the job and left him to it. After around forty minutes we went back outside to check on his progress. The builder was smiling, happily scrubbing away, no gloves, no goggles. Every part of exposed skin looked red and blotchy.

"*STOP!*" Jason cried, "You *must* wear goggles!" he pleaded.

"NO NEED!" José shouted, refusing the safety gear. "These are my goggles" He pointed to his wrecked red eyeballs and smiled as if he were too macho to wear protection. Jason left the gloves and goggles on the floor in case the builder changed his mind.

Once José had finished, his face burnt and pitted from the frequent exposure of acid drops, we handed him his last wages with an extra bonus inside. We waved him off as he sped out of the village on his newly-fixed motorcycle and his jumper of modest tools secured on the back. José had been such a regular part of our lives it was going to seem strange not to have him around anymore. But seeing him leave was as much a relief to our bank balance as it was to finally realise how much the house had developed - the end of the project was in sight.

The following afternoon the weather had stayed nice and dry so Jason took the opportunity to slide under the Land Rover to change the worn handbrake pads. I poked my head out of the old schoolroom window from the upper floor to ask if he wanted a drink and I noticed not two, but four feet sticking out from under the car. I recognised Oscar's characteristic open-toed boots, his blackened toenails sticking out as he shuffled further under the car on his back. It amused me to think how trapped Jason must have felt to have Oscar in such proximity. I could hear him telling Jason how to tighten the nut, so it was just tight enough and the clinking of tools being thrown to the ground, with just a hint of irritation.

What I didn't know from watching from above, was that Oscar was more of a stinking mess than usual. He had consumed so much alcohol over the fiesta period that he had vomited over himself and had not changed his jumper since. Jason had needed to hold his breath under the car and pretend he had finished the repairs, just so he could escape.

Weeks flew by and in addition to our renovation, Abuela's house was also developing. Her family came and went with such secrecy that we hardly heard or saw them enter into the village. Only Rico would occasionally be seen, hunkered down in the passenger side of his latest joy ride, entering the village from a narrow brambly covered lane. The evidence of these stolen cars lay everywhere, chopped up and abandoned in nettle-covered gullies at the side of the road.

Abuela had added to her animal collection by means of a donkey and a Friesian cow - both lived a lonesome existence in our eyes and we often wondered how Abuela had acquired them. I was sure the cow had been traded as part of some dodgy deal because it was confined to a small dark barn and rarely saw the light of day. The cow remained hidden until the day I spotted Abuela bringing it armfuls of dried grass, on my way to the communal bins. The door had been left open just enough for me to see her patting the cow as it ate but as quick as a flash Abuela slammed the door as if I had uncovered a money-laundering racket. *Perhaps she had every reason to protect her investment?* I thought to myself.

The donkey, however, was kept in a field that joined our access to the woods and we deliberately changed our dog-walking route just so we could give it some company. It was in a terrible state and we felt dreadfully sorry for the poor animal. A piece of blue rope made from rough industrial nylon had been knotted and strapped far too tight around its muzzle so that when the donkey moved, either when eating or shifting to a new grazing area - it tugged, cutting into the flesh. The protective fur had worn away, exposing open sores to persistent flies. The poor donkey was virtually being eaten alive. The only way it could relieve itself was to shake its head to be rid of the flies but only for the briefest of moments before they returned.

And in addition to this, despite our disapproval, Abuela still confined her dogs in the tiny cage under the hórreo grain store. They hadn't left that cage in all the time we had been there as far as we knew. I struggled to understand how any maltreatment of this kind was acceptable to the family. But knew that any intervention from us would have grave consequences for the animal. This was never more apparent than when we discovered a six-month-old puppy roaming the village, which had been gifted to little Zara.

The puppy, already emaciated in its young body, survived off a few pieces of scrap food a day. When I saw it for the second time it broke my heart, how it was left to fend for itself and beg for food when the family had plenty, was beyond me. The cruelty angered me to my core so we left food out for it in secret but even by then it had completely vanished, perhaps to scavenge elsewhere. It reappeared a few days later with a broken leg that was so badly mangled, it appeared to have tried to chew its leg off at the joint. Perhaps it had been caught in a hunters trap? I thought it was a cruel twist of loyalty that the dog had returned to its owners, desperate and skeletal.

We reacted with horror in front of Abuela and hoped that by bringing attention to it, would prompt her to have a conscience.

As we inspected the damage, to see if there was anything we could do, Abuela who had not cared about its condition before, suddenly reacted with concern. She quickly shuffled the dog inside her house. We heard a flurry of voices and moments later the dog was shoved back into the street with an old bandage wrapped around the wound in an attempt to show us that they did care for the animal after all. That same day Jason went outside with a small pot of dog food but there was no sign of it, in fact, we never saw the dog again. I had a nagging suspicion that it had died somewhere from infection or it had been terminated in the woods, away from prying eyes.

We took our frustrations to my parents' house where we talked about Animal Protection and what to do. As there wasn't a version of the RSCPA in Galicia at that time, which we knew of, our only option would be to denounce the family to the police. But without any proof, it was unlikely our complaint would go any further. My parents warned us that this could be dangerous. By reporting the family we might end up making enemies of ourselves. It would be obvious who had filed the report in the first place and I doubted the police would protect the source of the complaint. It was a tricky situation within a tiny community where everyone was willing to defend each other, right or wrong, and we were still very much the outsiders.

However, there was something we could do about the donkey. As soon as the donkey was alone, Jason sneaked into the field where it stood and loosened the tight rope knots around its nose. He cleaned the wounds with cotton and applied liquid iodine to sterilise them. It was then that Jason noticed that the donkey had far bigger problems. The hooves on all four feet had grown so long they looked like clowns' shoes. The donkey could barely stand, let alone walk – we had to do something to help him.

After a bit of research, we found a donkey organisation online and sent an anonymous email to the charity underlining the problem and the rough address of our neighbours. The website stated that a small team of volunteer vets travel to rural areas to educate owners on improving the health and well-being of livestock in poor rural areas. I got a reply a day later but not with the news I was hoping for. Unfortunately, the organisation were based a few hours south of the province and didn't have enough funding to cover travel expenses so were restricting their areas. It was a blow; we were hoping the charity would make a big difference and at least make a dent on an ongoing problem that blighted this beautiful land.

42. A MAURITIAN WEDDING

Joseph's chemo and radiotherapy treatment had left him with very little appetite for anything. During these moments he remained courageous and focused on getting through the day. After coping so well with the invasion of toxic medication his body had quickly grown tired so at home he lay slumped on the sofa wrapped in blankets, losing himself in nature programmes, or retired to his bedroom to sleep. I realised then, that so much of his active mind was still there and had plenty to give, and yet so much had already been lost. None of us had any idea that dealing with brain cancer was so up and down and my mother handled the torment of emotion as best she could. Joseph was always the strong healthy one - the backbone of our lives in Galicia so we struggled to accept that his future was so uncertain.

A month later, things were looking up. Joseph had gained some of his strength back and seemed to be recuperating. With that in mind, it seemed a good time to head back to Valencia and make a start on our wedding plans. My mother urged us that it would be good to have something positive to focus on.

Our initial research of getting married in Spain brought up all sorts of complications. Translations of documents and Marriage petitions were required which took a lot of time and organisation, a hassle when we were constantly travelling and living in two locations.

A stress-free option was preferred, coupled with an unforgettable honeymoon location and Mauritius seemed like the best choice.

We booked a package with a hotel where the onsite wedding coordinator organised everything for a fraction of the cost, of a UK wedding. No hassle, stress-free with two weeks to enjoy the warm breezy Indian Ocean for our nuptials backdrop and have cocktails waiting on the side.

As the wedding would only involve the two of us, due to our families being unable to travel so far, the plan was to throw a huge unforgettable pool party in Valencia and celebrate properly with our family and friends on our return.

When our wedding day finally arrived a few months later, we thought we had everything sorted. We arrived at the matrimonial entrance, hand in clammy hand and gave the waiter the nod to play the opening song so the ceremony could begin. It was not the beautiful ambient acoustic guitar number we had chosen but the panpipe version of Bryan Adams *'Everything I do, I do it for you'*. A song that had been played twice a day for every wedding at the resort and had become a bit of joke for its popularity. I groaned out loud but it was hilarious at the same. All those weeks of agonising over so many beautiful songs and it hadn't made the cut. We had to embrace our new wedding song with how our lives went – never to plan!

As cliché as it could have been - our waiters were our witnesses. In between supplying our nerves with drinks one of the waiters shakily filmed our wedding for our families back home, taking particular interest in panoramic shots of windswept palm trees as if a hurricane was on the verge of destroying us. Grinning holidaymakers stood and congratulated us from the side-lines of the beach. I found the attention of strangers taking photos of our most precious day, touching. Their presence and kind wishes were heartfelt – especially when our parents were absent and yet so desperately wanted to be there.

In the evening, after having changed into our formal clothes, we were seated at the VIP table on the restaurant deck overlooking the shimmering blackness of the sea. Having lit small lanterns on our table, our hosts silently presented beautifully prepared Mauritian food and supplied us with an abundance of colourful rum cocktails.

We shared our wedding cake with the hotel staff and only then did I feel a real hollowed absence for not having our parents and friends with us. Afterwards, we took a stroll on the beach which gave us a moment to reflect on our day. Despite the undeniable void of our families and the mess-up with the music, it had been a perfect day.

A week later back in Valencia, sixty-five invitees from three different countries made their way to our mountain village. It was late October and unusually wet and cold. The guests trickled in and checked themselves into the hotels we had reserved for them and for those who preferred to stay longer hired apartments.

With the help of our neighbours, we borrowed tables and chairs that we draped in linen and positioned around the terraced garden, creating intimate seating areas. Two band marquees were erected on the deck, ready for when the DJ and live band equipment rolled in. Taking inspiration from the mansion garden at the Blue Biker Bar we used the same lighting effects: snaked rope lights around the palm trees and lined the edge of the pool with oversized lanterns. Floating candles and battery illuminated lilies, bobbed on the surface of the swimming pool and to add the final touch, Jason meticulously strung thirty meters of multi-coloured bulbs from the pine trees, fit for a Mexican fiesta.

The following day - with just one day left to get everything prepared, Jason tested the electrics by powering everything up together. That's when we realised we had a problem and the power kept shorting-out. Men collectively came together to come up with the best strategy. But it was our neighbour Nicolás, who realised that if our big pool party was to go ahead, the entire length of cable from the electric box in the street to the house would need to be replaced. Stressful as it was, Jason, his father and uncle pushed on to get the job done, much to my relief.

All the while I received constant phone calls from guests that had gotten lost in the Valencian countryside and I had to go and rescue them.

At around lunchtime, just as we were exhausted from the preparations I got a grief-stricken phone call from my mother, informing me that Joseph had had an epileptic fit and collapsed while having lunch with his daughters. Although the doctors had warned us that epilepsy might be a side effect of his cancer, my mother wasn't prepared for the frightening convulsions that left her powerless to help him. They were a thirty-minute drive away and restaurant staff had already called an ambulance to take him back into the city. Joseph would be confined to a hospital bed so he could be monitored.

Everything had turned upside down and I didn't know what to do. I had guests turning up while we were in turmoil once again as I stood motionless in the kitchen not knowing which way to turn. My closest friends were right there to support me and I took great comfort in their reassurance that at least Joseph would be safe where he was for the night. The rest was simply out of my control.

On the afternoon of the wedding party, we put on our bravest faces. I hurriedly climbed into my wedding dress as guests were arriving and despite the dreadful worry for Joseph, managed to eat and catch up with family and friends who I had missed dearly.

As the evening drew in and my dad had dutifully embarrassed me with his brilliant speech, we took to the pool deck – now a stage buzzing with live music. The party had been chaotic from the beginning, freewheeling our party plans as we went. But the spontaneity of that worked in our favour and this was never more evident than when musicians, from all sides, came together on stage to jam. Jason's brother Gary and his friend Nick played old rock classics and blues on their guitars while Jason joined in on the drums. My university friends – the Banana Plantation Crew - joined in and together they all created some of the most memorable music that evening that literally had the deck shaking from all the dancing.

The next day, we were pleased to hear that Joseph was well enough to be discharged so my parents took a flight back to Galicia so they could see his consultant. It had been the most testing time for everyone involved and I was thankful that whatever would happen next, I had the love and support from some of the best people I knew around me.

43. A GALICIAN CHRISTMAS

December arrived in a heartbeat and it seemed only days since the last of the wedding guests had departed from our villa, leaving behind a field of beer cans and enough empty wine bottles to warrant our own recycling plant.

We packed some things and travelled north again, the animals quiet and seemingly prepared for the long journey back to Galicia.

The road was smooth and familiar and we were fortunate not to drive through any bad weather. We entered the north tunnel under a damp Madrid sky and chugged along the soot-smothered underpass for what seemed like a hundred miles. We eventually emerged on the other side to a bright flash of white, *a winter wonderland!* Where an unexpected snow-covered Narnia was waiting to be discovered.

We zoomed past fresh plantations of glistening Christmas trees and as we drove further north towards Lugo the temperature plummeted. We stopped overnight in a modern hotel and ordered some Caldo soup and crusty bread to warm ourselves. Jason was so tired that after half a bottle of wine he crashed out in the warmth of our hotel room. As he slept, I took a long soak in the bathtub where I savoured the boiling water that turned my skin lobster red. Feeling exhausted I flopped between the clean hotel sheets, drinking in the absolute luxury of it. It would be a long time until I would feel this clean again.

The next morning after passing more spectacular winter scenery, we pulled into our sleepy hamlet and quickly unloaded the car, releasing the animals to familiarise themselves with the house and the moist air. Our house seemed to have coped in our absence. It was still dry inside and nothing had collapsed. We refuelled with a quick camping-stove meal before unpacking our bags and setting off to my parent's house.

When we arrived at my parents, it was clear from my mum's downturned expression that Joseph was not doing well. His mood had become volatile, a side effect of the illness which he wasn't conscious of, or could control. His aggression left my mother frustrated and upset as to how to handle him when he snapped at her. His medication was supposed to stabilise his emotions and if they didn't – it meant they weren't doing their job.

The three of us took Joseph back to the hospital where the doctors ran a new series of scans. I sat with Joseph in his room while the doctor called my mother and Jason out into the corridor to update them. Jason's Spanish was better than mine and my mother was so dazed she needed Jason to translate the parts she couldn't.

When they returned a few moments later the look on Jason's face was so stunned, I knew that the news would change all our lives forever. He explained what had transpired in the corridor; another aggressive tumour had appeared – this time on the left side of his brain. Surgeons could operate but as the tumour was deep, entwined in a complicated area of the brain, it was unlikely they would be able to remove it completely. The operation would only gain more time and was not a cure. How much time, was anyone's guess.

The hope we had lugged around for so long diminished and grief took its place making me feel instantly sick. We were handed more prescription notes and an operation date was scheduled for the following week. Joseph was discharged and as we left to go home through the hospital corridors, we were saturated in a cloud of numbness.

Back at home that evening while Joseph was tucked up in his bed, an agonising family debate was discussed, how to break the prognosis to Joseph.

In the past our family debates over dinner had often taken us into the depths of such an unlikely conundrum, we had laughed about it then. But now, the irony of hypothesising those catastrophes had been useful after all. We knew what Joseph would have wanted – and that was to *not* know the real truth. Back then, he had been quite certain of that.

We quickly settled back into rural village life and it appeared that the dynamics had shifted since we had been away. Abuela's family seemed more at ease and were open about greeting us when we met in the street, although this wasn't often.

With Christmas creeping up and Joseph having undergone his second operation, we headed into town to pick up a few Christmas decorations to cheer my parents up. For now, all we could do was to try to make the best out of the bleak situation.

Old Manola had seen the local forecast for the Christmas week and dramatically announced that a heavy snowstorm was on its way, threatening to trap everyone in the valley. With snow looming and the house prone to freezing drafts, we had decided to set up camp in one area of the house where we could have a wood-burning stove to keep us consistently warm. But the only viable area that could accommodate a wood burner was to convert the old chicken coop – an open space at one end of the lower ground floor which was directly underneath our bedroom.

It was currently in a state of perpetual foulness thanks to the dried lumps of animal poo, mummified mice and rats' bodies scattered on the mud floor. The thick walls were bare laid stone and had once been filled with mud, hair and seashells that had long since crumbled and fallen out leaving vast gaps.

We swept out animal debris and put off-cuts of polystyrene insulation on the floor and into ceiling joists, then layered the floor with cardboard and rugs and stuffed newspaper into the draughty gaps in the walls. We squeezed in a bench and a side table, a lamp and a small boxy television. A little wood burner sat on a platform of breeze blocks so the dogs' baskets could be near it.

Now the room was ready we hoped that the heat from an evening fire would not only keep us warm and toasty downstairs but slowly heat our bedroom above until we were ready to retire to a warm and cosy bed.

For the Christmas period, I decorated the little coop with fabric hearts, candles and a sprinkle of tinsel on top of the TV. A thick bunch of reeds with twinkling lights was placed in the corner and acted as our contemporary Christmas tree - it could have looked better, but it was cheery enough to feel like we had made an effort.

Lastly, we sealed off the coop from the galleria room with a pair of thick grey curtains. By tying a long line of thin rope nailed to a beam, the curtains created a wall that was bound to keep in the heat once the stove was lit. I realised then with some irony that once the curtains were tied back, it looked nothing short of a nativity scene.

On Christmas Day we took six big rubber buckets of wood off-cuts to my parent's house to top up their winter supply. We ate chunks of bread, cheese and fruit for lunch, and opened presents by the afternoon fire and tried to put months of hospital visits behind us. Joseph seemed happy for the distraction and my mother was pleased to see him eating with a real hunger that he hadn't had for a long time.

We loaded the cars with the dogs and drove to La Vaca beach where we had a windy but refreshing walk. As I walked arm in arm with my mother I felt her relax in my company. Jason and Joseph strolled ahead to the crashing shore where they skimmed pebbles into the water to entice the dogs to swim. My mother tilted her head back to capture the fleeting sun's rays between the clouds. These past weeks had been the toughest yet and I hoped that the outing would benefit her in the way that she needed. Her future was so uncertain in many ways and so dead certain in others, so just for a few hours, I hoped she could have a respite from it all and feel supported by us being together.

That same evening my parent's friend's came over to have dinner and to see how we were coping. By midnight when we could see that Joseph was exhausted from the day's activities and needed some rest we all left for home. It had been a good night, almost like old times, and I took comfort in the closeness of our family and pleaded for a miracle.

At 5.40 am the following morning the phone rang its shrill and frantic tone causing my stomach to knot in instant sickness. I clambered over our tool-scattered floorboards and dived for the telephone knowing that this call wasn't going to bring good news.

My mother was on the other end stammering and trying to explain that she had held off calling me but could we come over to help her - Joseph had had another seizure.

We frantically pulled on our clothes from the night before, grabbed our coats and jumped in the car in the darkness.

When we arrived my mother was in the living room holding a mug of coffee and a cigarette while Joseph was tucked up in bed. Apart from my mother being up so early, everything seemed normal. I raced upstairs to find my stepdad quietly nestled in his duvet, the strong smell of coffee emanating from a pile of his clothes on the floor.

"I'm waiting for the ambulance to arrive but they should have been here over an hour ago," my mother explained as I raced back downstairs. I nodded and held my breath, waiting for her to explain more.

"He was up at three making both of us a coffee. I was asleep in my room and heard him making all sorts of noises downstairs. He was confused and must have thought it was already breakfast time but I think he had another seizure in his sleep and woken himself up. The next minute he was walking upstairs, bringing me a cup of coffee, but he fell up the stairs and spilt most of it on himself. I got up to check if he was all right, and then the dog did the strangest thing. She jumped between us and then pushed me away from Joseph."

"Coco must have sensed that you might be in danger on the stairs?" I suggested.

"Perhaps," she agreed vacantly and gulped her lukewarm drink.

Her eyes were bloodshot with exhaustion. She explained that the on-call doctor had already been and had arranged for an ambulance to come. By eight that morning the ambulance still hadn't appeared. We called again and were told the paramedics were lost somewhere between two villages and needed assistance. Jason drove out of the village to find flashing orange lights of the ambulance in nearby woods. When the crew did finally arrive at Joseph's bedside he was utterly confused to their presence and insisted he was fine, convincing them to leave. The paramedic frowned at us as if we had all been wasting their time.

"No, no," I stressed, "It's not true, he's had a seizure! *Oh God* – what's the Spanish for seizure?" I panicked, desperate to get Joseph taken away to the hospital and checked out.

The paramedics briefly consulted with each other and then turned to leave. Luckily, one of them spotted a note that had been left on the dresser by the on-call doctor, instructing the crew to continue with their pick-up despite the patient's resistance.

Daylight had not yet peeked over the thickly forested mountain as I sat, yawning, unimpressed at the dull cab interior of the ambulance. It was Boxing Day and it had been decided that I go with Joseph in the ambulance while Jason drove my mum to the hospital after locking up the house.

I had been instructed to sit in the front with the driver so I could direct them out of the village, Joseph had remained upbeat as he was strapped in the back. A moment later he got agitated and tried to unbuckle his seat belt and I thought he might need to be restrained, but a stern yell from the crew member made him behave himself. He took his tobacco out from his pocket and tried to roll a cigarette until he was told off again.

At the hospital, we spent an agonising day waiting for an update on Joseph's condition when finally he was released to go home with a just slight adjustment to his medication.

As if life wasn't gruelling enough for my parents, things in their house started going horribly wrong. We returned from the hospital that day to a house without power, which wouldn't have been a disaster if it wasn't during the coldest month so far, and Joseph was still recovering from his recent surgery.

"It's fine living abroad when everything is going all right, but a hell of a wake-up call when things go downhill," my mother said bitterly. It was clear my mother needed some kind of respite as she was struggling to cope and doing so with her own agonizing hip problems.

To alleviate the situation, Jason offered to fix the old fuse that had been crumbling away for years. But he was worried how this temporary fix might last, given the severity of the old electrics. The quick fix would give my parents light and heat for the next twenty-four hours but he warned my mother that if there was another electrical surge it was a fire risk, so it was of utmost importance they get hold of their electrician immediately.

My parents had called every electrician they could but much to their annoyance, no one would help, especially over the Christmas break.

The following day having settled down for a late brunch a loud pop came *not from the electric box* but from the toilet under the stairs, prompting the three of us to peer cautiously into the hallway. We stood there open-mouthed as gallons of stinking, dirty water and excrement floated down the corridor. My mum was too drained to give a hysterical reaction.

"I think you forgot to call the Shit Man out again," I said to my mother.

The Shit Man was a local farmer called Frank; who, once

every couple of months drained gallons of my parent's sewage from the two underground tanks under the front garden patio. The chambers had never backed up so much before and had certainly never exploded into the house. With a suspected blockage at the entrance to the tank, Jason bravely tackled the job armed with just a torch, a mop and a flimsy bamboo poking rod.

He soon found the culprit, and with one deep breath and a good shove he set the blockage free and we breathed a sigh of relief. We spent the rest of the afternoon mopping the entire downstairs, spraying perfume, bleaching the floor, and trying to get hold of Frank - *The Shit Man*

It was unprecedented how all these disasters were happening one after the other and just as we were recovering from that, the very next day the electrics box at my parent's house exploded and caught fire. Thankfully it had happened late morning during breakfast. My mother had been counting out Joseph's medication when the fuse box blew up into a fireball and ignited thick layers of paint on the ceiling that my mother reapplied every summer.

Joseph in his state was unable to react. My mother took charge by running the hose through the kitchen window and soaked the ceiling. Once satisfied, she dragged the hose upstairs and drenched the bedroom floor above the kitchen hoping to extinguish any remaining flames that might lurk under the floorboards.

My mother explained all of this to me down the phone, much to my horror.

"The flames, MY GOD! You have no idea quite how scary that was," And I thought to myself, *Oh but I do*. I remembered how frightened I had felt when I set our lareira on fire as I pulled on my coat setting off again for their house.

We arrived to find smoke puffing out of the open windows and doors. Joseph had gone back to bed, leaving my mother traumatised and paranoid that something else might happen. Jason felt terribly responsible given he was the one who had tried to help with the electrics. It was shocking to see just how much damage the fire had done in a short time. The kitchen ceiling was smothered in sticky blackened bubbles and a melted wall clock and various kitchen implements lay discarded in the bin. The whole kitchen would need to be stripped back and re-decorated. On the bright side, at least the fire had happened in the daytime. Had the fuse box exploded in the dead of night, I had no doubt that neither of them would have got out in time.

The stress of these events seemed to perpetuate through to us and Jason came down with a virus in the days that followed. It seemed we were all in a constant state of gloom when we had tried our upmost to remain positive over every hurdle.

We had faced many demands over the past year – the house build and the problems that came with it, the hospital visits and helping my parents out. We were so emotionally tied to everything that we felt as if we too had reached our limits on what we could handle.

I took the dogs out for a walk into the nearby woods to get away and clear my foggy head. As I passed under a dense area of eucalyptus forest, I wondered why life was so testing. I thought of my own family and the ripples that are formed from the bond we have so that from one person to the next we are all affected by each other's dilemmas. I concluded that we have all been emotionally broken so many times that there must be fragments still missing.

Perhaps it was our humour and positivity that kept us glued together, at least it was a comfort knowing we still had that.

The brisk walk was cathartic. Coco, my parent's dog, along with Teddy and Macey, were having a wild time jumping after water bugs in the streams which made me break out of my negative spell.

I was beginning to feel a strong attachment to Coco and wondered if we should have the responsibility of taking her on full time. It would lighten the load for my parents. My spirits were slightly lifted as I passed the quiet little church and breathed in the countryside air. I walked around the back of the towering graves and contemplated how much control we have of our lives, and how little control over our deaths. Before heading home I detoured slightly and turned towards Abuela's house. I passed her cattle shed, and noticed with surprise that the lone cow had gone, standing in its place a shiny white refrigerator. Perhaps the cow was still there but inside the fridge – its fate already decided.

Our New Year's Eve turned out to be a pitiful one but we tried to remain fairly cheerful. We sat in our squalid, dark chicken coop wearing long johns under thick jumpers and jeans, with hats and gloves on, and a sleeping bag over our laps. Three flatulent dogs stuffed full of Christmas leftovers sat at our feet in the glow of the coop.

Old Manola had been correct with her weather prediction. The temperature had plummeted so low we considered heading back to Valencia rather than brave it. We had imagined we would be roasting in our chicken coop every evening, but the small wood burner just about kept our bodies from freezing. On a flickering television set, we watched eye-watering bad Spanish reality shows and the fireworks display of the Sydney Opera house. We opened some wine and ate nutty turrón and at midnight we frantically munched through twelve grapes before the gong - the tradition in Spain for bringing good luck into the New Year if you could complete the task. We made wishes of health for everyone, and nothing more.

Drafts rippled through the house causing the plastic in the empty window frames to suck in and out like a pair of pneumonic lungs.

"At what point do we say enough with the suffering in these temperatures and head back to Valencia?" I asked Jason. He gave me a half-smile in response.

In the flickering candlelight I began to mend holes in a pair of my socks until I caught got a brief glimpse of my reflection in the television set.

"What the hell are we doing? Look at us. We're living an eighteenth-century life! I'm darning socks and wearing long johns, and there's mud and newspaper falling out of the walls!"

We talked into the night about how we would make it in Galicia if we kept the house. Perhaps this wasn't the right location for us after having got so used to life in Valencia? It had been a testing month, and maybe that had put a dampener on Galicia for us. But it also revealed just how the two provinces were worlds apart and in our view, in the dull candlelit room, we were coming to the conclusion that Valencia was winning when it came to the promise of a brighter future ahead.

44. SNOW ON THE HÓRREO

Those little demons - Chaos and Disaster, seemed to be under control at my parent's house and it seemed eventually things were settling down for them. The electrician had finally turned up to see what the fuss what about and had been utterly mortified that he hadn't come sooner when he saw the extent of the fire damage.

As my parent's lives got back on track, we were able to concentrate on ours and plough through the last of our rooms to a liveable condition.

Some of the rooms needed a paint with the earthy Scandinavian colours I had been experimenting with - which was always my favourite part of the renovation. Other areas needed a little more finishing off before I could get my paintbrushes wet. I put my efforts into varnishing the beams, painting the window frames and plastering areas of the kitchen roof beams with instant yeso to fill in the gaps.

Jason's to-do list was never-ending with kitchen cabinets to be made and worktops to be tiled. We were enthusiastic to reach one of the final stages of the build and soon Jason could re-wire throughout. We were feeling positive again, spurred on by how well our work was coming together.

While on a tea break we received a hasty phone call from Brenda, the lady who managed our Valencian villa rentals. Just as things were going well in Galicia it seemed all was not well with our new rental guests.

"Not to worry you," Brenda said in a gentle but concerned

tone. "Only the Dutch family we have been expecting all morning have just been robbed at gunpoint."

Great.

Brenda explained that the family had been on the motorway coming from Barcelona when a well-rehearsed group of robbers had forced their car off the motorway into a nearby petrol station. The robbers had banged on the passenger side window and gestured to wind it down. When the Dutch woman did so, one of the robbers had shoved a sawn-off shotgun through it and robbed the family of their jewellery and bags containing their wallets, cards and passports.

"They've been to the police but they are thinking of returning home as they're quite traumatised, they have two young children. I was thinking you might want to call them and convince them to stay," suggested Brenda.

It was a widely reported problem in Spain. Tourists with European number plates were targeted by gangs operating on the motorways. It was an unfortunate incident and I wasn't surprised they wanted to leave, although usually the Guardia Civil were pretty quick at capturing these highway robbers. Aside from the fact that the incident was a separate issue from our villa rental, we still felt as if we had an obligation to our holiday guests – and ultimately still wanted them to have a good time. It had become part of our new lives to juggle these unpredictable situations.

I called the family and reassured them that they had been very unlucky and that it would be a shame to let it ruin their stay. With the help of Brenda, we connected them to the Dutch embassy in Spain so they could file their report and claim for temporary passports. Three days later the family had put the incident behind them and were grateful for our support so they could continue their holiday.

The Snow in Galicia had fallen silently overnight so that when we awoke we experienced the wonderful childlike surprise of snow-capped trees and a fun-filled world we couldn't wait to throw ourselves into. Under this cold blanket, the white caravan became camouflaged as it blended in with the rest of the garden.

The temperature made it painful to work on the house renovation without having to wrap up in layers of clothes. Wearing fingerless gloves, I upholstered the antique priests' beds by using some wadding and pieces of striped fabric to decorate the bed ends.

It was a project I had been saving for a bad-weather-day and loved nothing more than to get stuck in, tacking pins to secure the padded fabric, and then painting the curved ornate ends and side panels in a glossy light grey. The bed looked wonderful under the chalky white window shutters and complimented the smoky-blue walls. The old schoolroom now looked good enough for a double-page spread in a provincial magazine.

That afternoon our bank manager from Valencia called us, casually disclosing that our funds in the bank were so low, we hadn't enough to pay the mortgage for the month. We couldn't understand how we were left with only a few euros, causing immediate panic as we downed tools and rushed to our nearest branch.

We knew we were heading into debt but we had been practical enough to leave a contingency just in case things had got out of control - *where had that gone?* As we stood in a disorderly queue for what seemed like days, waiting to speak to a clerk, my mind speculated to how we were going to complete the build but more importantly how we would make the long journey home?

During our financial panic, I tried to imagine myself on the real poverty line trapped in Galicia. I'd be dressed in typical Galician attire - just like the pigs in peasant clothing; a full-length blue apron dress with a green cotton fishing hat and heavy steel toe-capped boots. I'd be working in a "Pulperia" house washing the inky sucker marks off plates to earn my daily bread. Perhaps I'd be so hungry I would snatch leftovers as they plummeted towards the bin. My cheeks would be a permanent colour of rouge from the cold, my hands aching from peeling potatoes in fingerless gloves. Jason would be doing odd jobs for Oscar...being paid in eggs, which we'd be forced to eat, even though they'd be so rotten they would make us gag. When spring would arrive, Oscar would ask Jason to slaughter one of his lambs and out of desperation, he would do it even though it meant I'd be upset about it.

Dramatic as my imagination was, the picture was just too ridiculous. Things might be a struggle from time to time, but you'd never catch me in one of those aprons. And we would be more likely to adopt the lamb than touch a hair on its head.

After a couple of tense hours waiting, the bank informed us there had been a delay transferring our building money funds over to the mortgage account and we had enough cash to return to Valencia after all. We breathed a huge sigh of relief and headed back to Dos Rios to continue our work.

45. LAMB TO THE SLAUGHTER

We worked tirelessly on the restoration, cleaning and varnishing the vast wooden floor in the old schoolroom and filmed our progress to document it. At the end of another hard afternoon, we took the dogs for a walk to stretch our legs. We had kept our morning and evening dog walks short as we felt too physically exhausted to take one more step beyond sinking into the welcome mattress of our bed. But the dogs provided a sprightly excuse to blow away the day's dust as we followed little Teddy, Macey and Coco, into the forest.

We strolled over a bridge, towards our favourite stream, and ambled downwards on a muddy track, taking a left to loop around towards Oscar's sheep fields, and heard nothing but leaves crunching underfoot and running water from the many natural springs. Our relieving walk didn't last long.

Coco had tracked the aroma of something appetizing and in an instant, bolted through a brambly hedge and out to a field. We could hear her boisterous and demonic yipping, as she took flight in a field to which we couldn't get direct access. We heard the thudding of hooves and quickly realised she was chasing after the sheep, so we decided to split up to try and get the dog back before she did any harm. In the past she had been known to hunt prey; rats, mice and the occasional chicken - it was in her pack nature but nothing lager than that, until now.

At full sprint, my legs heavy and resistant, I pounded the muddy path leaving our other two dogs to trail behind. I paused and heard a lamb bleat causing my stomach to plunge with dread. I raced off again, this time cutting through a gap in the hedge, hoping I wasn't too late. I could hear Jason scrambling over a barbed wire fence that cordoned-off the lower field. He shouted at the dog to drop something. I charged through the slippery, overgrown grass, and caught up with him to see that he was standing ankle-deep in a stream, holding a tiny jet-black lamb upside-down by its hooves. He tried desperately to shake the water from its lungs so it might take a breath.

"She drowned it, I saw her. I can't believe it." he gasped.

Coco must have chased the flock and in turn, the flock had left the weakest behind. It was a classic case of survival of the fittest and we were outraged by what our dog had done. Jason gently placed the dead lamb on the grass as Macey sniffed at its lifeless body. Neither of us spoke for a while until I broke the silence.

"What shall we do with it? Do we tell Oscar?" I asked. But neither of us had an immediate answer to that question.

We glared at Coco, who stood there exhausted and dripping in river water. I attached the dogs back onto their leads and we headed in the direction of home, Jason carrying the floppy lamb in his arms. I wondered what to do and for a brief moment contemplated leaving the lamb in the field or burying it. I admit I had felt tempted to pretend it hadn't happened at all, but we knew that would be wrong. Coco was our responsibility and hiding the evidence wasn't the right thing to do, especially as Oscar depended so heavily upon his livelihood.

We realised we had no choice but to take the lamb back and tell him the truth. Perhaps it wasn't completely wasted? It was a fresh kill after all and I was sure Oscar would be able to make some kind of meal out of it which would be better than a rotten egg omelette. We arrived back to our house where Jason laid the heavy lamb on our makeshift bench. It looked so unblemished – as if it were merely sleeping. *What a tragic waste of a beautiful animal.*

We arrived at Oscar's carrying the lamb in Lidl shopping bag.

He peered into the bag and shrugged at our poor explanation of Coco's brutality. He was hard to read and wasn't giving anything away as to how he felt about it. I felt terrible and tried our apology once again.

"I feel bad, I am sorry, so very, very sorry. It is a very bad situation for you," I said in Spanish, putting my hand over my heart to emphasise my point as I had seen Oscar do on a few occasions.

He looked down at his feet and shook his head as if that wasn't enough. Jason and I looked at each other feeling the weight of our guilt double as Jason handed him the supermarket bag. Apart from Oscar's left eyebrow rising ever so slightly, he remained passive to his dead livestock. *He must be terribly angry with us*, I thought.

"Can you cook it?" Jason suggested.

Oscar's bloodshot eyes widened and a small tut escaped his dry lips.

"No," he said simply, "No good for nothing. The meat will be very tough. That lamb was only eight days old".

We walked away, our sorrow and guilt shadowing behind us like a weight shackled around our ankles. Not only did we feel terrible because the lamb was so young, but also because Oscar seemed so down, it was as if things happened like this all the time that he was resigned to it.

"We're going to have to muzzle Coco everywhere we go now. We can't risk her doing that again" I said as we reached our front door.

"Do you think we should pay him for the cost of the lamb?" asked Jason.

"I think that's the least we could do," I said.

Later on, as evening drew near and Oscar stood in the littered doorway of his house smoking a cigarette, we approached him again. I apologised once more but this time he nodded as if he was more accepting.

We had no idea how much a whole lamb would cost but hoped that fifty euros would be enough to cover it.

"We want to pay you for the lamb," Jason said.

"No, no," Oscar protested, as I aimed to stuff the fifty-euro note into his filthy shirt pocket.

"Take it, take it please," I tried again and managed to shove the note into his jeans and for the first time that day, Oscar seemed happy.

Oscar remained consistently drunk for almost two weeks on our fifty-euro compensation pay-out. When he wasn't hiding somewhere, drinking, he was putting his energy into planning how to get more drinking money. I imagined it was a draining task to keep the ideas original.

By the third week of his binge, Oscar must have been on the dregs of his vinegary wine as he came banging on our door.

"Bring a camera around to my house immediately," he ordered and scuttled off before Jason could answer.

When Jason got there, Oscar pointed to areas of his barn roof that had rusty holes in it. He wanted Jason to take some exterior photographs of the damage so he could get the council to compensate him for it. Jason agreed and took photographs, although in his opinion it was hardly worth bothering as the holes were so small. Jason offered Oscar some leftover corrugated roofing that we had lying around in our garden but Oscar declined it, not remotely interested in fixing the problem.

Feeling confident that we had restored our friendship after the lamb incident, things seemed back on track with Oscar. He even asked me to recommence my English classes with Maria, after I had to postpone them with all the disasters at my parent's house.

Oscar offered to pay, but taking payment from him just wouldn't have felt right and it was good timing to get back into teaching before our return to Valencia.

Maria's English grades had wavered at school and her teachers had warned her father that if she didn't keep up with the subject, she was likely to fail her exams. Since she had reached full adolescence she had lost interest in the subject and would only be taking the classes to please her father.

We scheduled our next lesson for the following day and I was relieved when she turned up. We sat in winter jumpers at the farmhouse table with her textbooks open. She giggled as she watched Maximus hunt birds in the garden - so easily distracted - as I supposed I had once been at her age. But with little patience on my side, I felt frustrated she had so little enthusiasm for the lesson. The last thing I wanted, was for her to feel that I had failed her. I hoped to make Oscar proud of her but equally, she needed to want that for herself too.

46. THE DOWNTURN

As we took ourselves and the dogs for a stroll on our favourite Galician beach one Sunday afternoon, my mother called me on my mobile to break the news that Joseph's illness had rapidly declined. I listened to her exhausted tone whilst walking along the cold sand and she cried, upset how she was unable to care for him at home. As there were few governmental care homes in Galicia, she had no choice but to find a private centre to deal with the palliative care he required. It was costly but with no other options available it was the only solution. With the help of a friend she had found a good a residential care home nearby and Joseph had been booked in for the following week.

As I stared into the lapping water, my mother revealed that the tumour was growing back again and there was nothing the doctors could do. She had been advised to tell friends and family to visit within the next three months.

My stomach somersaulted in sickness.

Two days after he was admitted, I visited him in the modern care home and he seemed comfortable and mildly unaware of where he was. Strangely, we were thankful that his cancer had numbed the reality of his condition for him. Others in the care home were not so fortunate - trapped inside dying bodies with alert minds. For my mother, it was a mix of emotions - relief for finally having the respite but utter sadness as he slipped further away from her. All we could do was to make sure he was comfortable and my mother was supported.

In Dos Rios, I continued teaching Maria but it was clear she had other ideas when she either turned up late or didn't arrive at all. I quickly realised I needed to stop trying so hard especially as I had other priorities and I hoped that one day I might get back into teaching.

Jason helped my mother by doing some home repairs for her. He increased the security on her front and back door now that she would be living alone and finished some jobs that Joseph had never got around to doing. She was heartbroken at how things had turned out but had a newfound strength thanks to a little more sleep that allowed her to keep moving forward.

Our funds were running worryingly low and didn't allow us much time to delay in getting the Galicia house up for sale. After much debate, we had decided this was the best move, so planned a brief visit back to Valencia so we could make a start in marketing it. My mother was calmer since Joseph had settled in at the home, but I worried constantly about leaving her, even for a short time. We locked up our house and left for Valencia once more. The dogs' tails' happily wagging sensing we were on our way back to a warmer climate.

On our way out of the village, we were thrilled to notice that someone had at last seen to Abuela's donkey. Its hooves had been clipped so that he no longer stood awkwardly. The cuts on his head from his harness had completely healed, and generally, his overall health looked promising. Perhaps the donkey organisation had made it to Dos Rios after all? Or maybe our meddling had been noticed. In any case, we could not have felt happier for the donkey as we chugged our way out of the village and headed to towards the flatter plains of Valencia.

***

The most simple of things, made me feel happy being back in Chulilla – the scent of warm pine sap that greeted us on the mountain, the red squirrels and dryness in the air. It was the welcome home we needed after months of worry.

The next day, we took a walk into our rural village and met our friends Alex and Kazimir for coffee. Since we had been away things seemed different. Usually, the village population was made up of retired people, but I noticed there were people of all ages when they should have been working or studying until I realised that they were most likely a part of the unemployed problem plaguing Spain. We kept abreast of the news and couldn't believe it as we watched other countries in Europe stumble from one crisis to the next with warnings that Spain would be sure to follow in the downturn. As the financial crisis deepened we watched television reports as it decapitated Spain. People were losing their jobs, starving, squatting in abandoned cities, giving up their cars, or throwing themselves off top-floor balconies, it was the first time we began to feel nervous of Spain's future. The economy had taken a turn for the worse and although property developing had always been a gamble, this time things were different.

We feared that if the country was so deep in political-ruin any chance of us selling the Galicia house now seemed slim, perhaps we had even missed our selling opportunity? The whole of Spain had never felt so divided between the rich corrupt politicians and the rest of us, it was a million miles away from the kind of 'belt-tightening' we were used to in Britain.

The cost of living abroad was no longer something we could boast about. We were threatened with the loss of our Valencia house if we couldn't keep up with the mortgage payments until we sold the Galicia house and in the meantime, we needed to earn money. I'd had an idea that I wanted to talk to Alex about, so the next day I rode my bike down the mountain to his guest house.

"You want to shadow me?" said Alex, as we sat gazing down

at the green valley from his balcony terrace.

"Yes, I know it's a big leap-," I interjected before Alex could protest, "But I thought it might be a good experience for me. I know I don't have any training or TEFL qualifications but I thought if I could just sit in quietly during a class and observe, it would be a start".

Alex nodded thoughtfully and lit a cigarette. The heat from the sunshine penetrated the top of my head and it felt wonderful.

"OK, yes, I don't see why not. I'll have to clear with it with the parents first. I shouldn't be too worried about having a TEFL qualification, though. It's not like anyone's going to ask you to present a certificate – this is Spain after all," said Alex, matter-of-factly.

Within a few days, it was set up and I joined Alex at his next private class. Shadowing him was an eye-opener for me. He was a naturally gifted teacher whose relaxed persona seemed to make teaching look effortless. I had bluffed every lesson I had given Maria back in Galicia and I was sure that even Maria could see through my spontaneous classes. But then Alex had many years of training and experience behind him and I knew that I could learn a lot from his techniques.

During the hour-long lesson with his young student Ángel, I sat and observed in silence. Alex calmly worked through the pages of the textbook, correcting any mistakes. There was a mix of English and Spanish in the conversation and lots of encouragement for the student's impending exams. Alex showed me which grammar books he thought were the best resources, kept close in a leather satchel at his side. I found the lesson interesting and intense as I jotted down notes and concentrated on the methods he used.

After the lesson was over and money had been casually paid. Alex chatted with Ángel's parents updating them with his student's progress so far. I felt a little overwhelmed at that moment, wondering if I could ever I live up to his level of professionalism?

Two weeks later Alex had been kind enough to recommend my services to the parents of a fourteen-year-old girl, whom he had taught from a young age in a local village school. She had wanted to continue with her English language education but Alex was so overbooked with students that Camilla was delegated to me.

I nervously snapped two pens during my first lesson as a paid teacher. Although I had already taught Maria in Galicia, this felt different. Having taken on one of Alex's students there was pressure on me to not let him down and I wanted to make a good name for myself in the area.

Camilla sniggered lightly but soon we were both giggling as I swept shards of the plastic pen from my lap, which made my first-day nerves filter away. She was sweet-natured and mature for her age. More importantly, she seemed to be a more willing student than Maria in Galicia had been which gave me a boost of confidence. As Camilla was painfully unconfident with the English language we started with word games and this seemed to particularly thrill her and hold her interest during our introductory session. For the following lessons I downloaded teaching material from various teachers' forums on the internet, and from thereon, I taught myself, how to teach.

47. GOODBYE

Almost three weeks later in July, the phone call I had been dreading finally came through and I withdrew into our bedroom to be alone. I realised then that grief is a kind of madness that takes hold of your heart, squeezes the blood into your head and fills your veins with poison. For a moment I think my heart might have stopped too. I can't remember much of the days after the death of Joseph, but I remember feeling numb and consumed with pain like nothing I had ever experienced before. Shrouded in disbelief that I would never feel his cuddles, hear him tell me he was proud of me, or hear his funny accented words again. I found it impossible to believe his existence was gone.

The funeral had been scheduled immediately for the next day, as was customary in Spain, and we had to act quickly if we were going to make it. Flights to Galicia only ran once a day so our only option was to drive, departing in the early hours if we were going to make it. Hurriedly we packed our car with the animals and headed on the long road back to Galicia in near-silence. So many times we had taken this journey across the country and been welcomed by my parents waiting patiently at the other end with open arms. So many times we had driven the familiar roads that chilled our bones as the temperature plummeted.

As we raced our way diagonally across the country, my distraught mother was comforted by my stepsisters, all coping with their own grief. It was soothing to know they were all there for each other but despite our most desperate efforts, we didn't make it in time and the funeral went ahead without us.

The days afterwards were like looking into the mouth of a waterfall. You understand that logically there is a noise that comes with the roar of the exiting water, and that water makes a sound as it crashes into the rocks below but somehow you have become deaf and the most naturally beautiful things we share on this earth seem ugly and pointless. You can feel the earth's gravity pulling you in and out, a relentless tidal-wave of grief. And just when you think you're doing OK, the smallest detail - a memory, pulls the floor away from you and will send you plummeting. In that instance, you will want to forget the memory of him but if you do, it's as if he never existed.

The strangest thing was that I heard his voice many times in the weeks and months afterwards. Little snippets of the way he used to poke fun at me. A nugget of his wisdom when I was restoring something; advising me on what I was doing wrong, holding his hands up, saying, *"Fine, don't listen to me. You're as stubborn as your mother!"* And I knew then that those precious memories were stored in the muscle lining of my heart.

The family would talk about him as if he were next door, in his workshop and in some ways we liked that. It kept him warm and alive with us, which was about the best scenario we were going to get.

We stayed to support my mother in Galicia for three long months after the funeral and took Coco permanently into our brood.

Although Joseph's death brought my family closer together, being in Galicia after he passed seemed somewhat wrong. As if being in certain bars and shops and favourite beaches was somehow a deceitful move. Often the guilt of being able to enjoy the things he no longer would was unbearable. Some things were a comfort, others were painful reminders of a joke we had shared, a conversation we'd had, or advice I was given. Sometimes I had the feeling that he was two steps behind me, rolling his cigarette as he paused in the street. This time though, he wouldn't catch up with me.

48. MOVING ON

Teaching my private class was a welcome distraction from thinking too much about Joseph. The drive to my student's house through the countryside felt cathartic and gave my mind some clarity which was better than being stuck at home, focusing on the negatives.

My once-weekly classes with Camilla had been going well enough to boost my confidence in teaching. But my standards would be put to the test when my student was to do her first English oral exam at school. The following week I was greeted by Camilla's grinning parents at the local supermarket, and they seemed delighted in bragging about their daughters latest test result. To my relief, she was one of two students at the top of her class so I hoped that she would continue to make great progress, especially as her parents had high ambitions for her future.

Jason had started his own handyman business, maintaining expats' villas and pools while the owners were absent. Before long these clients were requesting decorating services so they could sell their properties. It gave way to a whole new line of work, and occasionally with a little assistance from me, we overhauled these homes for the holiday rental market. A full service right through to getting them online.

The work was stimulating after the gruelling slog on the Galicia project and we felt a rebirth of enthusiasm that soon gained us a one-off interior design job that propelled us forward in doing what we loved best. A friend's daughter had purchased an investment property - a two-bedroom holiday apartment in Dénia, situated inside a popular German and Dutch expatriate urbanisation along the coastline. The owner wanted us to modernise the apartment from top to bottom so she could get it on the holiday rental market.

Compared to our hard Galicia project this was a creative, fun job that could be completed over two weekends. As the property was some distance away from us and unoccupied, we planned to make a working weekend of it, staying overnight so we could visit the beach and communal pool in our downtime. For an additional perk we would eat out at authentic Indian restaurant, a luxury we didn't have in our area. With a packed overnight bag, bedding, dogs and all the tools we would need for the job in the car, we headed to Denia to make an immediate start.

The client had given us an extensive list which included repainting the entire interior, ceilings, hallway, bedrooms and stairwell. Updating light fittings, moving sockets, hanging pictures and mirrors, putting together flat-pack furniture, co-ordinating soft furnishings and bedding. The balcony terrace doors needed stripping and re-varnishing and there were cracks above the internal door arches that needed to be filled before painting.

The best part about it was the free rein and trust we had from our client. The owner had been on a lavish triple-trolley shopping spree and dumped all the accessories - still in their packaging - on the table for us to use where and how we liked around the apartment. She trusted our colour scheme choices and there was a sense that whatever we did, would be loved by holidaymakers.

Over the first weekend, we discarded smelly salty rugs, sun-bleached pictures and warped furniture. Jason dismantled the exterior shutter doors and stripped off the varnish.

We clicked on the radio and let our ears re-tune to English speakers. It had been years since we had heard radio discussions in our own language so we listened intently to this new expat world as we cleaned years of salt and sandy grime off the floors and balcony.

The client had bought a stack of panoramic picture frames

but no photographs to go inside, so I planned to shoot my own and create a photo gallery along the hallway and in bedrooms. This would be a series of insightful photographic images of the area to inspire guests to go out and explore.

While Jason painted the ceilings, I slipped out to the beach with my camera. It was mildly cloudy - ideal conditions for black and white photography allowing me to capture scuffed and abandoned upturned boats and close-ups of disused fishing nets. I clicked away, capturing beachside cabins with their salt-worn façade, historic stone turrets, surfers with their dogs and lone fishermen teetering on the edge of a jetty with their fishing rods. It was a location rich with quirky details and within just forty minutes, I had all the shots I needed to create the gallery.

Later that evening near the harbour in Dénia, we gorged on curry and what we couldn't finish, the waiter boxed up for us. Back at the apartment we opened a bottle of red wine and carried on working into the night, sewing curtains and painting finishing touches, savouring the transformation.

By the end of the second weekend, we were done. It was a dream job with seaside perks that was enormously satisfying from living inland for so long. The apartment looked refreshed with its natural tones in the living room - bridging the apartment to the sea. Simple decorative accessories and bold prints from the textiles brought bursts of coloured texture to a tranquil palate.

The upstairs landing was uplifted by sleek glass turquoise lighting, transforming it to that of a modern hotel corridor, coaxing guests towards two clean, spacious bedrooms. But downstairs in the hallway was where I felt most proud; the photo gallery in their beech-wood frames depicted a lifestyle that was honest and enviable. Before locking up one last time, we stood back from our work and felt incredibly pleased with our joint achievements.

A few days after the completion of the Dénia job, I attended a job interview at a language academy in the centre of Valencia.

I was surprised when they offered me a teaching position on the spot, commencing immediately. The job offer seemed like a good opportunity until I read the zero-hours contract and realised it wasn't a good deal for me. The wages were hardly worth it, especially after deducting the academy's cut and taxes. They could only offer me two evening classes a week which wouldn't have been enough to cover my petrol for the hour drive in from the countryside. It dawned on me how tricky it was going to be to get any more teaching work when we lived so far out from the city. But I did wonder if it might be worth taking on just get my foot in the door. I told the academy that I would think about it.

Alex frowned worriedly when he heard about my interview as if I had made my first rookie mistake on the teaching ladder. He had a personal dislike to some of these establishments and warned me that teacher's contracts could be ambiguous and offered me a better alternative – more private one to one classes with another female student of his in the same rural village as Camilla. Accepting this immediately, I quickly set up a meeting with the new students' parents to secure the work.

Meanwhile, Jason was darting from one holiday-villa to the next with his handyman duties and had also noticed a gap in the market for a taxi driver in our village. The idea of being the local taxi driver had come to him a while back, during our wedding party. Not one taxi firm had operated in our area, and we had struggled to find anyone who would shuttle my drunk relatives and friends back to their accommodation.

Jason had long since sold his old bone-shaking Land Rover after our most popular tour location had suffered from drought and lost its appeal. Instead, he bought an affordable seven-seater people-carrier, ideal for taxiing clients from the local spa hotel to the village. With the help of our neighbour Nicolás – who also happened to work at the spa hotel - a meeting was set up with the hotel manager who was happy to permit the business even though

Jason did not hold a taxi driver's licence. The boss didn't want a cut of the profits – after all, Jason was offering a useful service - but insisted that if anything went wrong, or the police got involved he would deny he had given permission. Jason thought this was a fair agreement and so at weekends he rigged up a sandwich board advertising his set rates and operated his slightly illegal taxi firm venture.

Teaching became my vocation in life and I found it increasingly enjoyable the more work came my way. Before long a third student was added to my books. Marie was nineteen and the oldest student I had taught so far. Her bursting enthusiasm showed me what a pleasure it was to teach when someone devoted themselves to the language. Driving through the rural countryside to my student's houses, my passenger seat piled with books - gave me a sense of self-employed freedom that felt liberating.

My new student was so in love with the English language she ate it, slept it, read and listened to it and was always hungry for extra work. At times she challenged me and taught me things in Spanish so our professional relationship was wholeheartedly rewarding. And being mature for her age was a good sign that one day she would be living her dream and teaching a class of her very own. Marie would not only do her mother, a former teacher, proud, but she would also be able to take jobs outside her own country, something that during these trying financial times was a golden ticket.

All my classes were scheduled for late afternoon, to coincide with the students' return from school or college. It was ideal timing and would free-up my mornings to plan the lessons or continue other projects at home.

And then, just as I was getting my feet firmly under the tutor's desk, our good friend Christopher contacted me with an offer which was about to fast-track my teaching opportunities in Valencia.

Christopher had just accepted a full-time job in an international primary school leaving an opening for someone to step into his freelance shoes. These classes were held on a Thursday morning in in a quiet room, at the vast campus of the polytechnic university in Valencia.

The university was located on the outskirts of the city near the rice and vegetable plantations and, more importantly, right near the blue-flag beaches. It was an ideal post and a location I couldn't refuse and the hours would fit in with my other lessons out of town. I could work in the city in the morning and make it back for my late afternoon classes. But I wasn't confident I could do it. Again my lack of experience niggled at me. Would the class accept me as they had done with Christopher? Could I fill his very skilled and TEFL trained shoes?

Teaching young adult students was one thing but this job was slightly different - this time my students were the very teachers, the *professors*, who taught at the university. Teaching a group in a class setting was on a different level from what I was used to doing. I now realised that enrolling in some kind of teaching course might have armed me with confidence and a set of preparation skills. Luckily Christopher couldn't have been more supportive in helping me relax about it.

"It's all about the personal connection within the group rather than experience. They just need to speak a lot, and you'll need to correct them," he assured me over the phone.

"What if they don't take to me?" I worried

"Everyone takes to you. They're not scary people. Do you know that last week we spent our entire class talking about dream holiday destinations?" Christopher laughed. "Seriously, it's the easiest job in the world."

After a thorough briefing from Christopher, I felt less panicky about the teaching post. At his apartment he brought me up to date with the textbook his students had been studying, briefly outlining what I would need to cover in class and how I would use the subject matter to improvise further conversation.

"The rest," he advised "would happen naturally as the

conversation flows".

I was ready for my next challenge in Spain. After all, wasn't that what being abroad was all about - pushing our boundaries? The batten was passed, the door was open and all I had to do was walk through it with a confident smile.

Jason convinced me that it was worth trying and failing, rather than not trying at all. *You might even like it*, he suggested.

"But there's one thing we need to do first," he said.

I looked at him, wondering what else I hadn't prepared for.

"The drive," he said, knowing it would take a few test drives for me to get there safely.

I was still a reluctant driver in the city and there were areas I needed to be aware of. Security of the campus was tight and often cars were towed away if they were parked in illegal zones. The campus was based on the north side of the city and was vastly spread out, spanning an impressive two kilometres from one end to the other. There were multiple entrances to every department. If I got lost I could end up in another part of the city or, heaven forbid - the port, stranded in a maze of shipping containers.

Jason patiently accompanied me on several trips, navigating me over what seemed like a hundred and one roundabouts, until eventually, I got the hang of where I was going. It also allowed us to check out parts of town we hadn't visited before. The more we explored the more I fell in love with the city and couldn't wait to start my new job.

Thursday arrived and I was on the way to my first class with butterflies in my stomach from the olive fields to the university.

I parked alongside the allotments' - a dusty track road where the campus bordered traditional farmsteads. Students parked their cars and walked towards the main buildings forming a procession. I followed right behind, clutching my portable CD player and a heavy bag of books, excited to feel part of the crowd.

I took a short-cut between two buildings, passing a sculpture-class where students were cutting into blocks of granite using angle grinders. Further on, I came across a campus map that was nothing short of a holiday park. Students casually sauntered past me with books and folders in their arms as I gasped up at the diagram of this new world. It was a student's heaven. Modern halls of residences, two multiplex sports centres complete with indoor swimming pools, tennis courts, athletic fields, student art galleries, dance studios, parks, greenhouses, and even a parade of shops and restaurants. It was like being at a trendy island resort! Fifteen minutes after arriving, I entered the Technology department and found my classroom empty, giving me vital time to prepare my notes and write my name on the whiteboard. I was nervous but wanted this to work more than anything.

An hour later I walked out of the class grinning and feeling immensely proud of myself. Christopher had been right - I had nothing to fear. From the start, the teachers were kind and relaxed and even though they talked continuously I managed to weave in and out of the textbook with ease and some degree of professionalism. Most of all I enjoyed the interaction with the teachers and felt that I was learning a lot from them and the group environment. There was an energy in the room that gained momentum the further we progressed, enlightening me to the difference of one to ones. Teaching had stepped up a notch and I couldn't wait to have my next class to see where it would take me.

My conversational classes continued to be fast-paced and much more enjoyable than sticking to textbook grammar. The teachers explained how much pressure they were under to be at the top of their game, as they had to teach a proportion of their lessons in English to Japanese and Chinese students. They sat relaxed with steaming canteen coffees, open and engaged, loaded with questions for me at the start of every class.

Our discussions ranged from political or social issues, from which I could understand how they felt about Spain's current affairs, corruption cases and environmental situations. To their personal opinions on dating, divorce, children's education, movies or tennis elbow. Everything was up for debate, from to how to make the best paella to which football team was going to win that season. The conversations could go anywhere as long as I corrected their grammar along the way.

An hour's class seemed like only minutes and sometimes I grabbed a coffee and continued chatting whilst walking through the campus park with one or two of the teachers.

A month into my classes two of my teachers wanted additional one-to-one private classes. We formulated a schedule that could work around their teaching timetables and I managed to squeeze in half-hour sessions before and after the group class.

It worked especially well with the less confident teachers, one gaining such fearlessness that it prompted her to take centre stage and lecture in English at a conference abroad - a proposition that would have terrified her the summer before.

Occasionally, if the classes had been delayed or cancelled from unforeseen teaching circumstances, I would buy a coffee and explore my way through the campus gardens. I'd stop to admire enormous graffiti murals on the art department walls and spot new iron-cast sculptures. I liked the solitude of the landscaped gardens, where I would find a bench or some wide sunny space of grass to take off my blazer, sit and read or just close my eyes to the sun. But the main reason I liked the campus so much was the bizarre sight of a genuine redundant steam train, on a short section of tracks at the entrance of the engineering block. Between classes, students would clamber over it, or lean against the dark red and black rustic paintwork and pose for photos. The steam train was one of many lively installations on the vast campus and a great way for many of the students to interact.

Usually, by lunchtime, my classes had finished for the day and if the weather wasn't too hot and I had no need to rush home, I liked to hop in my Jeep and drive the four kilometres down the motorway to the beach. There I would sit on the stone wall that separates the sand from the pavement and watch the waves roll in as I ate my sandwiches. This was the best part of working abroad, not to mention how freeing it felt working for myself. I would take off my sandals and stretch my toes in the warmth of the sunshine while I thought to myself how fortunate I was.

49. BILLIONAIRES SUPER YACHT

Our new jobs suited us nicely, giving us the independence and income we craved. Summer was fully upon us and with it, an unexpectedly rare opportunity had materialised which would sweep us off our feet.

Tim, an old work friend of Jason's who had lost touch long ago, got back in contact. The last we heard was that Tim, an engineer in the Navy, had been posted in a remote location out to sea. So it was a surprise to learn that he had traded-in the Navy for more exclusive and lucrative work. Even more coincidentally, the luxury boat he was working on – a Russian billionaire's Superyacht to be exact - was moored in a marina in Valencia.

Tim was one of two engineers who worked on rotation, on-board the six-deck superyacht that had been moored for repairs for a couple of months. With the owner and captain absent, he wondered if we wanted to join the crew for their usual, end-of-week jetty barbecue.

We were incredibly excited to accept this invitation and as the evening crept in, we raced through the city towards the port, the fading sun streaking the sky in a blood-orange hue. We whizzed past the dry river bed and Valencia's iconic City of Arts and Sciences complex and headed towards the America's Cup port.

When we arrived, security waved us through the barrier towards the private mooring section. Armed with a bottle of wine for our hosts, we strolled along the path as yacht lights glimmered onto the darkening water. An assortment of uniquely magnificent vessels varied from classic wooden schooner sailing boats to enormous luxurious Superyachts - one could only dream of owning.

In the fading light, we could see Tim in his monogrammed blue boiler suit, wiping his oily hands on a rag, standing on the aft of the most spectacular white yacht I had ever seen. The rest of the crew were off-duty and dressed-down in designer brand clothing, loading a golf buggy to transport themselves and food to the other end of the marina. A crew member hopped in and stamped on the accelerator, whizzing past us along the jetty, the passengers having to hold tight as it veered dangerously close to the water's edge. It scuttled off to the far end of the mooring to a grassy area where the barbecue was being prepared.

Tim welcomed us with hugs and dashed off to get changed.

When he returned he gave us a tour of the Superyacht, making sure we had removed our shoes before setting foot on the bouncy ramp to the first level. On-board the yacht was even more impressive than I could have ever imagined. German designed with impeccable engineering that oozed sophistication with its solid outer wall casing and curved walkways, tinted windows and teak wood decked floors. We were shown the owner's outside gym and solarium area.

There was an elevator that ran up through the centre of the boat - a solid cylinder of glass, encased in ornate (real) gold railings. Our reflections peered back at us in immaculately polished wooden doors. Tim kindly took us on a full guided tour, instructing us on what we could and couldn't touch. Inside the owner's private suite, he pointed out that every tap, sink, toilet roll dispenser, and door handle was made with 22 Karat gold and could not be handled with anything but butler's gloves once they had been polished.

The rooms were garishly decorated with dark wood, cream leather and marble. It was the kind of wealth that only royalty or the super famous could afford or want. I clenched my hands in front of me, as we lightly padded barefoot along the decked galley and into the private living quarters of someone very powerful. Our feet sank into a meadow of pearly wool and I actually thought I had died.

"Nice isn't it?" whispered Tim, "I believe it cost 12,000 euros - *per meter*" Both our jaws dropped. I wanted to saviour the luxury of it but there was still so much to see to stop for long. At the far end of the room, a black grand piano waited to be played by a talented musician. We weaved around the ginormous cream leather sofa suites and the circular dining table taking in the fine wooden inlay detail beneath the lacquered varnish. The ceiling lights twinkled above us as we peered at enlarged photographs in their solid gold frames. We looked up at Tim with the realisation that this was no ordinary billionaires' yacht. In the photograph, the yacht owner, a businessman whom I didn't recognise, was shaking hands with the likes of Vladimir Putin and Russia's equivalent of the Pope. Here we were, standing in the living room of his yacht almost peeing ourselves in fear of making one wrong move. Tim told us that when the owner was aboard, the yacht was heavily guarded with personal security. It was rumoured that a member of the family had been assassinated some time ago so all members were fiercely protected. Up until that moment I had felt fairly relaxed about being on the seventy-metre super-boat but standing there then I felt on edge as if any moment we were going to get shot through the head. Still, it was exhilarating to be there and it didn't take long before I had convinced myself I could handle living a lifestyle of such utter wealth *and* I was sure I wouldn't take it for granted as these people might have.

Tim snapped me out of my fantasy.

"Come on," he said, "I'll show you the massage suite that overlooks the water."

Afraid to shed skin and hair as evidence of our presence we crept around the rest of the boat in silence barely breathing. I tried my hardest to combat the resistance to touch things but there were *so* many mineral surfaces to caress, sparkly areas of marble, jade and pearl.

Outside in the middle of the deck, a cocktail bar wrapped around a voluminous Jacuzzi with a retractable roof that could offer shade if desired. And just as I thought I could take no more, at the rear of this level a collection of polished chrome sun loungers lined the edge of the decked area that would give the sunbather infinite views out to sea.

We made our way to the front of the boat, where Tim showed us the huge polished anchor chain and allowed us to indulge for a moment in a Titanic-posed embrace as I held my arms out at the very tip of the bow. We moved on, through a porthole door and down a staircase.

The lower floor was just as impressive. The boat housed a garage where the wall of the hull could drop out and lie over the water. This garage compartment was vast and allowed another boat 'The Limousine boat' (as it had blacked-out windows and was the sea-version of a white limo) to be lifted and dropped outside the yacht for a quick exit to a nearby beach or restaurant. I felt sick with envy. Jason's eyes blazed at all the gadgets on board down in the lower deck. This area housed a raft boat, two whopping jet skis and a series of underwater jet-propelled gadgets that James Bond would be jealous of.

The lower floor just above the waterline was dedicated to the staff and provided six carpeted luxurious rooms with bunk beds where two crew members per room shared an en-suite bathroom, wardrobe, laptop desk and television.

We followed Tim further into the depths of the boat's heart, down a metal staircase which lead to the windowless engine room *Tim's office* and tool department as he liked to put it.

I had expected to observe grime and smoke, oily fingerprints on the handrails, torn weeping rags wrapped around pipes, an echo of a drip. Instead, aluminium and steel tubes gleamed. Coloured cables were tied and coded, immaculate machinery didn't appear to have a smudge of dirt on it, nor a single tool missing from its shadow-board.

We climbed up a level and sneaked into the staff's secret passageway through a wooden panel in the wall. I caught a delicious scent of washing detergent in the corridor as we cruised past a laundry room and further on, to the staffs' kitchen and main socialising area.

We stopped for a drink in the staff room where Tim handed us a beer and introduced us to his crewmates that we had seen earlier on the buggy. The staff wing was as extravagant as the rest of the yacht. Designer cooking gadgets lined the kitchen worktop, fridge draws pulled out to reveal a vast selection of canned and bottled drinks and more confectionary than you could ever desire. There were individual lacquered dining tables to the right of the room, in the middle, a cinematic plasma television on the wall where the crew could relax on a comfy sociable curved sofa or eat a meal freshly prepared by the boat's Michelin-starred chef.

After our refreshing beer, we walked along the plush corridor towards the captain's private quarters where we sneaked into the wheelhouse and Jason plonked down in the deep cream leather captain's chair. We all stared out towards the bow of the boat and imagined the overwhelming responsibility the captain had with such an expensive boat in his charge. The control room was minimal and sleek with a big glass navigation table, futuristic touch-screen buttons and a handful of polished switches. I was somewhat disappointed with the size of the steering wheel, however – it was as small as a racing car's and it seemed too modest in contrast to the ostentatious appearance of the rest of the superyacht.

Once our tour was over, we joined the crew members outside at the far end of the marina for the barbecue and gushed over the other beautiful moored boats as the water slapped at the edge of the jetty.

Under the heavily-starred sky, we listened to yachting stories' that captivated us about faraway places I could only dream of. The crew were from all walks of life, from privileged and humble backgrounds, hailing from Thailand, Canada, Britain, South Africa and Germany. Tim's colleagues were relaxed and welcoming, so I could understand why he referred to them as his work family who he enjoyed spending time with.

We indulged in their hospitality, munching on steak and fresh fish, grateful for Tim's invitation which lasted into most of the evening. When we departed we briefly met the captain, who had returned for his next shift. I wished we could have joined him on his next voyage or at least stowed away somewhere in the engine room.

It was a huge contrast to how we had spent our last few difficult months in Galicia. An insight into a preposterously wealthy world, in which I wouldn't have imagined we would have had the opportunity to experience.

50. HIP HIP HOORAY

A month later, I was on an internal flight heading north back to Galicia as my mother was having hip replacement surgery. She looked pale and thin when I walked into her hospital room.

"Can you believe this view?" she said in a shaky voice.

I looked towards the window and saw a plump seagull sitting on the ledge staring right back at me with its beady eyes. But she wasn't talking about the bird. In the distance, a chalky grey crematorium building dominated the landscape. It wouldn't have been such a traumatic sight if it weren't for the fact that her husband had been cremated himself in that very place.

"Well, that's going to make any patient who has a room on this side of the hospital very bloody cheerful," my mother said with her usual sarcasm.

We watched as a flurry of fresh incineration smoke drifted towards the sea.

"Maybe they've got a secret passageway for the ones who don't make it in hospital. They slide down a chute under the motorway and straight into the oven," I joked.

My mother laughed bitterly, which seemed to relax her. I know we shouldn't have even joked about it but grief finds irony in everything.

There was a dark shadow behind my mum's weak smile, it was obvious her hip surgery had been a traumatic experience for her. With trembling hand's she explained what had happened and I felt sickened to what she had been through.

She had been given an epidural to numb her from the waist down and a sedative to relieve any anxiety but the doctors had planned to keep her awake during the procedure. A green division sheet had masked the view at her waist, behind which the surgeons huddled. The surgical team opened up her thigh and began cutting the bone with a saw but halfway through the operation, she began to feel pain and panicked that she hadn't had enough drugs. She became acutely aware of the operative noises and listened as the surgeons drilled, tugged and chipped away, separating the hip joint. She lay there, paralysed as she tried to explain her terror to the nurses. They didn't seem to notice her descending into shock. She suggested that maybe they could stop, or put some music on to take the anxiety away.

"We'll be finished soon enough, relax!" was the curt response as they carried on. So she lay there like a helpless victim as her body rocked with the motion of the surgery, her blood splattering on the green sheet then falling to trickle across her abdomen. She was trapped in a nightmare.

Tears welled up in her eyes as she relived the horrific scene and I felt furious at how thoughtlessly she had been treated. I had always known she was resilient but this had pushed her to the edge. She would need weeks of attentive care and emotional support to make her feel herself again.

I nursed her at her home, cooking her favourite foods so she would put some weight back on. I soaked her feet in tubs of hot water, cleaned the industrial-sized staples on her hip with warm water and iodine and changed her dressings. We enjoyed our evenings watching movies and eating ice cream, trying not to think of her ordeal. I was pleased to eventually see her on her feet and walking with the aid of crutches confidently. She talked with friends over the phone and the more I heard her talk about it, the more I noticed acceptance in her tone as she began to put the traumatic scenario behind her.

We drove to Miño beach where we sat on a low bench facing the water, deeply inhaling the salty air. We watched couples and made up stories of how they lived their lives and giggled like schoolgirls when a wrinkly old man showered and gyrated seductively in front of us.

By the end of the first week, my mother was gaining strength and her wounds were healing quickly. Jason called me one morning to say he was on the yacht again, just visiting for the day but I felt a stab of jealousy and wished I too could have been there.

"Gotta run," he said, excitedly "they're getting the jet skis out from the lower deck for a maintenance check and I'm taking one out for a spin." He signed off saying, "Oh, by the way, I've been offered some work on the boat!"

Later that same evening Jason called again, jubilant after playing with the billionaire's gadgets all afternoon. He gushed about how they needed to take the superyacht out for a run and how he had become part of the crew prepping the boat for sail. I felt so envious of him while I was stuck in Galicia nursing my poor mother, peeling potatoes as another rainstorm lashed at the cottage window. The more I thought about Jason on that yacht the more disgruntled I felt. *He hated choppy seas.* It was *me* who had always wanted to learn to sail. Jason couldn't set foot on a kayak without being as sick as a dog.

I remembered a particular moment during our Mauritian honeymoon when we were on a day trip on a catamaran. I had pointed to a pod of baby dolphins as they leapt from the water, our catamaran slicing through the waves as it headed towards an isolated island.

"Look at the dolphins!" I had excitedly shouted but Jason couldn't hear as he retched over the side of the boat for the entire two-hour trip.

Ashamedly, I couldn't help but feel jealous of him on that beautiful boat. But it pleased me to hear he was having fun with Tim again after all the years they hadn't been in touch. Tim had been kind enough put in a good word to the captain, suggesting that as the boat was running behind its service schedule - Jason could assist Tim to speed things up a bit while it was delayed at the marina. The captain thought it was a great idea and the next day wearing a blue boiler suit to match Tim's, Jason was working alongside his friend as they squeezed between decks, cleaning, polishing, replacing and degreasing boat parts.

My mother's recovery was gradual but I put that down to the trauma she had endured in the operating theatre. The left hip had been scheduled to be operated on, in a further six months but at least she was halfway there and the operation had spurred my mother on, to move forward and not give up on life. We had talked about her future and getting her house on the market which was a good focus for her from now on.

When I knew she was able to fend for herself, I took the return flight back to Valencia and carried on with my university and private home classes.

Jason had thrown himself wholeheartedly into work on the superyacht and although the job was only temporary, he loved going off every day to work and always came home with interesting stories and lovely second-hand treats that the crew had thought would no longer befit a billionaire's yacht. Our freebies were wonderful. We sunk into beautifully fresh Egyptian bedding and cooked on the Michelin chef's cookware and barely used gadgets. Almost every day the crew tossed plants, un-used table linens, clothes and brand new deck shoes to shore, due to the yearly upgrading of the yachts' plush interior and uniforms.

Aside from assisting Tim with the engine parts, Jason took on a list of separate jobs. From sanding the engineer's workshop bench to refitting a delicate gold plated sink - one of many on-board. The level of detail and care on the boat's workings was meticulous so every task was undertaken with absolute precision.

The perks were top class too; the yacht's chef provided staff with three cooked meals a day served in the crew's mess. At dinner time, the cook laid-out a choice of meals, ranging from sirloin steaks, pork ribs, beef stew or whole cooked fish. Every meal was accompanied by copious amounts of expensive wine.

Once the yacht's maintenance was almost completed a new crew stepped aboard to take the place of others on leave and we were saddened when the boat finally pulled up its anchors and departed for warmer shores over winter. It was a shame to see such a nice bunch of new friends leave but it was good to know that Jason the old sea-dog had finally overcome his sea sickness.

51. ADEUS GALICIA

Our Galician restoration project took two years to sell which in Spanish terms was a fairly quick sale, especially when a second recession had hit the country harder than the first. Thankfully our jobs and the summer rentals had allowed us to keep up with the mortgage payments and finally with the money from the sale we managed to repay the loan on our Valencian house.

We hadn't unfortunately, made a single penny in return for our investment, but we had come out of the experience relatively unscathed, as other, similar houses struggled to sell. It had sold to a Galician couple after two dramatic price drops to get things moving and the relief was enormous now that the project was behind us. The buyers hadn't seemed phased about the one or two areas we had failed to complete but then the majority of the costly restoration had been done. Now it was over we felt sure that we would never do another restoration this big again in our lifetime.

On the day of the signing, we flew up from Valencia and hired a van to collect the rest of our things and say farewell to the other villagers. When we reached our hamlet later that morning the place was so quiet it seemed as if everyone had abandoned it. It was likely Maria was at school and Oscar was drifting somewhere. We had told them both that our departure this time would be final, so we hoped to say our final goodbyes.

In spite of his vagabond ways, Oscar had been a significant part of our lives in Galicia and it would be regretful to not tell him so, but with only a short window of time to pack the van before we had to sign at the notary, we couldn't afford to delay.

After packing up the essentials and having to leave most of the larger antique pieces behind, I packed a box of my old things to give to Maria. Illustrated cookbooks, clothes, candles, costume jewellery and perfumed toiletries. They might not have been of much interest to her but I wanted her to find the box and know that despite our hasty departure she had been in my thoughts. Having no possession of a phone, there was no other way to reach them so I scribbled my contact details in a little purple notebook, threw it in the box and left the items outside her front door with the hope that maybe one day she might contact me. I wondered if we had made an impression on young Maria and Oscar, they certainly had done so with us and we wanted to wish them a good future ahead.

As we loaded the last of the tools into the removal van and slammed its doors, we stood silently to say our farewell to the priest's house. I inhaled deeply, ingesting the memory of our dreams, right from the beginning to the very bitter end and just then Old Manola shuffled out from behind her door to join us. She gave me a sympathetic pat on the hand - silent condolences for Joseph's passing.

"It's understandable you are leaving," she said in a kindly manner.

I hadn't the heart to tell her that we would have sold the house anyway, even if Joseph was still around.

Galicia had proven to be a place in which we couldn't completely adapt to after having been in Valencia for so long. For five years we had lived between both provinces and hadn't remained faithful to either. We had been going back and forth from our fun Valencian mistress to our Victorian Galician wife knowing for some time which location suited our purposes. The financial aspects had been tough in Galicia, but somehow we always managed to find work in Valencia. Perhaps this was because tourism was more favourable in warmer Valencia thus more work opportunities. I couldn't see those opportunities in the north-west of the country, either side of the summer.

But despite the awfulness of recent events, I felt a deep-rooted fondness for Galicia that couldn't ever be erased from my heart. We had made a handful of lovely friends, had some great memories, eaten extraordinary food and submerged ourselves in the culture and explored the area. Having spent so much time here as a teenager, I felt lucky to have got to know it again as an adult, to understand its heritage and traditions.

Now that Joseph was gone I felt pleased that I had spent quality time with him too over the last few years. Galicia would always remain with me and now there was a little part of me that would remain with it - in the walls of the house and the trees growing in the garden.

Sadly there were some things I wanted to forget about Galicia too. The hard times with my family and the loss we all suffered. Too much had happened for us to stay. Life seemed too arduous and we wanted nothing more than to see the back of it, for a while at least.

After handing over the giant key to its new owners at the solicitor's office, we drove to my mother's house where she had prepared a celebratory lunch. She had, at last, started to regain some of the weight she had lost, but as long as she was alone here she would remain a constant worry to me. Since Joseph's passing, it had been hard for her to make new decisions alone. Should she stay in Galicia or return to England to the company of her good friends? Part of her concerns was the guilt that she would be leaving Joseph behind, although he was already gone. For quite some time we had sat and talked about her options and decided that after she had allowed enough grieving time she would find a place in Britain – after all, that's what Joseph would have wanted her to do. Once some decisions had been made she became a little more clear-headed, somewhat stronger inside. She herself had seen first-hand how in a moment, even the most unlikely and healthiest life can be taken. As we hugged and kissed my mother goodbye I realised that if it was hard for us to be in Galicia without Joseph, his absence must have been unbearable for her.

52. A SHIFT IN THE WIND

I taught my adult group at the university for a further year alongside my private one to ones. The younger students weren't always as reliable so I had to adapt, finding replacements as quickly as possible to keep the momentum going. It was a reminder to how a young person's life moves so fast, the unpredictable change in direction that makes life so exciting.

And over that time my group of university teachers changed too as their schedules altered and I embraced the new energy of their replacements. I enjoyed the classes until the moment they ended when the faculty had a complete reshuffle. I held a meeting to try to work around the teachers' new timetables, but it seemed impossible for the group to share the same availability and so eventually, to my huge disappointment, my university classes came to an end.

My experience of being a teacher abroad was like being caught in a current - students in, students out. Sometimes leaving me feeling battered and washed up when they no longer needed me. But that was the nature of freelance teaching - there was no security to it and if you wanted to be in control of your freedom, you had to motivate yourself to bring in the next student.

During that summer we had been staying at a retired friend's holiday villa - Casa Rosa. It provided everything we needed as a temporary home and was conveniently located in a small town only twenty minutes from our own place, which meant we didn't require the use of Freddie and Brenda's management services during the rental period.

Casa Rosa was surrounded by orange groves and was situated in a pretty quiet cul-de-sac, known for its mixed Spanish and English retired community. When September arrived, we were thankful we'd soon see the close of another holiday rental season, and return to our mountain retreat. It would be a relief, especially as the heat was still unbearably suffocating. On our departure we packed our pets and gear into both cars and having swept the floor, we locked up and returned the key to the British neighbours.

We arrived back to our mountain house to the distinct aroma of suntan lotion and sweat that lingered in the bedrooms.

Our last party of guests had left us a note and bottle of wine - thanking us for a delightful stay. I was pleased that over the summer, we only had a few breakages: a wicker chair and a toilet seat had been destroyed by an extremely overweight Danish family. Someone had been stupid enough to squeeze two bottles of fire-lighter fluid into the barbecue causing mass incineration to a row of rosemary bushes in the tinder-dry garden.

Jason got busy fixing burst irrigation pipes, scrubbing oily residue from the edges of the swimming pool and deflating abandoned pool toys while I cleaned and mopped inside the bedrooms, checking if any guests' items had been left behind.

Once we had stripped every trace of paying guests from the villa, it was ours. And there we remained for the duration of the weekend, splashing about in the pool, enjoying every morsel of what we had.

At the beginning of a new week, the thermometer read thirty-six degrees, which was unusually hot for the time of year. The heat was beginning to feel unpleasant, causing my joints to ache from the intensity of it. I squinted up at the beating sun, sighed and looked at my watch, dreading the next hour. The vet was due to arrive any minute at our house and no matter how much we tried to busy ourselves, nothing would take away the guilt with what we were about to do. After seven good years with us, Teddy our beloved spaniel would be put to sleep after a long battle with Leishmaniasis - a disease carried by the female sand fly. He had endured injections to slow it down but eventually, the parasite had migrated into his organs and we knew he had entered the final phase when his fur began to fall out. It wasn't fair to keep him hanging on despite our reluctance.

We sobbed uncontrollably as the vet left us and Jason buried Teddy in a plot in our garden. The vet had remained for some time, crying in her car outside our house and I had wondered if it was because our grief for the little dog had been too much for her to witness.

That same week my best friend Jo came out to visit with her husband and new adorable baby. Their visit worked wonders to cheer us up from the sad cloud in which we had found ourselves. There was noise in the house again that had seemed so absent without Teddy. We went out to explore, cooled off in the pool and played games under the shade.

"Is it always this *ridiculously* hot in September?" my glamorous friend snorted as she slapped low-factor sun oil over her ample cleavage and arms, enjoying the prickly-heat sensation.

Our friends' visit uplifted me, proving that spending quality time together was the tonic I needed to get out of my depression over losing Teddy. I was surprised to find myself laughing again, which just a couple of days before had seemed unimaginable.

By the time our friends departed it looked as if the summer was going to drag into winter when we longed for rain to turn the parched mountains green again.

The dryness plagued me, and deep down, I knew there was substance to my fears. Only, what I feared would be worse in reality than I could have ever predicted.

53. HELL ON EARTH

Sunday 23rd September 2012 – It was still there. That fiercely-hot air that burned your throat every time you took a breath. There was a quietness in nature too. An eerie absence of usually active red squirrels and forest birds added to my unease.

As I prepared a roast for our Sunday lunch I couldn't help but feel a cloak of impending doom around my shoulders. It was such a dominating feeling as if someone were tapping on my shoulder whispering, '*Psst! I reckon these are the perfect conditions for a forest fire, don't you?*' I shrugged off my concern and carried on peeling potatoes.

Outside, Jason was tidying the contents on his tool shed. Apart from the pinging sound of his tools hitting the concrete floor, there was stillness, even our dogs remained subdued in their baskets, sniffing the dry air for clues.

The persistent nagging finger would not leave me alone. Putting the roast lunch aside, I walked out to our balcony terrace and stared at the valley below. I wondered when we might next have rain. It had been three months already, so in the back of my mind, I knew that if all the right elements were in place, a forest fire could be a reality.

It had happened here eighteen years ago when the entire mountain had been wiped out and the villagers had to be evacuated. All the wild shrubbery and pine trees that dotted the mountainside had been burnt and only now had the area fully grown back, restored and rejuvenated. But the locals had never forgotten about that day when their mountain turned to ash. Tales floated about and were retold every summer to grandchildren who were old enough to understand the devastation it caused. Heaven forbid we should go through that.

Fine! I said to myself so my instinct would hear me, *I'll pack an emergency bag, just in case.*

I headed down to the storeroom under the house, threw open the door and was confronted with a mound of – mostly my own – hoarded things. Sighing loudly, at a loss as to where to start, I grabbed a holdall to pack only necessary items and began to fill it with family photo albums. I feared that if my intuition could force me to act, then perhaps it was a fate I couldn't ignore. I hoped my prediction was wrong.

I dragged my mother's vintage leather suitcase off a shelf in addition to the holdall and packed some ancestral objects, books and jewellery that could never be replaced. I threw in hard-drives, cd's and important documents; deeds to the house, insurance and other vital paperwork that had taken months of bureaucratic hoop-jumping to get hold of. Once it was full I placed the bags by the door and put Joseph's guitar with it.

Back inside the house I packed a satchel of our most important things: bank cards and passports for us and for the pets, a phone charger and whatever cash we had. I placed the open satchel by my bed so that I could add things daily if I wanted.

Was I being completely absurd? Paranoid even?

I washed the dust off my hands and continued preparing our food. At least the nagging feeling had weakened slightly.

After a leisurely lunch, I settled down to write some emails while Jason had gone outside to clean the swimming pool.

At four o'clock strong gusts of wind stirred the dust from our track road, prompting me to close the windows to stop the dirt from entering inside. Just then, Coco barked her loud alarm, her tone urgent enough to make me race onto the balcony.

"THE MOUNTAIN'S ON FIRE!" Jason yelled as he pointed

to a gigantic wall of flames on the other side of the valley - no more than a kilometre away. Terror engulfed me and momentarily pinned my feet to the spot. I could not believe the intensity of the heat, aided by the wind from this distance. And that was when I heard it through the trees – a most fearful sound that as long as I live, will never forget; a thunderous, hollow roar as if the devil himself had opened up a cremation furnace and was saying,

Hey step inside, we've been waiting for ya!

"What the hell do we do?" I panicked.

As Jason stood there, unsure and open-mouthed. I ran inside and called my mother - which wasn't probably the best move because not only does my mother love to talk but I shouldn't have worried her when she couldn't do anything about it all the way from Galicia.

We called the fire department just in case nobody had spotted the huge flaming mountain but it turned out the fire crews were already on their way. Before long we heard rotating blades from a helicopter above chopping through the smoke-filled clouds.

Two men drove up to our road, spectators we assumed - to get a higher viewpoint. They sat watching the smoke and filmed the event on their phones.

Within minutes the entire far mountainside was ablaze. Black and yellow smoke billowed into the sky, fuelled by hot wind that chomped its way through the dry shrubs and knee-high grasses. Unkempt rosemary bushes instantaneously caught alight from the heat alone and carried the great wall of flames further towards us. The mouth of the fire howled relentlessly as if it were a tornado. As the wind spun, so did the fire, causing it to jump across roads and leap from the tops of trees obliterating what it could. The fire carried on finding fuel as it picked up speed, continuing on its destructive journey.

We decided to leave. I was sure that as we were on the outskirts of the village, we would be the last people to be evacuated.

Within seconds I had packed my car with the belongings I

had pre-packed in the storeroom, which gave us enough extra time to herd the dogs into Jason's car and the cat in mine. We made a dash back into the house to grab any last-minute things but at that moment my brain turned to jelly and instead of grabbing useful supplies I ran about mindlessly stuffing possessions into my rucksack and pockets as I tried to make practical choices; a bikini, chewing gum, cat toys and winter boots which were totally impractical in the present climate. No underwear, no water, no toothbrush.

I looked about the house in a panic. *How could we lose all this?* All our hard work, our whole life was in this house. What if we never saw it again? When we returned it might be a blackened heap of ash, our belongings unrecognisable. We would be homeless.

I grabbed my laptop and my keys and charged for the car.

As we evacuated our mountain retreat we could see the fire getting closer to our patch of forest. I followed Jason as we headed to our friends Alex and Kasimir's guest house for safety. The village was further away from the base of the fire and for the time being, we thought that going there seemed the safest option until we could work out our next move.

By chance, the couple were away on holiday and had left us a spare set of keys. From their ground floor bathroom window we observed yellow amphibious planes above depositing thousands of litres of water from its belly in one drop. From this distance, the amount of water didn't seem to be enough to extinguish anything.

We could hear agitated neighbours rushing about, shouting as car doors slammed. To gain a better view of the situation, Jason rushed to the top floor terrace where he noted the wind was continually changing. This caused the fire to split off in separate directions so it seemed like the fire was being pushed away from our neighbourhood. With this in mind, Jason decided to risk going back to our house for food supplies and speak to the locals for information while I waited at the guest house with the pets.

I could hear the amphibious planes drift off – I assumed to refill from one of the lakes where we had once taken our tours.

On the way back to the village Jason called me. He had stopped to speak to spectators who thought the fire wouldn't be brought under control for days. *Evacuate* - was the general advice by the bystanders. The police were going door to door, checking no one was left in danger as they whizzed by on mopeds.

When Jason returned, he told me that some residents had refused to leave their property when the police had asked them to go. They argued that they were prepared to battle the fire themselves, using garden hoses if necessary to soak the houses down.

Smoke billowed, the roar continued. So we ran upstairs again to Alex's balcony to get a better look to see in which direction the situation was intensifying. In the distance, flames grew to an immeasurable height as it consumed and roared with constant hunger. This engulfed patches of untamed forest areas both sides of the main highway towards Valencia. It burned on and grew, twisted and turned and headed towards more residential houses.

As we prepared to leave the guest house someone banged on the door, sending our already nervous dogs into a barking episode. Alex's neighbour had seen the lights on and thought it best to make sure that whoever was inside was ready to leave, or the police would start to arrest people to force them to safety.

For a second time, we collected our things, got in our cars and joined the queue of escaping residents as more planes flew in overhead.

Elderly people were rounded-up in wheelchairs and police helicopters used their air sirens to flush out the remaining residents. The road in and out of the village was being cordoned off by the army. Once out, nobody would be able to get back in until the village was deemed safe. That could be days or weeks, for all we knew.

Waiting in line, in an evacuation convoy felt totally unreal. Smoke had blanketed any remaining sunlight disorientating residents as they scuttled back and forth. I sat there with few possessions, which no longer seemed as important as having our dogs and cat safely with us. As my car idled behind Jason's van, images of our burnt mountainside raced through my mind. How horrendous it was that a fire could take hold of one of the most stunning and precious areas in the Valencian province. Was the fire deliberate or an act of nature? And where on earth would we go next? Would any of our friends offer us a place of refuge? Just as I had that thought, a man whose hands and arms were covered in black soot stepped into the street and called out to all the waiting cars.

"Go to the shelter!" He said calmly as he pointed in a northerly direction. We had no idea where, exactly, the shelter was but we were sure it would be obvious if we followed the crowd. Scores of cars that were usually so intent on getting into the village for the weekend were desperate to get out. I looked at the battlefield unfolding around us, the sun now masked behind the mountain leaving an eerie glow of the fire beyond flickering and projecting onto the clouds.

Petrified elderly people waited for coaches to collect them as children cried and mothers wiped away their own frightened tears.

The Red Cross had arrived - which was a serious sign. The local priest stood at the rear of a van, helping to load emergency blankets and foam mattresses, which I assumed were also destined for the shelter.

Helicopter sirens above bleeped in short deafening bursts from somewhere deep in the sky. It all seemed so apocalyptic.

I noticed then that my hands on the steering wheel had begun to shake uncontrollably and my jaw was so tense my teeth were starting to ache. I took in deep breaths of smoke-tinged air as the line of cars started to move forward. It was an impressively organised evacuation operation and I was grateful that everyone in the village seemed safe for now. All I wanted to do was to flee to safe ground. We drove away, out the back end of the village for a good twenty minutes, heading north towards the main highway with a convoy of bright headlights behind us. And as we did so, wondering if any part of this landscape would look the same on our return. We reached an area where Jason pulled his car into a layby and we could consult each other as we seemed to have lost the main flow of traffic. The other residents had turned off somewhere unexpectedly and we had just kept going, leaving a trail of countryside darkness behind. We didn't mind though, we weren't sure that we wanted to end up in the shelter – an unfamiliar school gymnasium with eight hundred other villagers and their agitated pets. We agreed we needed to calm our nerves with alcohol and to sleep somewhere quiet. We considered finding a hotel but we didn't want to leave the pets in the car. And then we remembered the house that we had rented for the summer, Casa Rosa. As far as we knew it was still empty and the neighbours still had the key. I immediately tried to phone the key holder but they weren't answering. We would just have to go to their home and knock on the door - it was an emergency after all.

Jason kept a steady course as I followed behind in my little car. Maximus started mewing loudly in fits. As I didn't have Jason to talk to, I manically chatted to the cat, mostly to calm my nerves and quash the negative thoughts about our house burning to the ground.

As we drove further away from our village the road inclined so that in the darkness I caught an extraordinary sight - both sides and the top of the mountain were consumed in an orange fireball as if a meteor had struck it. Even with all the help, the fire seemed unstoppable. It wouldn't be long before the fire crew and pilots would have to stop for the night and let it burn.

A mass exodus of dotted headlights fled Chulilla. *How would the town survive this?* I thought of all the wild animals caught up in the flames. I pitied the foxes, rabbits, red squirrels, woodpeckers and owls. I felt numb at the thought of their world being destroyed as much as ours.

We had a good fifteen-minute journey ahead. Keeping one eye on the road I wiggled my finger through the front mesh of the cat carrier to soothe Maximus but he bit my finger and I swore at him. As we drove away at a fast and steady pace, army trucks and fire engines hurtled into the fire zone. I realised that the more distance we put between ourselves and the fire was the most sensible thing to do.

I thought back to the moment when my intuition had led to this. All along it had been destined to happen. How strongly I had felt it, grateful now that I had listened to it.

I hoped that we could get into the villa for the night, otherwise we would both be sleeping in our cars. As I drove on I could feel my optimism running dry. *Everything has completely vanished. Why bother stopping at Casa Rosa after all? What's the point of hanging around in Valencia when we might not have a home to go back to? I have our passports with us, including the pet's. We could keep driving on through the night see where we end up.* I had become completely irrational.

Panic swelled my chest leaving me drained and exhausted as I tried my best to concentrate on the road ahead. I wondered if Jason was sitting in his car having the same thoughts.

At precisely nine-thirty that evening we pulled off the main highway, over a dry riverbed and through orange plantations before arriving at our safety zone. We drove along a quiet, dimly lit gravel road with only the cicadas in the tree's to welcome us. It was calming to be away from the mayhem.

We supposed that the key-holders were out at their usual expat pub quiz night judging from the quietness of the street but it turned out to be quite the opposite. We heard a cork pop followed by *Oooh!* From a gaggle of voices. The key holders – June and Nick were hosting an outside dinner party, which explained why they hadn't heard their telephone. As we stood at the gate waiting for a pause in their raucous laughter, I felt bad about ruining their evening with our sad news. June had decorated the garden and ivory marquee beautifully in white fairy lights, her guests seated and on their second helpings of curry. We announced our presence with a weak *hello* from behind the gate and must have looked a sight as virtually everyone got to their feet to see who the two pale-faced, charcoal smelling gate-crashers were.

June and Nick comforted us just as our own parents' might have, and I tried my hardest not to cry as we retold our story of the fire. Nick rushed off into the house to fetch us some left-over curry while June poured me a generous glass of wine to calm my nerves.

I was offered whiskey and diazepam tablets - which was tempting but I refused both, preferring to guzzle wine instead.

There were eight other guests around the dinner table, all curious to know the details of what had unfolded. As we each retold our parts of the story I realised how unbelievable it sounded. If you hadn't experienced the magnitude of it with your own eyes, how could you possibly understand how frightening it was?

I picked at the food in front of me. June's curry was delicious but I had no appetite at all. At midnight we hugged our friend's goodbye and then retreated to the familiarity of Casa Rosa. We showered before collapsing into bed, the fresh sheets a comfort as I drifted in and out of sleep, the sirens still ringing in my ears.

Our slumber didn't last long. At four-fifteen in the morning, I awoke to the familiar smell of smoke and sat bolt upright in bed. I thought at first I must have been reliving the nightmare but then Jason got up and ran up to the roof terrace. There, yet again, was a wall of fire consuming the lush orange groves and dry grass, climbing closer towards us. Jason ran back downstairs to the bedroom to find me sitting stunned in the moonlight.

"Get moving," was all he said and rushed out of the room. At least all our stuff was still in our cars.

Just as I was pulling on my clothes we heard Nick's voice in the darkness, warning us to get out.

"The fire has spread to this village now! Everyone's evacuating from here – we don't have long. I've got to get our dogs into the car but we'll meet you by the town hall," he yelled.

This was becoming ridiculous. I was now convinced the fire must be following us. *How far would we have to go to get away from it?* We were already twenty-five kilometres away from Chulilla, it seemed whichever way we turned we couldn't outrun it.

For the third time, we evacuated away from the fire. I stuffed the cat back into his travel box, threw myself into the car and followed Jason through the identical sugar-cube white villas that dotted the town. We parked both our cars on the main street and waited as fire trucks and police cars rushed towards the orange fields.

Over the following hour, we stood in front of the local Ayuntamiento - town hall, listening to the negative conversation of expats that had joined us from surrounding areas. Someone suggested that the village community centre was being prepped to accommodate the catastrophe.

We knew we should be in our own temporary shelter back in Chulilla - if we could have found it - but it didn't make a difference, the situation was still the same in this town. We waited under a dimly lit street lamp as volunteers from the village moved quickly to set up chairs and tables and offer hot drinks. It took no time at all for the helpers to drag, carry or wheel residents towards the refuge, helped by the fact that the village was less populated.

An English lady called Lesley kept up the chatter with annoying persistence.

"Oh, you know, we'll all be living on the streets in no time at this rate. I'll be lucky if I can salvage anything from my garden. All my plants will be ruined, it was that near. I think the woman over there is upset because they wouldn't let her go back and get her dog." She pressed her lips together.

We all looked over at the woman in question. She was an elderly local resident, who looked to be in her nineties. She was dressed completely in black apart from her electric-blue slippers. The woman was clearly tormented. She covered her eyes with her bony fingers and rocked back and forth, screaming and then crumbling into floods of grief-stricken tears as she raised both arms up to the sky. I felt a stone drop inside my stomach in sympathy for her. Surely someone had gone back for her dog?

The wind stirred, sending a warm wave around my legs, reminding me that I didn't have a change of clothes and that the shorts and t-shirt I had on might now be the only clothing I owned.

Lesley's negative chatter twittered on for an hour and it clearly made the others nervous. I realised I needed to let go of the stress and be on my own to process the last twelve hours. I muttered an excuse about checking in on our pets so I could retreat to the sanctity of my car.

There I sat in the driver's seat my head numb, I squeezed my eyes shut and took in deep breaths. I reclined the seat back as far as it would go and pulled the blanket I had snatched from the rental house up to my chin and tried my hardest to relax, settling into the soothing quietness.

I looked back to see how Jason was getting on. He was standing patiently with the other expats and I wondered why he was tolerating that Lesley woman.

Another deep breath to relax should do the trick.

I realised that wasting energy worrying about the things in life I couldn't control was pointless. Even if I had in some way predicted the fire, no one could have stopped it. As I tried to let go of the stress I felt the car began to shake. I looked about to see if Jason was playing a practical joke - rocking the car back and forth. But it wasn't him shaking at all, it was me. My whole body was convulsing with the kind of shock I imagined one would feel after a near-fatal car accident. I was aware of my own shuddering, but there was nothing I could do to stop it. As I closed my eyes again Jason hopped in the passenger seat.

"That woman is a nightmare. She's got everyone freaked out." He paused. "What's wrong with you?"

"I can't stop shaking. I'm trying but I can't stop." I held out my hand to show how demented it looked.

"It's just post-traumatic shock – you'll be alright in a minute."

He patted my knee as if I were a pensioner and pointed over to the local café.

"When that place opens we'll go and get a nice breakfast. You probably need to eat."

He was right, it felt like we hadn't eaten properly for days. But then I hadn't felt capable of eating anything. Jason snuggled down inside his jacket and closed his eyes. The sunrise was emerging but inside the car was still chilly from the night air. I pulled my blanket up to my chin and relaxed - on the edge of switching off.

By the time sunrise broke through the blackened sky my shock had subsided and had been replaced with a desperate feeling of hope. While the other expats and Spanish residents drifted into the now open community centre with their dogs, we ate breakfast at the café and waited for news.

Inside the café, locals shushed one another as they crowded around a wall-mounted television. Spanish news reporters gave out further details as the locals scrambled to see live pictures of our devastated village. I could barely watch the images as more yellow water planes dropped water on our burning mountain and exhausted, soot-covered firemen, shed clothing that they had tied around their waists. The fire had now been burning relentlessly for eighteen hours and still seemed to be out of control. Villagers around us shook their heads vigorously and explained to the hard of hearing that things weren't looking good at all.

I checked my emails on my mobile phone. I had a hundred worried messages from friends and family back in the UK who had seen the report of the fire on British news channels and imagined the worst. I posted status updates on social media to keep my friends informed.

For now, we had nowhere to go to. We had left three residences and couldn't go back to any of them. We had no choice but to drift around the streets and wait for news.

We drove to Losa, a tiny town that neighboured ours, where it seemed all the other displaced residents had ended up as well. The police protectively guarded the road into our village, stopping anyone who tried to pass through. After stopping for a drink in a bar, I called our neighbour Isabel hoping for any vital clues as to how our neighbourhood had fared. After a lot of questioning and phone calls later we finally got word that our house was unscathed. The relief that came with the news was immense - I suppose I had braced myself for the worst. We were told that the wind had directed the fire to a patch of forest behind the house where we had rescued Teddy from. Miraculously the fire had circled all around our area without burning through it, leaving our area of pine forest untouched.

We parked our cars in a residential road near the police boundary and stretched our legs at a nearby viewing point. Spectators had gathered at this spot as it had clear panoramic views to the fire scene. The fire was still consuming bushland and had been forced back by firebreaks. If the wind didn't change direction again, it could with any luck, burn itself out.

Along with the small crowd, we eagerly watched the army churn-over soil with heavy machinery creating a deep ditch so the fire had nowhere else to go from the base of the mountain.

Further along the fire line, a dedicated team of volunteer's outsmarted the flames by directing it one way and then beating it with bushy branches and rubber paddles. I had enormous admiration for those who confronted it.

As the day drew on and we grew tired, I hopped into Jason's more spacious car to try to catch up on some sleep. He tipped his head back and instantly fell into a restful slumber while I tried my best to disengage my active brain. The positive news that our house was still standing was enough for me to shut off my fight or flight mode and give into what I needed most of all.

An hour later I woke from my doze, hungry and alone. Jason had vanished from the car, along with the dogs. I got out to stretch my legs just as he emerged from the top of the road with a spring in his step.

"We need to buy the paper tomorrow," he said as he put the

dogs in the back of the car.

"Why?" I asked, wondering if there was a lead on how the fire had started.

"Because *I* happen to be in it. A reporter from El Mundo just interviewed me. I guess I'm the foreign perspective of the piece. He mainly asked questions on us and how long we've lived here. I managed to explain that our house was on the other side of the burning mountain and we had been evacuated three times, which the reporter couldn't believe. He wished us luck and took my photo, seemed like a nice guy."

"Well, that's more to add to our life story – at what point is life ever dull in Spain? I thought we moved out here for a quiet life, but there's hardly been a dull moment." I added.

We both chuckled with enormous relief. Not only because our house had made it through, one of the worst fire's in the Valencian province, but also because everyone else was safe too. There were no reports of anyone being injured thanks to the hard work of the emergency services.

At three o'clock local gossip bounced around that the fire was now under control but regardless of whether or not this was true, the police still weren't lifting the cordon.

We decided to drive the twenty-five kilometres back to the village where Casa Rosa was, to see how our friends were coping. When we arrived volunteers at the community centre were cooking an enormous paella and there was a lot of food to go round. We joined the Spanish and the Brits seated at the long table listening to their theories of how the blaze had started. Volunteers dished rabbit, chicken and steaming yellow rice onto flimsy plastic plates. Perhaps it was because we were particularly hungry but we thought the paella was the best thing we had ever eaten in our lives.

More information emerged as the conversation drew back and forth to the events of the fire. The fire had definitely started in our town of Chulilla and it had run through at least six other small rural villages, covering such a vast distance it was hard to know the magnitude of the devastation.

As the sun fell to darkness, police left the scene and for this village at least, residents were able to return back to their homes.

Our village, however, was still out of bounds so we stayed another night at Casa Rosa, which seemed a more comfortable option than our cars.

A row of singed orange trees, close to the property was evidence of how close it had come to us. Thankfully the fire had halted at a row of white house's just a hundred yards away, but not before decimating orange groves, olive and almond trees.

Later that evening, huddled together with our furry family, we munched on takeaway pizza and guzzled red wine. At last, we could have a full night's sleep and with any luck, we would be home in the morning.

54. RESURRECTION

Finally, three days later after the fire had destroyed our beautiful landscape, we received the news that we could go back to our house.

Vehicles slowly crawled back into Chulilla, all eyes on the aftermath before us. The sight was so devastating that I was on the verge of sobbing over my steering wheel as we returned. The fire had changed our once green, wooded parks to an eerie and decimated moonscape. Road signs had melted, hit by extreme temperatures where the fire had jumped its path. Nothing looked the same and as we drove further into the mountains the more evident the obliteration. Just around a sweeping bend, we came upon an area that was crawling with reporters. There must have been journalists from at least six separate news channels doing their bit for the camera. Large vans adorned with satellite dishes had been hastily parked at the side of the road, reporters at the ready. They spoke into microphones, gesturing to the blackened remains behind them explaining that this once beautiful picnic park had been annihilated into a lunar landscape of ash and smouldering rocks. They gave viewers details of how five and a half thousand hectares of the countryside had been claimed by the fire, dramatizing how it had swept through six other villages in just twenty-four hours.

I couldn't help but feel annoyed at the spectators who poured in to see the destruction. Curious tourists arrived in hire cars just for a photo opportunity and it felt horrible at how instantly the place had become a freak show. Leaving our cars by the roadside, I got out to get a closer look at the remaining evidence. I tried to find familiar ground as I plodded along a crunchy charcoal path. The sensation under my trainers felt alien as each step formed a stickier, thicker sole. Dazed by the geographical change I lost my bearings and walked into a sunlit space, formerly dark from the shade of so many trees. Mature trees lay fallen as wounded soldiers, their bark blackened and split open, heat rising from their root holes.

I was surprised to see some trees still alight, a gust of wind caused the smoke to spiral upwards, forming a ghost-like soul dancing in the sunlight.

We drove up the mountain track road towards our house and arrived to find it as we had left it - perfectly intact, we both sighed with enormous relief. *How* this was possible when there was so much devastation around was hard to understand. Our relief was short-lived however when we noticed smoke coming from the clifftop behind our house where a tree was still on fire and sent my guts churning in fear that our section of remaining forest could go up in flames. I called a fireman friend in the village who reassured me that this was normal - *a fire doesn't just go out – its core can burn for days*. Obsessively I checked on that lone burning tree, every half an hour throughout the entire afternoon, but by early evening our fireman friend must have listened to our concerns and deployed a plane that swooped right above our house, almost touching the tops of our trees, and dropped a bright red powder over the area to extinguish the flames. It made a return journey with another load, just to make sure. At last, after every tree had been double-checked and extinguished beside our house I could finally rest easy.

The next day we bought a copy of the newspaper El Mundo, to read Jason's interview and see the photo of him snapped from behind as he watched the fire being battled, along with other spectators. In the paper's centrefold, an aerial map illustrated how the fire had travelled with the wind, at seventy-three kilometres per hour, utilised forty-two aircraft, and had taken eight hundred ground crew and twenty-nine fire units to bring it under control.

The source of the fire remained under investigation but the newspaper article suggested that the most conclusive evidence pointed towards an electrical spark from an electric tower. The fire had cost the village dearly and tourism would suffer now that the landscape for which it was so famous for had been destroyed.

As I began to process the enormity of what we had been through, I realised that it had been most the most terrifying experience of my life and over the following weeks I experienced traumatic flashbacks that made me relive it. Even though I had consciously put the episode to bed, my subconscious mind had other ideas. The incident had penetrated so deep into my psyche that the aftershock manifested itself in my dreams.

In these nightmares, I was either trapped at the foot of the mountain inside a circle of flames, while the firemen on the outside of the circle were unable to hear my screams. Or I was desperately searching for our beloved dogs, who were trapped in the burning forest, my throat was too dry to call them back. In both cases, I woke up panting and pulling the bed covers off frantically, trying to cool myself down.

For months every time I awoke, I would sit up convinced I could smell smoke in the air. Whether it was simply a wood-burning fire from one of the villas in the valley, or food being cooked, the waft of charcoal made me overwrought with worry. Jason reassured me he couldn't smell anything.

How could it smell so real, if I had imagined it? In my paranoia, I wondered about the possibility of someone deliberately starting a fire with the flick of a cigarette. If the temperature had cooled down it might have eased my mind but the heat and wind continued for a further two weeks. Even when the first smattering of rain lightly fell onto the ashen ground, it barely dampened the black surface or my fears. Only then, when the gift of torrential rain finally fell for two days straight, did it put an end my suffering.

55. TRADING SKIES

By the following year, the landscape was beginning to blossom with patches of fluorescent green regrowth. Ash from the fire had kick-started nature's cycle all over the mountain and it thrilled me to see baby shoots sprouting up from within dead trees and plants. Thankfully our beautiful mountain was beginning to heal and regenerate.

As March arrived we had decided to start renting our little cabin in the woodland area of our garden as a holiday let. Jason had built it on a level of short stilts, due to the volcanic terrain. This elevated position made it appear larger than its five-by-four-metre dimensions and because it was situated at a distance from our villa, it gave guests' the privacy they needed and the thrill of being secluded in the forest as the pine trees enveloped them.

Technically speaking, the cabin was a garden summer hut but it was much more than that once we had transformed it into the ultimate glamping accommodation for the kind of clients who loved the outdoors.

We painted the exterior of the cabin in a pastel green so it camouflaged in with the trees that surrounded it and whitewashed the interior walls. The floorboards got a generous coating of dark battleship grey paint before being simply furnished with a double bed, small sofa, cosy blankets, DVDs and a TV. A kettle, toaster, and other basic kitchen equipment were housed inside an antique dresser along with maps, travel books and yoga magazines.

The cabin roof overhung, offering a generous shelter at the entrance and allowed the perfect opportunity for Jason to build a porch that would be protected from the weather. This porch platform ran the full front length of the cabin where guests could sit and eat meals outside if they wanted, this was accessed by two wide steps made from reclaimed chestnut floorboards we had brought back from Galicia. A handrail was created from a single thin pine tree, specially selected for its straightness from the nearby woods. Jason stripped its branches and bark, sanded, varnished and notched holes into one side to accommodate thirteen spindles, also left over from the Galicia project. Guests had their own private bathroom - a wooden built lean-to attached to the side of the cabin, accessed by a wooden path of sunken pallet-wood.

In addition to the accommodation, guests also had exclusive use of the barbecue, swimming pool and our services if they needed us.

Our goal was to create a magical rural retreat, targeting an audience of professional couples, backpackers and single travellers who longed for the tranquillity of the mountains. Guests could unwind by the pool, explore the lagoons and hike across the rope bridges all year round.

And it was perhaps for this reason that the cabin rentals became an instant hit over the following two years, attracting artistic guests from every corner of the globe; Choreographers, photographers, musicians, actors, film-makers, and novelists. We were attentive but not annoying, giving as much privacy as they wanted to celebrate birthdays, honeymoons and anniversaries.

Sometimes guests preferred to be in our company, to use our local knowledge of the area or show them the wonder of the many fiestas the region had to offer. On other occasions we would simply share stories over a smouldering barbecue and good fresh food. We took to hosting like we took to renovating – pulling our efforts together to create an environment that would stay with people in years to come.

Very occasionally we hosted guests who we suspected were having affairs, which wasn't difficult to spot as they tried so hard to cover their tracks. They usually arrived from separate destinations as tense as a coiled spring pretending to be a regular couple but clearly awkward around each other. It was their private business and we remained at a distance to give them the secrecy they required but it was still an indiscretion, hard to avoid.

It was almost impossible to ignore the lusty whimpering, grunting and unreserved squealing that emitted from the wooden cabin walls as we skimmed the surface of the swimming pool or swept the pine needles from the deck. A cheery *whistle, while we worked*, did nothing to hide our embarrassment while they submerged themselves in their happy place.

When it wasn't occupied with guests, I liked to use the retreat for myself. My cabin of solitude where I could read snuggled under a blanket on the sofa, or to nap while the rain hammered down on the roof. But most of all it was my place to write, a place where I could listen to the wind chimes that hung in the trees and let go of my imagination.

Hosting our fabulous guests over those years opened up our world in a way that we found hugely rewarding. We felt envious of the stories our visitors exchanged with us and eventually we realised we too wanted to travel and explore new destinations. As much as we loved hosting and being in Chulilla we felt a strong sense of wanderlust to be somewhere else. So we came to the painful decision to put the Chulilla house on the market and see - once again - what fate had in store.

We evaluated our decision for months, determining that since the fire our lives had never been the same. The village had regenerated well but our recovery was not without fear of it happening again. After that fateful day, I had an awareness that having all our capital in one property was risky. If we had lost our house and everything in it, the insurance pay-out would have only been enough to build the bare bones of it or they might not have paid out at all. We considered renting the house so we could travel further afield, but that was a vulnerable option and secluded villas were often a target for thieves who would strip the place bare right down to the electrics and light switches.

Our friends in both Spain and Britain had warned us that selling up would be a mistake. If we were to return to the UK did we want to go back to all that rain after we had traded our sky for a brighter one? After a decade of being in Spain, it felt like the right time to move on. We had worked tirelessly out of financial obligations and had experienced an actual *life* in the process. How many people we knew could say they were lucky enough to be in such a position?

It felt rather exciting to think of what adventures lay ahead, what other options could we seek, what other countries we could explore. I thought to myself what a positive step that was, coming out to Spain in the first place. It didn't take a lot for that first seed to take root and now I wanted to see what could come next.

56. BOUNDLESS POSSIBILITIES

Our villa had been on the market for a few months when we got a call from a British-run estate agent in Valencia asking us if we were interested in taking part in a new BBC2 daytime series *Escape to the Continent*.

The estate agent had been approached by an independent production company, seeking a selection of properties in the Valencian province for their show. This was to be a follow-up from the hugely successful *Escape to the Country* franchise which would be televised all over the world.

Our villa had caught the eye of the researchers stating it fitted the criteria of the contributors' - the couple who got to have their sixty minutes of fame while property searching in the glorious sunshine, all expenses paid.

We accepted the offer immediately – any promotion was good promotion and it was the perfect way to record our achievements. We knew of the production company, they were well-known for filming *Grand Designs* – a show we watched with envy, dreaming to build our own house one day.

The producer of the show got in touch and we set up a midweek meeting at our villa. They had made it clear that this first meeting was to shortlist our house with no assurances that our property would be featured.

The following Wednesday, two men from pre-production turned up; a producer called Jono, in his mid-thirties and Salvador, a very tall, handsome cameraman from Madrid who looked just like

Lenny Kravitz. We chatted while I filled-out forms and Salvador marched about our property looking for suitable spots from which to take sweeping exterior shots. They left an hour and a half later and said they'd be in touch with their decision – although we knew the production company would be reviewing properties all around the area of Valencia, we hoped ours might be a contender. As Jono left I wondered then just how genuine *were* these couples who participated in these shows. We had often watched these programmes and never heard of anyone purchasing a house when it came to it.

Two days later on a Friday afternoon, the telephone rang while I was fishing out leaves from the pool and hoped this might be the call we had been waiting for. It was Jono with the news that our property had been selected, along with two others to appear in the episode.

"I think your place has a lot to offer our contributors. So really I'm calling to just to make sure that you're both still happy to be part of the show?"

I agreed and silently punched the air trying not to squeal.

"Our presenter is flying in early next week and so we're hoping to start filming at yours by the end of next week if that's all right?" Jono asked.

"No problem, we'll be ready in a week." *That should give us plenty of time to clean up and perhaps touch-up the flaking paint in places,* I thought to myself.

"Oh but before that, we'll need to take some exterior shots of the garden, deck and pool area first if that's OK. Should be in and out in an hour or so. That will probably happen in the next few days." Said Jono.

"Sure," I said, and immediately regretted the commitment.

After I put the receiver down a flood of panic fell over me. We only had a few days to make our place look as presentable as it's ever been, how would we manage that?

Over the following three days, wearing our shabbiest decorating clothes we painted, cemented, swept and scrubbed inside and out. Using an electric compressor Jason spray painted all the retaining garden walls, the barbecue and anything else back to a blinding, bright white. He cleaned up buckets of dog mess in the garden and pruned the shrubs while I de-cluttered the shelves, cleaned windows, polished surfaces, rearranged furniture, made all the beds with my nicest linens and filled bowls with fresh colourful fruit. I mopped floors, threw curtains into the washing machine and even scrubbed the oven – *just in case it was caught on camera and I'd watch it back in horror.*

On the final afternoon, before the crew arrived, Jason spent hours sweeping pine needles off the drive and tidying up the storerooms. Once we could do no more I threw open the living room shutters to reveal panoramic views of the regenerating mountain and collapsed on the sofa. We were exhausted and it certainly gave us some perspective as to how much effort goes into the presentation for these shows.

The next morning a youthful crew arrived including Tom, the director - who would be filming the exterior garden shots himself as the other half of the crew were on another job further along the coast.

The plan was to get the sweeping shots done outside - *at least I thought that was the plan* until the tripod and camera ventured inside and I felt grateful we'd taken the precaution of cleaning-up the inside of the house as well. These shots lasted just a few seconds while we jumped out the way and remained quiet.

They filmed in short bursts, constantly testing the natural light with a handy little gadget before moving their equipment around for a different angle. These images were to be the ones used during the contributor couple's 'thought process' as they ponder on their options. I hid around corners, eavesdropping as the director spoke gently into a microphone stating where he was in the house - I imagined this was for continuity or editing purposes.

The scenes featuring the couple would be taken on the second day of filming along with the presenter.

A few seconds of footage here and there took hours to compile, and I hoped they weren't doing any close-ups of the stubborn red wine stain on the white kitchen cupboard doors or focusing in on the gigantic spider that I had only just noticed abseiling down from the ceiling.

While those shots were being taken the producer asked Jason if he knew of any other interesting areas to shoot and not a minute later they had jumped in Jono's hired jeep to make their way up the track road to the top of the mountain behind our house, any further and they would have to haul the equipment up the mountain on foot. It was a fine day for hiking and panoramic shots so the team managed to capture exactly what they were looking for.

After they left and we walked back into the house, we were struck with the realisation that we couldn't touch or move anything inside or outside the property. Before each take, the director had set up the room by adjusting the sofas, repositioned cushions and nudged items a little to the right or left so they sat perfectly within the frame. In the kitchen, Jono had hidden or rotated branded products so that the labels wouldn't be advertised on television.

I was afraid to move almost everything, fearful that things would be out of place for continuity. For the next few days until the full crew returned we lived in our own 'studio'. Perched on the edge of furniture and didn't dare eat any fruit from the overflowing bowl. When we did have to move something I photographed it first so that I could put it back exactly as it was. I couldn't wait for the next filming session just so I could relax in our home once again.

A few days later, a film crew in a convoy rolled in, this time escorted by the local policeman on his moped who looked very proud to be part of the theatrics. Several black SUVs screeched to a halt in succession outside our house, making it seem as if the FBI had arrived. A full crew had turned up this time and it was exciting to feel the tension of their energy as they hurriedly clambered out from cars to unload their equipment for the shoot. Salvador, Jono and Tom gave us a warm welcome as they stretched their legs and breathed in the warm pine tree scent.

TV presenter, Anita Rani, hopped out of her car looking styled, refreshed and ready for a morning's work. She wore a perfectly tailored black dress with wedged shoes as she strode confidently towards me with her hand extended in warm greeting. Her glossy black hair was professionally styled in a long plait that fell past her tiny waist and I wondered if she had done that herself. She was engaging and more petit in reality than I had expected but more surprisingly was her passionate spirit, it was nice to see someone who clearly loved their career. We were swept away a little at first, not only by having a celebrity in our home but by the flurry of equipment that was instantly set up, our property now a stage.

Under the guidance of the director, we were soon immersed in this marvellous experience. We had additional paperwork to fill in; consent forms giving the crew permission to film on our property. Jono explained that we had exactly thirty minutes to brief Anita on the important selling points of the house and any potential income opportunities that she could add to her script. Once we were done we would need to vacate the property while the crew would send for the remaining car to bring the contributors up to the house to begin filming their part. They needed not to meet us at this stage nor see the house before the cameras were rolling so every emotion could be captured naturally on film.

A sound man appeared with rods and two compact bags of equipment: tripods, cameras, leads, lighting and small gadgets. Time was passing by in a flash and Anita's easy-going and professional nature made us feel relaxed about how they were going to tackle the filming. She dashed from one end of the patio to the other, coming up with possible ideas for opening scenes. Her eyes widened in delight as she poked her head inside the cabin door. She stated that it was just what the couple were looking for, a magical writers' retreat in a unique part of Spain.

"They're going to *love* this house!" she gushed enthusiastically.

The producer checked his watch. Time was beginning creep up as the remaining SUV containing the contributors pulled up and sat waiting on our dusty road building up the tension.

"Ten minutes, everyone!" called the director to warn us that the camera would start rolling soon. Anita pulled her shoulders back and darted towards the barbecue. I had no idea that presenters put so much into their work – she was like a well-oiled cog, and everyone else fell into her rhythm with just as much vigour.

For now, our time was up, it was the house's turn to shine until we received the signal to return. Jono, thanked us continuously as we herded the dogs into the car, he seemed embarrassed at asking us to leave our own house but we assured him we didn't mind. As we manoeuvred the car around to exit, we could see a crew member instructing a mature couple to keep their backs turned and their eyes closed as to not spoil the surprise.

We drove off through the village and out towards the olive-rich mountainside where we pulled into a track road at the foot of a mountain. We took the dogs out for an hour-long walk through the olive groves and orange plantations, our minds constantly occupied with the filming.

We wondered what the couple's reaction would be. *Had they found their dream house and was it likely they would make us an offer?* Were they serious buyers or was the programme just a way for them to get a free holiday? After all the preparation we had put in, we hoped our efforts would pay off. As we strolled up a dried muddy track we talked about the spontaneity of our lives and how things seemed to always fall into place eventually. After our walk, we headed into our village for a coffee in the town square where we sat with the dogs under our feet, sipping our drinks under a large parasol to shield us from the brilliance of the sun.

The producer called us an hour and a half later to tell us they were pleased with how the filming had gone and were packing up. According to Jono, the couple had adored the house and had requested to meet us so they could pursue their interest. Excited that the contributors had fallen head-over-heels for our home, we raced back to the house to find the crew packing up and were promptly introduced to Amanda and Mike. They seemed genuinely impressed with the house, actively seeking tranquillity and plenty of green space so the location seemed to fit all their criteria.

They peppered us with questions, barely giving us time to reply before each taking one of us aside – Amanda with me, and Mike with Jason.

Amanda was keen to know more about the age of the property and the possibility of building more cabins on the surrounding land. They asked about the climate in winter and the overall costs for living. Once satisfied with all the answers they thanked us and said they would be in touch.

The presenter, contributors and crew left us shortly after midday, spinning off in their executive cars. It was a relief to be on our own and to have the house to ourselves to mess up again.

As the dust settled on the road outside, the sudden quietness drew out a young red squirrel who scuttled across the desert-dry ground. Their numbers had declined since the fire so I was pleased to see they were returning to our forest once again. As I stood on the terrace balcony watching the squirrel, I wondered how life always seemed to have a way of surviving the most unfathomable situations, and how we ourselves play a part in that fate.

"What do we do now, then?" I asked Jason as I flopped back onto the sofa kicking off my shoes.

"Well, I guess we'll just have to wait and see," he replied.

EPILOGUE

It took the contributors a couple of weeks to think about the house, the production company stating they were 'considering their options'. I knew they were just buying time, and had never been serious about making such a big step as to move abroad. The estate agent had divulged that their UK house wasn't even on the market and they didn't have any other collateral to make a move.

However *Escape to the Continent* was aired on BBC2 the following April and had a loyal audience, giving our property the exposure it needed. We listed the house online and within days, interest flooded in so much so, that it became a full-time job responding to emails. The following month the series ran a repeat causing a further flurry of online activity and prompted a family from Oxford to get in touch. They had fallen in love with the house the first time the show aired but had assumed the contributors had bought it - going from their on-screen enthusiasm.

The family couldn't believe their luck when they stumbled upon it online so were serious buyers from the start. Our relationship with them strengthened over weekly phone calls until a viewing could be arranged. As the couple had childcare and work commitments only one of them could fly out at one time, they got around this by coming out individually and filming the viewing so they could share the experience back at home.

However strong our commitment was for a smooth sale, it was a still painful transaction. The English estate agent we used to process the paperwork wasn't happy that we were dealing directly with the buyers and although we had agreed on a flat fee, the agent pulled out without informing us and disappeared. That left us, and the buyers stranded when we needed them the most. Thankfully our good business relationship had built up enough trust that this didn't derail the sale, and through sheer determination, we quickly found a local reputable agent and eight months later the house had sold. It felt wonderful to plan for a fresh start back in the UK - not the ideal choice and climate but after a lot of consideration, we felt we needed some stability that Spain could no longer give us and if we were back on the UK property ladder mortgage-free, that would be an ideal financial position to be in.

Sadly we lost Macey to gastric-flu just before the move and travelled back with the crazy cat and Coco, who both lived happily with us for a few years before passing at around fourteen years old. I found loosing Max particularly hard. His companionship on my lap during all of my writing days, in the cabin in Spain, writing from the many temporary homes that we rented during the summers – he sat with me as I relived and reworked this book right to the end.

I like to think we are temporarily settled, with an option to do what we want, when we want. Where we now spend precious time with our families and travel to countries inspired by our cabin guests.

Jason set up his own handyman business (legally this time) which has been an enormous success and at times, I assist him and it reminds me of the good old days in Galicia...but with less interruption from the neighbours.

I find the time to write when I can, either side of working and doing the things that make me happy but I'm always searching for that next great adventure or a place that inspires me.

I reminisce of our Spanish adventure with great fondness and am thankful that we embarked on the adventure together. Without it, we wouldn't have known how it felt to have grafted so hard to achieve our dreams and then in some cases to have almost lost everything. We wouldn't have helped, rescued and lost animals without knowing the love we could give *and receive* from them.

But most of all we wouldn't have been motivated without the encouraging people we met along the way and those who took the journey with us from the very beginning who believed that with a little, *Salud, Amor y Dinero* we all can make that step towards our next adventure.

ACKNOWLEDGEMENTS

It is to my husband Jason that I want to express my deepest thanks and whom without our Spanish adventure would not have been possible as we broke free from one world into another. Who put up with my incessant questioning during the writing process, encouraged me and helped pull the pages together for the final edits while supplying endless cups of tea over the years that it has taken me to write this book. For believing that "If you build it, they will come" you did build it, and yes those cabin guests came - to whom I am still grateful for their friendships today. It is your story as much as mine and so I hope, I have done you proud.

To Beth Harwood, thank you for undertaking the first round of epic edits for me in exchange for a crate of Rioja. You introduced me to the hideous process of re-writing and supplied me with editing knowledge when I was flailing. You also humbled me when you knew I could do better, and so your faith encouraged me to be the best I could possibly be.

To my mother *and biggest fan* who opened my eyes up to what was missing. Your persistent belief in this book that has driven me all the way, along with your endless encouraging support, laughs and bedspread disasters. Who allowed me to tell parts of your story, no matter how difficult it was for you to relive the memories, this book is also for you. The Carter's & Pickard's for your love and backing on all our projects and endless support over the years in Valencia and Galicia. You were behind us every step without a doubt and ready to give us a hand when we needed it. Your advice and love meant the world to us as it still does today.

To our Spanish and English friends who have asked constantly when the book will be finished, you know who you are and I hope you won't be disappointed. Special thanks to graphic artist and friend Caroline Burton for bringing my story into life in her cover design.

And finally – a closing word about how long this book has taken me to write. When I embarked on this it took me three years of collating everything I had. From notes written on scraps of paper to emails that eventually became this book six years later. A memoir is a particularly brutal book to write because I had to relive the moments I'd rather forget, I cried throughout but also laughed at the memories and situations I found ourselves in. At the time of writing, I had no idea that one of my main characters and real-life stepfather was going to pass on and at that point, I had to put this book down and leave it to rest. After a year, only after my grief had weakened did I find the inner strength to continue. So to Joseph, where you rest peacefully in my heart - if it hadn't been for your love of the place, there would have been no beloved Galician adventure. Lastly, Thank YOU, all my readers who I hope will find your own adventure where ever it may be.

ABOUT THE AUTHOR

Georgina Carter Pickard is a
freelance writer from Teddington,
South-West London. She has
written marketing campaigns,
renovation blogs and contributed
to *Home Building and Renovating
Magazine.* She specialises in Interior
& Garden design but her work
extends to wellbeing and mental
health issues for *Fertility Road*
magazine.

©Photo by Katrina LETAILLEUR

She currently lives in Wiltshire
with her husband Jason and
rescue- dog Luna, where she enjoys
upholstering and restoring furniture
from her workshop. Forever and
Olé is Georgina's first novel.
She can be found on Instagram,
Twitter @PickardCarter.
Or visit:
www.georginacarterpickard.com

Printed in Poland
by Amazon Fulfillment
Poland Sp. z o.o., Wrocław

59850754R10221